Critically
engaging CBT

Critically engaging CBT

Edited by Del Loewenthal and Richard House

Open University Press

Open University Press
McGraw-Hill Education
McGraw-Hill House
Shoppenhangers Road
Maidenhead
Berkshire
England
SL6 2QL

email: enquiries@openup.co.uk
world wide web: www.openup.co.uk

and Two Penn Plaza, New York, NY 10121-2289, USA

First published 2010

A catalogue record of this book is available from the British Library

ISBN 13: 978 0 335 23829 3 (pb)   978 0 335 23830 9 (hb)
ISBN10: 0 335 23829 7 (pb)   0 335 23830 0 (hb)

Library of Congress Cataloging-in-Publication Data
CIP data applied for

Typeset by RefineCatch Limited, Bungay, Suffolk
Printed in the UK by Bell and Bain Ltd, Glasgow

Fictitious names of companies, products, people, characters and/or data that may be used herein (in case studies or in examples) are not intended to represent any real individual, company, product or event.

*The **McGraw·Hill** Companies*

Contents

Other books by the editors

Richard House

Implausible Professions: Arguments for Pluralism and Autonomy in Psychotherapy and Counselling (co-editor, Nick Totton), Ross-on-Wye: PCCS Books, 1997

Therapy Beyond Modernity: Deconstructing and Transcending Profession-Centred Therapy, London: Karnac Books, 2003

Ethically Challenged Professions: Enabling Innovation and Diversity in Psychotherapy and Counselling (co-editor, Yvonne Bates), Ross-on-Wye: PCCS Books, 2003

Against and For CBT: Towards a Constructive Dialogue? (co-editor, Del Loewenthal), Ross-on-Wye: PCCS Books, 2008

Compliance? Ambivalence? Rejection? – Nine Papers Challenging HPC Regulation (co-editor, Denis Postle), London: Wentworth Learning Resources, 2009

Childhood, Wellbeing and a Therapeutic Ethos (co-editor Del Loewenthal), London: Karnac Books, 2009

Del Loewenthal

Post-modernism for Psychotherapists: A Critical Reader (co-author, Robert Snell), London: Routledge, 2003

What Is Psychotherapeutic Research? (co-editor, David Winter), London: Karnac Books, 2006

Case Studies in Relational Research: Qualitative Research Methods in Counselling and Psychotherapy, Basingstoke: Palgrave Macmillan, 2007

Against and For CBT: Towards a Constructive Dialogue? (co-editor, Richard House), Ross-on-Wye: PCCS Books, 2008

Childhood, Wellbeing and a Therapeutic Ethos (co-editor Richard House), London: Karnac Books, 2009

Contributors

Ann Casement, LP, is a Senior Member of The British Association of Psychotherapists, an Associate Member of the Jungian Psychoanalytic Association (NY), and a New York State Licensed Psychoanalyst. She served on the executive committee of the International Association for Analytical Psychology from 2001–2007, and is currently the Honorary Secretary of its ethics committee. She has published widely including articles for *The Economist* and other professional journals.

Windy Dryden is Professor of Psychotherapeutic Studies, Goldsmiths, University of London. He is a Fellow of the British Psychological Society and of the British Association for Counselling and Psychotherapy (BACP). He began his training in rational-emotive behaviour therapy (REBT) in 1977 and became the first Briton to be accredited as an REBT therapist by the Albert Ellis Institute. Windy is perhaps best known for his voluminous writings in REBT/cognitive-behaviour therapy (CBT) and the wider field of counselling and psychotherapy; to date he has authored or edited over 170 books. He has also edited 18 book series including the best selling *Counselling in Action* series. Windy was the founding editor of the *British Journal of Cognitive Psychotherapy* in 1982, which later became the *Journal of Cognitive Psychotherapy: An International Quarterly*. Windy was co-founding editor of this journal with E. Thomas Dowd. In 2003, Windy became the editor of the *Journal of Rational-Emotive and Cognitive-Behavior Therapy*.

John Heaton is a psychotherapist in private practice. He is the author of *The Eye: Phenomenology and Psychology of Function and Disorder* (1968), *Introducing Wittgenstein* with Judy Groves Illustrator (1995, 4th edn, 2009), *Wittgenstein and Freud* (2000) and many papers in medical and philosophical books and journals. He has written *The Talking Cure: Wittgenstein's Therapeutic Method and Psychotherapy* due to be published in 2010.

Jeremy Holmes MD FRCPsych BCP, a retired psychiatrist, is visiting Professor of Psychological Therapies at the University of Exeter, where he set up and co-runs the qualifying course in psychoanalytic psychotherapy at the University of Exeter. In 1998–2002 he was Chair of the Psychotherapy Faculty at the Royal College of Psychiatrists. He has authored, edited or co-authored 15 books and over 100 articles and book chapters in the field of psychoanalytic psychotherapy and attachment theory, including the best-selling *John Bowlby and Attachment Theory*. In 2009 he was awarded the Bowlby–Ainsworth award for contributions to the field of attachment theory. His most recent book is *Exploring in Security: Towards an Attachment-informed Psychoanalytic Psychotherapy* (Routledge, 2009).

Richard House PhD is Senior Lecturer in Psychotherapy and Counselling in Roehampton University's Research Centre for Therapeutic Education, a publishing editor with Hawthorn Press and a trained Steiner teacher. A campaigner for childhood with the 'Open EYE' Campaign, he writes regularly on childhood and psychotherapeutic issues. With Sue Palmer, Richard co-initiated the Open Letters on 'toxic childhood' and play to the *Daily Telegraph* in September 2006 and 2007, respectively, which have precipitated a global media debate on the place of childhood in modern technological society. His books include *Therapy Beyond Modernity* (Karnac Books, 2003) and *Against and For CBT* (edited with Del Loewenthal, PCCS Books, 2008).

Del Loewenthal is Professor of Psychotherapy and Counselling at Roehampton University where he directs the Research Centre for Therapeutic Education and the doctoral programmes in Psychotherapy, Counselling and Counselling Psychology. He is also a Chartered Counselling Psychologist and Analytic Psychotherapist in private practice. His books include *Against and For CBT* (with Richard House, PCCS Books, 2008), *Case Studies in Relational Research* (Palgrave Macmillan, 2007), *What is Psychotherapeutic Research?* (with David Winter, Karnac Books, 2006), and *Postmodernism for Psychotherapists* (with Robert Snell, Routledge, 2003). Del is currently interested in the development of post-existentialism, and is founding editor of the *European Journal for Psychotherapy and Counselling* (Routledge).

Stacey Millichamp is Director of Clinical Services for the charity Children Our Ultimate Investment (UK). Additionally, she teaches and supervises on the MA Psychotherapy at the Psychosynthesis and Education Trust primarily delivering training on 'The Transpersonal Field' and 'Depth Work', and works in private practice as a psychotherapist and supervisor for individuals and couples in north London.

Ian Parker is Professor of Psychology in the Discourse Unit (www.discourseunit.com) at Manchester Metropolitan University. He is a practising Lacanian psychoanalyst. His books include *Revolution in Psychology* (Pluto Press, 2007).

Howard A. Paul is a Professor of Psychiatry at the University of Medicine and Dentistry of New Jersey, Robert Wood Johnson Medical School where he lectures to both psychology interns and psychiatry residents on integrative, empirically informed treatments with a CBT focus. He is also a field supervisor for the Graduate School of Applied and Professional Psychology of Rutgers University. He is the Book Review Editor for the *Journal of Child & Family Behavior Therapy*. He maintains an active private practice. He has contributed over 80 articles, studies and book reviews in his 40+ years of practice.

Michael Proeve has an MA degree in clinical psychology and a research PhD He has moved between professional practice and academia several times during his career. He has practised as a clinical psychologist chiefly in forensic mental health settings and has managed two treatment agencies in this area. He has taught psychology in three universities in the areas of clinical, forensic and general psychology. He has taught clinical psychology and conducted research at the University of South Australia since 2003.

Anthony Ryle was born in 1927. He was educated at Oxford and University College Hospital, qualifying in medicine in 1949. Until 1964 he worked in a group practice in Kentish Town, London where he carried out research into the prevalence of psychological disorders in his patients. In 1964 he went to the new University of Sussex, initially as Director of the University Health Service and subsequently as a Senior Research Fellow. From 1983 to 1992 he was Consultant Psychotherapist at St. Thomas's Hospital, London. From the 1960s on he was active in psychotherapy research and was increasingly involved in the development of cognitive analytic therapy (CAT) and he continued these activities after retirement from the NHS.

Peter Stratton is a Systemic Psychotherapist with broad research interests and substantial involvement in statutory processes that affect the provision of psychotherapy. His own research includes development of an outcome measure for families in therapy (the SCORE project); the effects of basing training on concepts of active learning and the dialogical construction of self; the relationships of humour and creativity during psychotherapy; attributional analyses of family causal beliefs and blaming; public attitudes to terrorism by combining attributional coding with metaphor analysis; and fostering practitioner research networks. His current positions include: Editor of *Human Systems*; Academic and Research Development Officer for the Association for Family Therapy; Chair of the UKCP research committee; Chair of the European Family Therapy Association Research Committee.

Keith Tudor is a qualified and UKCP registered psychotherapist. He was a founding director of Temenos, an independent training organization in Sheffield, UK. In July 2009 he emigrated to Aotearoa, New Zealand where he is a Senior Lecturer and Programme Leader in the Department of Psychotherapy at Auckland University of Technology. He is a widely published author/editor in the field of mental health, psychotherapy and counselling, with over 100 papers and 10 books to his name. He is on the editorial advisory boards of three international journals and is the series editor of *Advancing Theory in Therapy* (published by Routledge).

Acknowledgements

We would, first and foremost, like to thank our contributors for the way they have helped us in critically engaging with CBT, and not least for their impeccable keeping to our schedule. Our three CBT contributors in particular responded with remarkable speed and quality to especially stringent copy deadlines. We would also like to thank Professor Arnold Lazarus, Dr Nadine Pelling and Professor Windy Dryden for their help in advising us on developments in North America, Australasia and Europe, respectively, and staff and students from the Research Centre for Therapeutic Education, Roehampton University for many stimulating conversations, and in particular Rhiannon Stamp for her help throughout the project. We would also like to thank Dr Chris Gilleard, Dr Roslyn Law and Jane Street from South West London St George's NHS Mental Health Trust, for their help in developing our IAPT-based programmes and research. And last but not least, grateful thanks to our publishers, Open University Press, for their commitment, guidance and support throughout this project.

Del Loewenthal and Richard House
London, October 2009

1   CBT and the other psychological therapies in an age of happiness

Richard House and Del Loewenthal

Introduction

In this book, we intend to begin a long overdue conversation across the richly diverse psychological therapies field, in which eminent representatives of the different therapy modalities explore their approach's world view and praxis in relation to that of cognitive behaviour therapy (real or perceived). The seemingly inexorable rise of cognitive behaviour therapy (hereafter, CBT) in modern Western culture has been perhaps *the* central talking point in the profession-centred conversations that can routinely be found in both professional and informal therapy circles. Certainly, the various schools of counselling and psychotherapy might be expected to have very diverse 'takes' on the rise of CBT, with relatedly distinct ways of making sense of that ascendancy, and with their own distinct theoretical responses to the ontological assumptions and world view underpinning CBT theory and praxis. To our knowledge, and somewhat to our surprise, there exists to date no substantive literature that attempts to 'compare and contrast' the various therapy modalities with CBT, in terms of the broad philosophical and practice-based assumptions that underpin and inform them.

A *psychoanalytic* perspective, for example, might highlight the impact of CBT's rise on the unconscious phantasies of practitioners, whose very livelihood and professional survival might be felt to be under imminent threat, as CBT is increasingly legitimized by the state as *the* 'treatment' of choice for many presenting problems. Such a perspective might also highlight the *competition* and 'battle of ideas' that, arguably, are always raging in the psy field (e.g. Dryden and Feltham, 1992; Feltham, 1999; Clark, 2002), but which is perhaps particularly acute at times of unusually scarce resources and the associated struggles for hegemony and power, whether overt and conscious or otherwise. A *humanistic* approach might bemoan the relative downgrading in importance of 'the emotional' that seems to be accompanying the rise of the (allegedly cognitively biased) CBT with, for example, its common emphasis on the primacy of 'the cognitive' (thinking) over 'the emotional' (feelings) (e.g. Padesky and Greenberger, 1995). A *postmodern* therapy perspective (e.g. Loewenthal, 1996; House, 2003; Loewenthal and Snell, 2003) might focus on the assumptions about 'the self', the human subject and the nature of human relationship that are necessarily entailed in CBT praxis, and might crucially deconstruct those assumptions, and the very status and nature of the 'scientific' knowledge to which CBT claims to give rise. And a *transpersonal* approach might not only assume a world view that explicitly acknowledges the efficacy of the ineffable (Klein, 2003) and the spiritual in human experience (Margitics, 2009), but it might also question at a very deep level the very nature of human suffering itself. And it would also tend to embrace a very different philosophical view about what constitutes valid 'knowledge' (e.g. Polanyi, 1966; Puhakka et al., 1997; Hart et al., 2000).

The latter perspectives, then, offer just a flavour of the kinds of issue that this book attempts to address. We believe that these comparative modality positions constitute crucial questions with which a rapidly maturing therapy field is surely now ready to engage in a relatively undefensive way, rather than the modalities continuing to snipe at (or ignore) each other from their schoolist bunkers (Clarkson, 1998), and in the process generating far more heat (and collateral damage) than light. This is most certainly not to argue, however, for some kind of 'lowest common denominator' eclecticism or naïve integrationism, whereby substantive, and even philosophically *incommensurable* differences (Kuhn, 1962; Chang, 1998) that exist between CBT and the other modalities are politely (but misguidedly) ignored.

This book is part of a larger project we are engaged in at Roehampton University, exploring the place of theory, forms of knowledge and research within the psychological therapies. We first attempted to open up a conversation regarding CBT and the other psychological therapies, particularly in terms of paradigmatic, epistemological, political and cultural perspectives, in the *European Journal of Psychotherapy and Counselling* (House and Loewenthal, 2008b), and in the book *Against and For CBT: Towards a Constructive Dialogue* (House and Loewenthal, 2008a). This book's level of sales and positive reception provided one early indication that we had had some success in opening up a conversation in the field. A relatively small proportion of that book was given over to what we termed 'clinical perspectives', and it is this initial exploration that we have made the entire focus of this book.

There is one further aspect, common to both books, that we would like to mention here; namely, our own positionings in relation to the issues we are raising here. For while we hope that our own position has become more open to self-examination and reflexivity as a result of this work, it is important for the readers (and ourselves!) to have some understanding of our own relationship to CBT – not least, so that they can judge for themselves the extent to which the arguments and approach we have adopted really lead to a genuine opening up of a dialogue, or whether they are merely an attempt to establish more favourable grounds for our own position on which to base an apology for an authentic dialogue.

In this regard, in *Against and For CBT*, we stated:

> ... we of course have our own views about CBT, which are located toward the critical end of the debate – ranging between, on the one hand, the view that CBT as *one approach amongst many* within a rich plurality of different approaches is fine – particulary for those who cannot bear the thought of thoughts coming to them – though disastrous as *the* main approach for a whole society (DL); and on the other, to the fundamental questioning of the assumptive (modernist) worldview that underpins CBT's foundational theory and practice (RH). Yet, we would like to think that we are both also committed to embracing a questioning, deconstructive sensibility in our work – and not least toward our own cherished and taken-for-granted assumptions and prejudices; so in this book, we have actively welcomed an open and mutually respectful dialogue between some of CBT's most articulate critics, and several of CBT's many able theorists and practitioners. It will not serve either 'side' if each merely snipes at the other from deeply entrenched positions and defences, without each, at the very least, making a genuine effort to understand the other's position.
>
> (House and Loewenthal, 2008a: 7–8, original italics)

It is in this spirit, then, that we introduce the reader to the structure and content of what follows.

The book's outline and structure

In deciding how to structure and organize what follows, we wished to strike some kind of balance between a book that was sufficiently coherent such that common comparative themes could be traced and followed through across the different therapeutic modalities, on the one hand, and on the other, a book that left the contributors sufficient latitude such that the distinctive attributes characterizing their approach had the opportunity to be expressed. We certainly have some doubts about overly formulaic books, and we hope that the delicate aforementioned balance has been achieved, at least to a good enough extent.

While endeavouring to make our suggested contributors' chapter template as inclusive as possible, then, we also accept that there will exist very real 'paradigm incommensurabilities' between modalities, such that some approaches will place very different emphases on different headings, and with some even rejecting some of the suggested headings we laid out. Thus, for example, as Ian Parker states in his chapter, Lacanian analysts tend to eschew any idea of a 'model of the person'; they also carefully avoid any attempt to generalize about human experience on the basis of their modality approach; and they also 'refuse the lure of "objectivity" and "evidence" ' (Parker, Chapter 6).

While there is therefore some inevitable unevenness in the ways in which contributors have interpreted our suggested comparative framework between each modality and CBT, we were impressed by the extent to which there does exist a good enough coherence in the comparative themes addressed in each chapter. Moreover, we certainly see any diversity between chapters that does exist as a strength rather than a weakness, not least because it pays due honour to the importantly distinctive 'voice' that each modality holds and represents in the field.

While wishing to give our contributors at least some flexibility in fashioning their chapters in accordance with a broad organizing framework, then, we proposed to them the following generic questions, for each to draw on in fashioning their contributions:

1   The world view underpinning your approach; for example:
    - Model of the person
    - Can we generalize about human experience on the basis of your approach?
    - The possibility of objectivity?
    - Does your approach have a distinctive view on 'evidence'?
    - Does your approach have a view on, or an approach to, 'intersubjectivity'?
    - Where does your approach sit on the materialism/transpersonal continuum?

2   What are the advantages and disadvantages of your approach in relation to CBT?

3   What is your approach's view regarding the alleged 'cost-effectiveness' and evidence/research-based 'efficacy' of the CBT approach?

4   Your approach's conception of therapeutic change?

5   How well, if at all, does or can your approach cohere with so-called 'medical-model' thinking?

6   What place do the notions of 'happiness' and well-being hold in your approach?

7   How could or might your approach respond to the 'Layard thesis' that many hundreds of thousands of people are needing relief from psychological/emotional distress and unhappiness?

8   To what extent, if at all, would it be possible for your approach to align itself with, or even create a hybrid with, CBT?

Questions of 'evidence' and research

It is important to declare at the outset that we both tend to take a critical, postmodern perspective on questions of evidence and research in counselling and psychotherapy (e.g. Loewenthal, 2007; House, 2010) – at least some of which viewpoints are shared by our modality contributors; so in the service of balance and pluralism, we particularly welcome, in Chapters 10–12 inclusive, the responses of our eminent CBT contributors to these critical viewpoints. Thus, for us, the rise of such 'modernist' totems as 'outcome research', 'clinical *audit*' (House, 1996, 2008b; Power, 1997; Loewenthal, 2010), empirically supported/validated treatments, systematic reviews, randomized controlled trials (RCTs), the National Institute of Clinical Excellence (NICE) guidelines and 'evidence-based practice' has come to dominate much recent research in the psy field, and to become directly associated with CBT – certainly within National Health Service (NHS) contexts. With statutory regulation of the UK psy field via the Health Professions Council increasingly dominating psycho-politics, a new hegemonic language has arguably come to create a new 'regime of "scientific" truth' in the field (House, 2003), preoccupied as it is with notions like 'standards', 'quality assurance', 'audit' and 'cost-effectiveness' – a language that practitioners increasingly simply *have* to use (Lees and Freshwater, 2008) (or at least go through the motions), if they are to be taken seriously in the modern super audited NHS (Power, 1997). For many if not most psy practitioners, these are quite alien, 'managerialist' concepts that simply do not belong in anything approximating values-congruent practice (House, forthcoming). Moreover, these developments also represent a critical shift in the locus of power away from the professional autonomy of practitioners themselves, and towards managerial and administrative bureaucracy (Lees and Freshwater, 2008).

It is within this (for us) disturbing context that this new book should be located, with the editors forcefully arguing that practitioners should just as legitimately be viewed as researchers as are academics and service managers, and advocating a Feyerabendian line (Feyerabend, 1975) that no one ('scientific') paradigm should be assumed to be dominant or more valid than a multiplicity of others that are available. We agree with Lees and Freshwater (2008) in their wish to establish what they term an 'epistemology of practice', which they hope will help to redress a balance that has tipped far too much towards the kind of 'technical rationality' that drives the dominant positivistic paradigm.

So beyond the limitations of empiricist/positivistic science, how *do* we ascertain the advantage and disadvantage of various competing approaches? This question can be posed from both an individual as well as from a policy-maker's perspective – though if one agrees with the research that is being used, it would appear that there may well exist far greater variations *within* a given modality (under the influence of all kinds of confounding variables) than there are between them (e.g. Stiles et al., 2007).

There are also all manner of complex questions that arise around the issue of 'cost-effectiveness'. There can, for example, exist very different bases for assessing costs, and not least, in relation to the ontological assumptions one makes regarding what might constitute a 'cost'. Certainly, defining precisely what a 'cost' might consist in is far from being unproblematic, and perhaps inevitably entails the incursion of unquantifiable *values* into the discussion. There are also important social and political questions about who should pay for society's cultural embracing of the psy therapies, and related questions about the legitimate role (or otherwise) of the state in extensive psy provision and evaluation.

Further, from an epistemological and research perspective, what is currently regarded as the nature of evidence and research in our field, and is it sustainable epistemologically, when subjected to searching and deconstructive interrogation (e.g. Slife and Williams, 1995)? Questions of *ideology* inevitably rear their inconvenient head in any such discussion. There is arguably a need to consider other forms of evidence from research activity that may be more suited to the psychological therapies (Lees and Freshwater, 2008), yet contradict the current dominant evidence/research discourse. Interesting things have recently been happening in France, for example, where it seems to have been accepted politically that psychoanalysis should not be subject to prevailing, positivistic (Anglo-Saxon?) notions of 'evidence-based practice', but rather, should be allowed to develop in its own way (Snell, 2007).

Such a discussion inevitably leads into fundamental questions such as 'What is the nature of psychological therapeutic knowledge?' It would appear that we do not really know how such therapies work – or, indeed, what therapists are actually doing in their work (Spinelli, 1995; House, 2003). Furthermore, notwithstanding phenomenology's compelling arguments against theory (Heidegger; Merleau-Ponty; see House, 2008a), it is increasingly being questioned whether various competing theories might exist more to take the psychological therapists' minds off their problems than necessarily to be of any direct benefit to their clients/patients themselves (Craib, 1987; Heaton, 2000; Loewenthal, 2008).

A further interesting consideration is the compelling and potentially revolutionary proposition that there may be some *common factor (or factors)*, or so-called *non-specific factors* (Bergin, 1982; Orlinsky and Howard, 1986; Frank, 1989; Shepherd and Sartorius, 1989; Frank and Frank, 1991) that are helpful and therapeutically potent in *all* the psychotherapies, with 'the relationship' (however we might define the term – which in turn perhaps begs all the questions! . . .) being foremost among them (Beutler and Harwood, 2002). We must be very careful here, however, because if it *were* to be widely accepted that there are relational 'common factors' across all of psychotherapies that constitute the main factor in therapeutic change, then from a political-economic standpoint, what better rationale could there be for embracing the cheapest possible training in creating an 'army' of therapists across the land (and currently, of course, that would suggest CBT)? So there are many complex levels of argument that need to be teased out in all this, and we see this book as just the beginning of those crucial conversations.

There might also be a 'schoolist' influence here (Clarkson, 1998), in that most people involved in psychological therapeutic research aren't perhaps so much interested in research *per se*, as they are in proving that their particular approach is a winner (see, for example, *European Journal of Psychotherapy and Counselling*, 2009). The psy institutions are also increasingly running conferences partly in order to encourage the use of research, but also to show the government that they can talk the conventional 'evidence-based' language (Lees and Freshwater, 2008). At a more overtly political level, in the UK, the two largest professional organizations involved with counselling and psychotherapy are both prioritizing research within their organizations and within their training courses in an attempt to 'stay in the game', at least until the government reduces their influence through their plan for the Health Professions Council to take over statutory regulation of the various psychological therapies (Postle, 2007; Parker and Revelli, 2008), and the Department of Health, through a policy entitled 'Skills for Health', approves only those therapeutic approaches in the public services that are deemed 'evidence-based'. And there is also the funding of the government's new 'improving access to psychological therapies' (IAPT) programme, which avoids both these professional bodies – and which is, again, based on CBT.

We have written elsewhere about CBT's apparent ability to incorporate anything that research has proved to work (House and Loewenthal, 2008a, b). There are many other reasons for CBT's current popularity, of course, including the fact that it costs much less to train therapists, and that both therapists and, more importantly, society, can condone, and indeed encourage, the prevention of disturbing or unwanted thoughts coming to them (Loewenthal, 2008).

Cioffi (1998) has argued that it is, at least sometimes, a major category error to proceed as if a phenomenon calls for empirical enquiry when what is really wanted with regard to it is 'clarity as to the sources of our preoccupation and, where appropriate, untroubled contemplation of it' (Cioffi, 1998: 1). He claims that James Frazer, in his account of human sacrifices and other human rituals, makes this mistake, and so does Freud himself: that is, they try to explain, when what is needed is 'clarification' of the significance for us of these phenomena. Perhaps what Cioffi is arguing is less *against* empirical research, and more about the importance of questioning its appropriateness, and in particular with our difficulty with seeing when this is not what we need. Or put even more radically, perhaps we should begin the task of radically deconstructing the very modernist and previously unquestioned notion of 'research' itself (House,

2010). Perhaps we therefore need to re-examine questions on, for example, the ideology of 'outcome research' in terms of what we regard as ontology, epistemology and methodology (e.g. Gadamer, 1975), and the idea that research can be a tool of ideological dominance (Schostak and Schostak, 2007; Stainton Rogers, 2009). On this view, then, we urgently need to open up theories and methods, both in the psychological therapies and in the way we attempt to research them, not only epistemologically, ontologically and methodologically, but also *ideologically*, in order to enable that which we cannot and may not ever be able to measure (Klein, 2003), so that it can flourish.

Currently, a dominating positivistic research seems concerned not only with narrow notions of evidence, but with narrow notions of *method* as well. For one grave danger is that the use of research as an attempt at professionalization, and political game-playing in the name of professional survival, will in fact constrict the nature of the psychotherapeutic endeavour. We might also consider whether there is any possibility that we could work and genuinely search for 'truth' with all its associated and unavoidable problematics – to look at whether what we are doing is helpful and how we might improve – rather than attempting to prove that what we are doing 'works' in some 'instrumental-reason' sense. We need, perhaps, to return to the many devastating radical critiques of positivism with which the social sciences were awash in the 1970s and 1980s, and consider more the relationship between truth and method (Gadamer, 1975) – and, in particular, how the current dominant cultural ideology, as well as underlying *modality* ideologies, attempt to set up research methods that spuriously masquerade as 'independent' and objective.

With specific reference to research and CBT, it can be argued that the state, through its regulation of the psychological therapies, is expediently focusing on symptoms rather than on societal causes (Loewenthal, 2008). In the challenging world of Realpolitik, of course, it is appropriate to have some sympathy with policy-makers who wish to make the best use of their (our) resources; yet how can we do this if we do not really know how 'psychotherapy' even works? What seems to have happened is that the research methods that have come to the forefront are those that sustain this managerialist ideology in favouring those modalities which are the cheapest to provide (House, forthcoming), and which take our minds both individually, and as a society, off the causes of our problems (Loewenthal, 2008).

The age of happiness?

Previously in this chapter, we discussed our own positionings, as authors, in relation to the (clinical and cultural) 'CBT question'. We had originally decided to include the phrase 'the age of happiness' in our book title, but soon discovered that several of the book's potential contributors questioned this gesture towards the sociological. Nevertheless, some of our contributors have, in the event, very much responded to what might be termed our current cultural preoccupation with 'happiness'. We consider that it is not by accident that the meteoric rise of CBT, including the increasing difficulty of defining what 'CBT' actually is, together with related developments such as the UK government-sponsored IAPT programme, has occurred contemporaneously with happiness becoming a key consideration in our culture (cf. Pilgrim, 2008).

This culturally fashionable notion of 'happiness' is thus given particular emphasis by several of our contributors, especially John Heaton (Chapter 4) and Keith Tudor (Chapter 7). John Heaton takes us on an unusual philosophical journey in investigating just what 'happiness', as construed within a specifically therapeutic discourse, might (or might not) consist of. Certainly, the swathe of relatively uncritical literature on 'happiness', and the specifically CBT-relevant literature in this field (e.g. Seligman, 1991, 2005; Layard, 2005) has met with refreshing challenges from a number of quarters (e.g. Vernon, 2008; Wilson, 2008); and the jury is still very much out on whether it is even possible or appropriate for modern society to have, or to construct, a culturally accepted understanding of what 'happiness' consists of – and indeed, whether its pursuit is at all helpful or appropriate (Vernon, 2008). These are surely arguments and discussions to which the psychological therapies, from their privileged vantage point of working at relational depth with the human condition, can and should embrace (for a beginning, see Fisher, 2009); and the contributors to this book are making the first welcome steps in this regard.

Introduction to the modality chapters

The following chapters address these and other questions arising from a comparative (and, we hope and intend) constructive engagement of CBT with some of the other main therapy modalities. The particular modalities we have chosen for critical engagement with CBT are an attempt to provide as broad a range of perspectives as possible from across the richly diverse psy field, without sacrificing depth for the sake of quantity. We are certainly aware of many more modalities or approaches (some would say well over 400!), which we have had to leave out, due to considerations of space. We are also aware that there are significant differences *within* these modalities, including CBT, which we have also not been able to represent. There might even be a legitimate discussion to be had, for example, regarding the extent to which it is meaningful to speak of 'coherent enough' comparative responses to CBT emanating from relatively self-contained therapy modalities. However, we do think that whatever the particular focus or interest of the reader, the modalities that are represented in the book will, at the very least, stimulate thought, whatever the reader's way of working, or modality label under which they work. We are delighted to be so fortunate as to have commissioned contributors who are international leaders in their respective fields.

In Chapter 2, **Jeremy Holmes** looks, first, at psychoanalysis. Some psychoanalysts have been arguing that contemporary enthusiasm for CBT reflects our longing for swift, rationally based help for, or succour from, psychological suffering (e.g. Milton, 2008). For this reason among others, competition for funding is threatening the presence of psychoanalysis (and psychoanalytic therapy) in the public sector. Psychoanalysts have suggested that, compared to a psychoanalytic model, a cognitive model is commonsensical but less complex, with less potential explanatory and therapeutic power (ibid.). At the same time, it is acknowledged that cognitive and 'integrated' treatments have a key advantage, in that they are often less intrusive and emotionally challenging, and hence more acceptable to at least some patients. It appears that brief, time-limited psychotherapies of either a cognitive or psychoanalytic modality have a similar, modestly favourable outcome, and it is claimed that this may be based more on the 'dynamic' than on the 'cognitive' elements of therapeutic process. Psychoanalysts are also arguing, however, that formal outcome studies of the more widespread psychoanalytic psychotherapy, and also of psychoanalysis itself, suggest that these long and complex treatments are effective in ways that are claimed to be more comprehensive than CBT.

Anthony Ryle introduces cognitive-analytic therapy (CAT) in Chapter 3. CAT constitutes an attempt to take what is best and most efficacious from what seem, to many, to be very different, even incompatible therapy approaches – cognitive therapy and psychoanalytic therapy – and melding them into a new 'hybrid' approach that draws on what is most therapeutically potent from both traditions. Clients are encouraged to think about themselves and their relationships, and to formulate and continuously monitor, with the therapist's help, what is repeatedly going wrong in their lives. Classical CBT approaches may be used, while, at the same time, psychoanalytic transference phenomena are interpreted as they arise. CAT is founded on the observation that CBT-type approaches may be acceptable to some clients/patients in a way that a more 'purist' psychoanalytic therapy might not be, with clients avoiding areas that they may have good reasons to protect. Whether it is possible to combine all the advantages of the different techniques without losing therapeutic power is open to significant question, however. What position this hybrid approach takes in relation to CBT will be interesting and revealing.

John Heaton introduces an existential perspective on CBT in Chapter 4. From an existential therapeutic standpoint, the client is viewed as a totality, and not as the sum of constituent parts, as might sometimes be suggested in or implied by at least some versions of CBT. Existentialists have argued that the psychotherapist is someone who interrelates with the client as if she or he was someone existing in a life-world that is as personal and individual as the client him/herself. In comparison to CBT, an approach informed by existentialism does not seek to solve problems; rather, its aim, through a philosophical investigation of one's life, is to further one's understanding of, and insight into, the many paradoxes that are unavoidable by virtue of living a human life. In his chapter, Heaton takes a strongly philosophical approach, focusing in particular on the nature of what 'happiness' might (and might not) consist in (cf. Loewenthal, 2008, 2009).

Peter Stratton introduces family/systemic therapy in Chapter 5. This modality approach is often associated with postmodern ideas and philosophy, as well as with systems theory, and with constructivism, narrative approaches and social constructionism; and from these perspectives alone, it might be expected to have a very different take on the therapeutic process compared with what is arguably a quintessentially 'modernist' therapy modality, CBT. *Prime facie*, it might be important to consider the existence of quite distinct 'schools' of family therapy in deciding on how the field *as a unity* might relate to CBT praxis and its underpinning worldview.

In Chapter 6, **Ian Parker** brings us to Lacanian psychoanalysis. Lacanians commonly take a radical position, arguing that CBT is a therapy that tends to serve market-driven societies, where 'the self' is seen as an effort to get better, rather than having some kind of intrinsic truth. If the theory of the human mind that underpins CBT has got any value, Lacanians argue, it needs to be able to explain human cultural production. The key Lacanian concern is that CBT is seen as 'the cure' for everyone, as though changing thoughts alone will make everything better. On this view, the sense that each analysis is unique, as are we all as individuals, can sometimes get lost in the 'one answer fits all' mentality of much therapy the occurs under the 'CBT' label.

Keith Tudor then introduces us in Chapter 7 to a person-centred/Rogerian take on CBT. Some person-centred therapists have recently begun to question the politics surrounding CBT, and also its research bias, as well as the 'evidence' that favours CBT over other therapies, including person-centred therapy (PCT) itself (e.g. Tudor, 2008). As a counterpoint to the claimed dominance of CBT in the psychology of cognition and behaviour, Tudor argues that the behavioural and cognitive aspects of PCT are at least as fully articulated, theoretically speaking, as they are in CBT. On the basis of the research evidence of comparative studies and meta-analyses, PCT legitimately claims equivalence of therapeutic effectiveness; and in terms of client/patient choice, it also strongly advocates the promotion of equal opportunities for equal access to a choice of therapies in the public sector.

In Chapter 8 on analytical/Jungian therapy, **Ann Casement** looks at the differences between a Jungian analytical approach and CBT. The Jungian approach to psychodynamics has both similarities to, and crucial differences from, a more orthodox psychoanalytic approach, represented in Chapter 2 by Jeremy Holmes. While both approaches share an understanding of a 'dynamic unconscious' and its efficacy in human experience, they part company particularly with regard to the role of sexuality in human development, and also regarding the role of what Jungians term the 'collective unconscious', which is normally understood in a transpersonal way that is usually missing from both orthodox psychoanalysis, and from CBT. A Jungian 'model of the person' is clearly very different from one informed by CBT, and this difference alone will have major implications for the extent to which there is any commensurability between the two approaches, and the ways in which each makes sense of the therapy experience and process.

In the final modality chapter, **Stacey Millichamp** looks at psychosynthesis in Chapter 9. Psychosynthesis embraces an explicitly *transpersonal* approach to therapy and therapeutic change which, in its theoretical detail and world view, seems to bear very little resemblance to CBT. Although generalizations must be offered tentatively, CBT is commonly seen as a quintessentially 'modernist' therapy modality that tends to at the very least downplay, if not ignore completely, the spiritual or transpersonal dimension in human experience. A stark comparison between the theoretical foundations and metaphysical–cosmological assumptions of the two modalities illustrates the chasm that separates them, both in terms of 'model of the person' and approach to praxis.

In Chapters 10–12 inclusive, three internationally renowned CBT practitioners offer authoritative and penetrating commentaries on the eight preceding modality chapters. The first of these respondents is **Howard Paul** who, in his chapter, 'Critically engaged CBT' (Chapter 10), offers an interesting, historically informed perspective on the rise of CBT from its behavioural and cognitivist roots; and like the other respondents, he argues that there is an ongoing misunderstanding of the current nature of CBT. There is a refreshing openness in this chapter to discussing some of the theoretical problems and challenges that CBT has encountered – not least, the relative primacy of affect and thinking; and there is also a welcome willingness to look at what other, previously alien approaches (e.g. a dynamic one) might have to offer CBT. There is also a refreshing honesty about some of CBT's limitations (e.g. around what Paul terms 'the 70 per cent conundrum'), and also CBT's crucial embracing of the importance of 'the relational' which, it is admitted, had perhaps been unduly neglected in earlier manifestations of the approach. There is notably no attempt in this chapter, however, to engage with the broad *paradigmatic* issues that many of the book's contributors, including ourselves, have flagged up in the book. Yet the preponderance of medical-model terminology in Paul's chapter does indeed suggest that he is writing from a paradigmatic position or world view – albeit an unarticulated and largely unspecified one. Yet we were also delighted to see poetry being used in the CBT approach that Paul describes.

What comes across strongly, again, is the extent to which one can meaningfully still call an approach 'CBT' when, if one were to compare its procedural details and theoretical underpinnings with earlier approaches that have previously existed under the same label, the differences are such that one would be very hard pressed indeed to argue that they should come under the same modality label, and so be referred to by the same name!

In 'CBT, happiness and evidence-based practice', **Michael Proeve** argues in Chapter 11 that a least some of the pictures drawn of CBT in the modality chapters are 'overly mechanistic and coldly cognitive'. His approach is therefore to give an account of some of the changes that have occurred since the original CBT approaches were first articulated, focusing in particular on the role of cognition in CBT, the therapeutic relationship in CBT, and moves towards integration within CBT. Proeve then helpfully discusses those areas in which CBT is arguably less than fully developed; namely, in case formulation, personal experience by therapists, the question of meaning, responsiveness to research and CBT's adaptability. Proeve also considers the engagement of CBT with the 'happiness' agenda that several of the book's modality contributors address, including a discussion of evidence-based practice. There is also some emphasis on what Proeve terms CBT's 'eclecticism'; and he finishes his chapter with some reference to the so-called 'third-wave' behaviour therapies (BTs) like dialectical behaviour therapy (DBT) and (ACT) acceptance and commitment therapy, which Proeve sees as being 'related but separate from CBT'. He interestingly concludes that 'Useful approaches to the question of meaning may be borrowed from other approaches such as existential or analytic therapy' – which approach does at least suggest the possibility that there might be a wider meta-cultural movement occurring within the evolution of psychotherapy praxis towards integration, perhaps in the kind of direction that Arnold Lazarus was advocating back in the 1970s. It remains to be seen, however, just how impervious to such integrative developments the various schools of therapy will continue to be in the short and medium term.

As editors, we welcome **Windy Dryden**'s attempt, in Chapter 12, 'What can CBT therapists and other psychotherapists learn from one another?' to define CBT, and particularly his robust challenges both to the authors of the modality chapters and to some of the editorial directions taken, including the effects these may have had on the coherence of this book. (It may well be that coming from our more critically 'postmodern' perspective, the criterion of consistency is of less importance to us than it is to Dryden.) Without, we hope, being unduly defensive, we respond to what we see as Dryden's main challenges in Chapter 13 (**Loewenthal and House**) when we attempt to draw out some central issues for this important debate.

Some concluding remarks

In this discursive editorial introduction, we have not touched on a number of issues that we have asked our contributors to address – for example: how do we begin to go about ascertaining (what might be the very subtle – Atkinson and

Claxton, 2000) advantages and disadvantages of various modality approaches? What do the various modalities claim on the basis of psychotherapeutic change as seen from their particular modality vantage-points? What position do the various modalities take in relation to 'the medical model'? How do notions of 'happiness' vary across the modalities? – the answer to which question has obvious and crucial implications for the nature of the 'therapeutic offer' that each modality makes. What is the best way of meeting the needs of the rapidly increasing populations who, it is claimed, are suffering inappropriate unhappiness and emotional distress in 'late modernity'? (Richard Layard's [2005] work is particularly interesting and important here in terms of the use of population-based medicine, thus raising questions about state intervention, and whether the problem being addressed is not more sociological than it is psychological and clinical.) Should psychotherapy be seen more as a means of helping people's adjustment to the prevailing societal status quo, or as an intrinsically subversive, counter-cultural praxis, which seeks to take forward human consciousness on individual, interrelational and cultural levels? How can we determine whether other modality approaches should consider aligning themselves with CBT in some way?

We are not by any means assuming, finally, that the balance of argument in all this is a simplistic calculus that assumes 'CBT = naïve; existential etc. = profound', as there are a number of new initiatives within the broad field of CBT that are taking CBT practice far beyond the previous, highly limited view that it is merely about 'changing faulty or dysfunctional thinking' (see, for example, Crane, 2008; Gilbert and Leahey, 2009; Rhodes and Jakes, 2009; Gilbert, 2010). Though we should also note in passing that we are then left, perhaps, with a growing sense that it may be increasingly difficult, if not impossible, to speak of 'CBT' as a remotely conformable, internally consistent category or therapeutic modality (House and Loewenthal, 2008a, b) – a key issue that at least some of our contributors address in what follows.

We hope that the following chapters will serve to open up an essential and relatively undefensive, post-schoolist conversation across the psy field about CBT, and its advantages and discontents, which we have already started in House and Loewenthal (2008a); and we invite the reader to take a full part in what promises to be one of the most important conversations in the psy field for some years to come.

References

Atkinson, T. and Claxton, G. (eds) (2000) *The Intuitive Practitioner: On the Value of Not Always Knowing What One Is Doing*, Buckingham: Open University Press.

Bergin, A.E. (1982) *Comment on Converging Themes in Psychotherapy*, New York: Springer.

Beutler, L.E. and Harwood, T.M. (2002) 'What is and can be attributed to the therapeutic relationship?', *Journal of Contemporary Psychotherapy*, 32: 25–33.

Chang, R. (1998) *Incommensurability, Incomparability and Practical Reason*, Cambridge, MA: Harvard University Press.

Cioffi, F. (1998) *Wittgenstein on Freud and Frazer*, Cambridge: Cambridge University Press.

Clark, J. (ed.) (2002) *Freelance Counselling and Psychotherapy: Competition and Collaboration*, London: Routledge.

Clarkson, P. (1998) 'Beyond schoolism', *Changes*, 16(1): 1–11.

Craib, I. (1987) 'The psychodynamics of theory', *Free Associations*, 10: 32–56.

Crane, R. (2008) *Mindfulness-based Cognitive Therapy*, London: Routledge.

Dryden, W. and Feltham, C. (eds) (1992) *Psychotherapy and Its Discontents*, Milton Keynes: Open University Press.

European Journal of Psychotherapy and Counselling (EJPC) (2009) Special issue on the allegiance effect, issue 11(4).

Feltham, C. (ed.) (1999) *Controversies in Psychotherapy and Counselling*, London: Sage Publications.

Feyerabend, P.K. (1975) *Against Method: Outline of an Anarchistic Theory of Knowledge*, London: New Left Books.

Fisher, S. (2009) 'Is it moral to offer happiness?', *Therapy Today*, February. Available online at www.therapytoday.net/index.php?magId=24&action=viewArticle&articleId=65 (accessed 1 March 2009).

Frank, J.D. (1989) 'Non-specific aspects of treatment: the view of a psychotherapist' in M. Shepherd and N. Sartorius (eds), *Non-specific Aspects of Treatment*, Toronto: Hans Huber Publishers, pp. 95–114.

Frank, J.D. and Frank, J.B. (1991) *Persuasion and Healing: A Comparative Study of Psychotherapy*, 3rd edn, Baltimore, MD: Johns Hopkins University Press.

Gadamer, H.-G. (1975) *Truth and Method*, New York: Continuum Publishing.

Gilbert, P. (2010) *Compassion-focused Therapy: Distinctive Features*, London: Routledge.

Gilbert, P. and Leahey, R. (eds) (2009) *The Therapeutic Relationship in the Cognitive Behavioral Psychotherapies*, London: Routledge.

Hart, T., Nelson, P. and Puhakka, K. (eds) (2000) *Transpersonal Knowing: Exploring the Horizon of Consciousness*, Albany, NY: State University of New York Press.

Heaton, J. (2000) *Wittgenstein and Psychoanalysis*, Cambridge: Icon Books.

House, R. (1996) ' "Audit-mindedness" in counselling: some underlying dynamics', *British Journal of Guidance and Counselling*, 24(2): 277–83.

House, R. (2003) *Therapy Beyond Modernity: Deconstructing and Transcending Profession-centred Therapy*, London: Karnac Books.

House, R. (2008a) 'Therapy's modernist "regime of truth": from scientistic "theory-mindedness" towards the subtle and the mysterious', *Philosophical Practice*, 3(3): 343–52.

House, R. (2008b) 'The dance of psychotherapy and politics', *Psychotherapy and Politics International*, 6(2): 98–109.

House, R. (2010) ' "Psy" research beyond late-modernity: towards praxis-congruent research', *Psychotherapy and Politics International*, 8(1): 13–20.

House, R. and Loewenthal, D. (eds) (2008a) *Against and For CBT: Towards a Constructive Dialogue?*, Ross-on-Wye: PCCS Books.

House, R. and Loewenthal, D. (2008b) 'CBT in question' (editorial Introduction), *European Journal of Psychotherapy and Counselling*, 10(3): 181–6.

Klein, J. (2003) *Jacob's Ladder: Essays on Experiences of the Ineffable in the Context of Contemporary Psychotherapy*, London: Karnac Books.

Kuhn, T. (1962) *The Structure of Scientific Revolutions*, Chicago, IL: Chicago University Press.

Layard, R. (2005) *Happiness: Lessons from a New Science*, London: Penguin Books.

Lees, J. and Freshwater, D. (eds) (2008) *Practitioner-based Research: Power, Discourse and Transformation*, London: Karnac Books.

Loewenthal, D. (1996) 'The postmodern counsellor: some implications for practice, theory, research and professionalism', *Counselling Psychology Quarterly*, 9(4): 373–81.

Loewenthal, D. (2007) *Case Studies in Relational Research: Qualitative Research Methods in Counselling and Psychotherapy*, Basingstoke: Palgrave Macmillan.

Loewenthal, D. (2008) 'Post-existentialism as a reaction to CBT?', in R. House and D. Loewenthal (eds), *Against and For CBT: Towards a Constructive Dialogue?*, Ross-on-Wye: PCCS Books, pp. 146–55.

Loewenthal, D. (2009) 'Childhood, wellbeing and a therapeutic ethos', in R. House and D. Loewenthal (eds), *Childhood, Wellbeing and a Therapeutic Ethos*, London: Karnac Books, pp. 19–36.

Loewenthal, D. (2010) 'Audit, audit culture and *therapeia*: some implications for wellbeing with particular reference to children' in C. Moutsou and L. King (eds), *Audit Cultures: A Critical Look at 'Evidence-based Practice' in Psychotherapy and Beyond*, London: Karnac Books.

Loewenthal, D. and Snell, R. (2003) *Post-modernism for Psychotherapists*, London: Sage Publications.

Margitics, F. (2009) *Handbook of New Spiritual Consciousness: Theory and Research*, Hauppauge, NY: Nova Science Publishers.

Milton, J. (2008) 'Psychoanalysis and cognitive behaviour therapy: rival paradigms or common ground?' in R. House and D. Loewenthal (eds), *Against and For CBT: Towards a Constructive Dialogue?*, Ross-on-Wye: PCCS Books, pp. 101–17.

Orlinsky, D.E. and Howard, K.I. (1987) 'A genetic model of psychotherapy', *Journal of Integratic and Eclectic Psychotherapy*, 6: 6–27.

Padesky, C.A. and Greenberger, D. (1995) *Mind Over Mood: Change How You Feel By Changing the Way You Think*, New York: Guilford Press.

Parker, I. and Revelli, S. (eds) (2008) *Psychoanalytic Practice and State Regulation*, London: Karnac Books.

Pilgrim, D. (2008) 'Reading "happiness": CBT and the Layard thesis', in R. House and D. Loewenthal (eds), *Against and For CBT: Towards a Constructive Dialogue?*, Ross-on-Wye: PCCS Books, pp. 256–68.

Polanyi, M. (1966) *The Tacit Dimension*, New York: Doubleday.

Postle, D. (2007) *Regulating the Psychological Therapies: From Taxonomy to Taxidermy*, Ross-on-Wye: PCCS Books.

Power, M. (1997) *The Audit Society: Rituals of Verification*, Oxford: Oxford University Press.

Puhakka, K., Nelson, P.L. and Hart, T. (1997) *Spiritual Knowing: Alternative Epistemic Perspectives*, Carrollton, TX: State University of West Georgia.

Rhodes, J. and Jakes, S. (2009) *Narrative CBT for Psychosis*, London: Routledge.

Schostak, J. and J. (2007) *Radical Research: Designing, Developing and Writing Research to Make a Difference*, London: Routledge.

Seligman, M.E.P. (1991) *Learned Optimism: How to Change Your Mind and Your Life*, New York: A.A. Knopf.

Seligman, M.E.P. (2005) *Authentic Happiness*, London: Nicholas Brealey.

Shepherd, M. and N. Sartorius (eds) (1989) *Non-specific Aspects of Treatment*, Toronto: Hans Huber Publishers.

Slife, B.D. and Williams, R.N. (1995) *What's Behind the Research?: Discovering Hidden Assumptions in the Behavioral Sciences*, London: Sage Publications.

Snell, R. (2007) 'L'anti livre noir de la psychoanalyse', *European Journal of Psychotherapy and Counselling*, 9(2): 231–9.

Spinelli, E. (1995) 'Do therapists know what they're doing?', in I. James and S. Palmer (eds), *Professional Therapeutic Titles: Myths and Realities*, Leicester: British Psychological Society, Division of Counselling Psychology, Occasional Paper 2, pp. 55–61.

Stainton Rogers, W. (2009) 'Research methodology', in D. Fox, I. Prilleltensky and S. Austin (eds) *Critical Psychology: An Introduction*, 2nd edn, London: Sage Publications, pp. 335–54.

Stiles, W.B., Barkham, M., Mellor-Clark, J. and Connell, J. (2007) 'Routine psychological treatment and the Dodo verdict: a rejoinder to Clark et al.', *Psychological Medicine*, 38(6): 905–10.

Tudor, K. (2008) 'Person-centred therapy, a cognitive behaviour therapy' in R. House and D. Loewenthal (eds), *Against and For CBT: Towards a Constructive Dialogue?*, Ross-on-Wye: PCCS Books, pp. 118–36.

Vernon, M. (2008) *Wellbeing*, Stocksfield: Acumen.

Wilson, E.G. (2008) *Against Happiness: In Praise of Melancholy*, New York: Sarah Crichton Books.

2 Psychoanalysis and CBT
Confluence of theory, watershed in practice?

Jeremy Holmes

Prelude

Let us start well away from the consulting room, in what is rather quaintly known as the 'real world'. It is my local sub-post office, in the middle of a notoriously rough housing estate. Ahead of me in the queue are: a very young-looking father with a baby in a pushchair, and a couple in their early 40s, scantily clad, hair dyed respectively blond (male) and shocking pink (female), both with an opposite-sex moniker tattooed on their necks, presumably of each other.

'Cheer up darling it may never 'appen; got the 'ump or something?' shouts the man to a rather glum-looking shop-girl across the aisle. 'Nothing to be cheerful about' comes the reply. At this rebuff, his female partner comments, sotto voce: 'She's *breathing*, ain't she; that's all the 'appiness you need'. She turns to the pushchair baby: 'what lovely long hair; mine were all bald as coots. Oooh, but I do prefer pink ones to blue ones. Far less trouble'. 'No they ain't', retorts her man, 'you don't 'ave to say to them in a few years time – no you *can't* sleep with 'im!'.

This woman seems to be an enlightened being. She knows that for contentment one need look no further than an in-breath, offering the insights of mindfulness-based CBT to the depressed shop-worker, the 'patient' in this example of folk therapy. Meanwhile, there is an inescapable sexual ambiance generated by the oedipal confluence of man, woman and baby – the latter's infantile sexuality projected forward into her adolescence, the physicality and mock-aggressive banter of the couple suggesting somehow that bed is not far from their minds.

While none of the characters in this mini-drama would seem ideal candidates for therapy, it would be hard to deconstruct it without the help of *both* Beck and Freud. The girl needs immediate help with her misery. Focusing on the positive, while detaching herself from bad feelings through breathing meditation, may well be the first aid she requires. But ultimately, there will likely be 'characterological' sexual/oedipal ramifications to her unhappiness – she hasn't got a boyfriend and wants one; she's got one but wants a different one; she is pregnant and wishes she wasn't, or isn't and wishes she was.

Theoretical non-incompatibility

My aim here is to 'negate the negation' that typifies cognitive behaviour therapy's (CBT) and psychoanalysis' view of one another. Both are adept at 'othering', straw-man debating points, special pleading, polemics and tendentiousness (see, for example, Samuels and Veale, 2009).

Psychoanalysts tend to dismiss CBT as a superficial, quick-fix, 'fast-food' therapy which, while it may temporarily remove symptoms, is often followed by relapse, leaving fundamental dysfunctional character structures unchanged. The unconscious and its manifestations in the transference – the key province of psychoanalytic work – is ignored, glossed over, denied, or seen as irrelevant.

Equally, from a CBT perspective, the following is typical:

> The scandal is that GPs can't access CBT so they continue to send patients for outmoded treatments that don't work. When a severely health-anxious patient is told to 'lie on a couch and tell me about your relationship with your mother', he doesn't see the relevance and he drops out.
>
> (Salkovskis quoted in Brearley, 2007: 20).

Implicit in this slur is the following: psychoanalysis (a) is trapped in a fossilized past; (b) is ineffective; (c) lacks a collaborative culture; (d) patients are made to do things that don't make sense to them; (e) has high drop-out rates; (f) practitioners are slightly mad and mother-preoccupied; and (g) is generally absurd and contemptible.

Conversely, psychoanalysts characterize CBT practitioners as therapeutic terriers, oblivious to personal and temporal boundaries, insensitive to client disappointment and hostility, obsessed with questionable psychiatric diagnoses, form-filling, homework and handouts at the expense of spontaneity and emotional expression, and blind to the interpersonal difficulties of their clients, especially those that arise in the therapeutic relationship itself.

Despite all this, a good argument can be made for a degree of theoretical compatibility between the two approaches (cf. Power, 2002). As Kuyken et al. (2005: 114) put it: depression is characterized by 'maladaptive beliefs about the self, the external world and the future, shaped through formative developmental experiences'. Common ground with psychoanalysis here includes: (a) targeting mental phenomena of which the client is at presentation unaware; (b) focusing on the combination of affect, wish and belief that typify a people's fundamental view of themselves and others, and the relationship between them; (c) the avoidance of psychic pain by defence mechanisms; and (d) the anachronistic persistence of such defences into adult life.

Through diary-keeping and pedagogic instruction, CBT helps its clients identify the 'automatic thoughts' that underpin depressive affect – 'I am useless', 'nobody would want to be friends with someone like me', 'I'll never get better'. Until they are elicited in this way these thoughts remain latent, out of conscious awareness. Psychoanalysis uses different means to a similar end: dream analysis, free association and transference analysis. The distinction between preconscious and unconscious thoughts can be used to mark a radical divide between the two modalities, but in clinical practice is often of little significance. Similarly, CBT's 'maladaptiveness' of depressive thinking is consistent with psychoanalytic defence analysis, in which patterns of self-protection appropriate to childhood persist into adult life to the subject's disadvantage.

CBT picks out typical predetermined patterns of inappropriate thinking in depression: overgeneralization, catastrophizing, black-and-white thinking, and so on. Each of these is potentially translatable into psychoanalytic meta-psychology. Overgeneralization illustrates Matte-Blancoian (1975) symmetrization, the conflation of differences typical of the unconscious thought processes. Catastrophizing arises when a single setback is taken as a signal of general disarray. It can be seen as a failure of Bionic 'K' – the lack of processing of beta into alpha elements due to the absence of an internalized 'thinking breast' (Bion, 1967). CBT protocols and excercises aim to instil this skill in the depression sufferer. Similarly, black-and-white thinking exemplifies pre-depressive-position defensive splitting of the world into good and bad, in order to protect the former from the aggressive aspects of the latter.

From an etiological perspective, the Kuyken et al. quote shows that CBT readily acknowledges the childhood origins of depressive psychological difficulties at a theoretical level even if, in practice, less emphasis is placed on the past than on correcting current maladaptive tendencies. Contemporary psychoanalysis is more concerned with the 'present transference' (Sandler, 1976) than reconstructions of a putative past. Linehan's (1993) dialectical behaviour therapy (DBT) model of borderline personality disorder (BPD) sees 'invalidation' in childhood as the key to pathology in adult life. Psychoanalysis may have a more detailed and nuanced theoretical account of infancy and childhood, and work with the ways in which subjects of invalidation, trauma or neglect may at an unconscious level contribute to their own victimhood, but it would be hard to find points of major theoretical disagreement here.

CBT arose in part from a dissatisfaction with certain aspects of psychoanalysis, the dominant paradigm in US psychiatry and psychology in the 1950s and 1960s: the cost and length of time needed to complete an analysis, lack of diagnostic precision, absence of scientific evaluation and overvaluation of the unconscious as opposed to the conscious mind. However, the other main strand in the emergence of CBT flowed from the 'cognitive revolution' in which theoretical psychology began to acknowledge the limitations of stimulus-response psychology and to recognize an inner world characterized by mental models and maps (Westen, 2005).

In a typical acronymic fashion, CBT focuses on these in terms of 'expectations, assumptions, rules, schemata' (EARS). Young's (1990) 'schema-focussed therapy' develops the idea of early maladaptive schemata (EMS); that is, unconditional beliefs about the self, and the self in relation to others, which form the core of a person's identity. These representations are a precipitate of early experience and the growing child's ways of coping.

One difference between the two disciplines is CBT's focus on the subject's relation to him or herself, while contemporary psychoanalysis, especially in its interpersonal, relational and intersubjective variants, homes in on the self in relation to others. However, Safran and Muran (2000) move CBT's intrapsychic tack in an interpersonal direction, building on schema-focused approaches by suggesting that EMSs influence behaviour in such a way that a person's environment is shaped to respond in ways that confirm core schemata. Typical borderline sufferers may have EMS suggesting they are worthless and bound to be rejected by those with whom they try to establish emotional contact. Their unpredictable behaviour in intimate relationships then provokes and confirms the very rejectingness that lies at the core of this self-belief.

EMS seems to resonate easily with, and is no doubt in part derived from, the notion of the internal world as conceptualized by the object relations school, a fundamental constellation of self in relation to significant others, instantiated in infancy and childhood and often persisting into adult life, with maladaptive consequences. There are, of course, important differences in emphasis. Psychoanalysis tends to emphasize the sexual and ethical (in the sense of splitting the 'good' and bad' aspects of the self and other) aspects of core beliefs and the representational world, rather than staying with the beliefs and assumptions themselves. But schema-focused and object-relational formulations map one to the other without too much awkwardness.

There is an ever-shifting dialectic between experience and the language and narrative structures used to represent it. The stories people tell about themselves are 'representations of representations' in that they are attempts to encapsulate the mental structures that underlie them. The latter are 'unconscious', either in the descriptive sense of being out of awareness until activated through therapeutic dialogue, or in the formal psychoanalytic sense of being repressed or split off in order to avoid the mental pain they embody. In either case, a developmental perspective suggests that these self-narratives derive from representations of actual relational events (cf. Stern, 1985); representation of interactions that have been generalized (RIGs). The 'dialectic' refers to the way in which one's view of oneself determines experience, both literally (if one is expecting to be abused one is more likely to 'choose' a potentially abusive partner), and in the narrative sense that the sense one makes of those experiences will be accommodated to fit pre-existing meaning structures ('the fact that men exploit me proves how useless I am').

Schema-focused approaches concentrate on the *consequences* of this dialectic, while psychoanalysis on its *antecedents*. A CBT therapist would try to elicit the dysfunctional guiding principles/propositions by which a person lives – 'uselessness', passivity, unwantedness, and so on – and then help her or him to find ways to generate experiences that disconfirm them, including implictly the therapeutic relationship itself, which honours the intrinsic value of a human life, and of a person's right to attention and respect. The main drive would be towards examining the client's current situation and relational constellations, and trying rather directly to change them.

A psychoanalytic approach would focus more on the abusive events themselves, and their possible affective meanings for a child beset with external trauma and inescapable developmental priorities of establishing a gender identity, a sense of efficacy and ways of dealing with 'normal' oedipal envy and rivalry. The mutative agenda here entails attending to 'mentalizing' (Holmes, 2010) these thematic repetitions/manifestations in the transference. Both CBT and psychoanalysis adhere to Freud's dictum that 'effigies cannot be destroyed in absentia', but in CBT's case the transcendence of these false Gods take place outside the consulting room, through 'experiments', while psychoanalytically they are brought to life and then reworked in the therapeutic relationship.

'Mechanism of action'

CBT's theory of action rests on two planks: (1) cognitive change, replacing dysfunctional assumptions with more appropriate and realistic ones, and (2) exposure, in imagination, and/or vivo, to phobically avoided thoughts and affects. Translated into psychoanalytic terminology, the former corresponds to Freud's dictum of 'where id there ego shall be', or the acquisition of mentalizing skills or 'alpha function', via interpersonal exploration in therapy sessions (cf. Holmes, 2010); the latter with the benign presence of the therapist providing a secure enough base for the patient to acknowledge and face disavowed feelings.

These ideas are at present no more than speculations. When it comes to testing them in the laboratory of psychotherapy research, the results tend to be confusing and contradictory. A core CBT mantra holds that changes in cognition result in changes in mood in depression. However, comparing outcomes in people with depression receiving CBT or pharmacotherapy, Imber et al. (1990) found that in both groups cognitive change followed rather than initiated mood changes. It is entirely possible that 'non-specific factors' in CBT – therapist attention, the attachment relationship, restoration of hope, and attribution of meaning whatever that meaning may be – are what produces change, not the supposedly 'active ingredient' of cognitive restructuring.

Similarly, great stress is placed on the role of accurate transference inter-pretations as a mutative element in psychoanalysis. Yet a much quoted study found that the more the interpretations, the worse the outcome of psycho-analytic psychotherapy (Piper et al., 1999). Recently, researchers looking at the role of interpretation versus support in psychoanalysis found in one instance that transference interpretations made things worse for people with low quality of object relations (QOR) and better for the less disturbed (Piper et al., 1999), while another found they were associated with sustained better out-comes in low QOR clients (Hoglend et al., 2008). Capturing the subtlety of therapeutic interaction, both 'horizontally' in the minutiae of a session and 'longitudinally' in the overall strategy of a therapy, remains a huge research challenge (cf. Kächele et al., 2008).

To make a rather grandiose comparison, psychotherapy currently finds itself in a place comparable to Darwinian evolutionary theory in the 1870s. Evolution by natural selection was an established fact, but, pre-Mendel, pre-Watson and Crick, its mechanism of action remained obscure. Similarly, we know that psychotherapy 'works', but how change comes about is still unclear. Subtle dynamic models, encompassing both unconscious and con-scious ingredients in the therapeutic relationship, are needed to tease out the mutative elements in psychotherapy. Disinterestedness, a genuine spirit of scientific enquiry, openness to 'soft' as well as hard data, not to mention generous doses of research funding, are preconditions for advancing the field, all of which currently are in short supply.

Technical non-compatibility

Despite the lack of serious theoretical dissonance between the two disciplines, when it comes to practice CBT and psychoanalysis could hardly be more divergent, although as we shall see, recent developments mean that even this must be somewhat qualified.

One striking difference is the ratio between meta-psychology and tech-nique. CBT is mainly concerned with clinical practice; it is relatively unconcerned about developing itself as a general theory of the mind. By contrast, there is a distinct theory–practice gap in psychoanalysis. As Fonagy (2006: 26) elegantly puts it, 'clinical technique is not entailed in psycho-analytic theory'. The edifice of psychoanalytic theory is vast and diverse. Detailed accounts of what to do and when in psychoanalytic sessions are, with notable exceptions (e.g. Gabbard, 2004) relatively rare (but see Roth and Lemma, 2008).

Whatever the theoretical overlaps, CBT is keen to differentiate itself from psychoanalysis as a practice. It claims to be transparent, 'problem-focused', 'collaborative' and 'scientific'. It relies on 'experiments', imparting 'portable skills', setting homework tasks, time-limitedness and close evaluation of outcomes. However, although the proverbial prurient fly on the wall in the consulting room of a psychoanalyst and CBT practitioner would undoubtedly notice differences, these might not be as marked as either side would claim.

The opening and closing moves of sessions would likely be divergent; the psychoanalyst waiting for clients to 'bring' thoughts and feelings into the session, while the CBT therapist might ask what sort of week they had had. The implicit 'job' of the psychoanalytic client is to attend to his or her inner life, to freely associate and to bring dreams for consideration in sessions. The more directive CBT therapist, in collaboration with the client, typically sets an agenda for their hour together, unlike the psychoanalyst, who is alert to spontaneously emerging themes.

The middle sections of both sessions might be less dissimilar, with the therapist listening to clients' account of some episode in their week, and/or its connections with past difficulties. Meaning-seeking interventions might also be comparable. Psychoanalysts undoubtedly make 'cognitive' comments, for example, about the ways in which people's negative views of themselves become self-fulfilling prophesies, paying particular attention to how this plays itself out in the transference. Equally, CBT therapists allow free-wheeling periods in sessions characterized by listening and speculation about the client's affective states.

There is a tension in any therapy between spontaneity and formulation. Meaning-making is central to any therapeutic activity (Holmes, 2010). Therapists need a guiding formulation that will help the client understand an individual's difficulties. But too rigid adherence to a formulation inhibits the emergence of the uniqueness of an individual's experience. CBT therapists tend to work to nomothetic, rather general, formulations about the origins of depression, while psychoanalysts, schooled in 'Keats' 'negative capability' (i.e. tolerance of uncertainty), probe for the idiographic specificity of a person's life trajectory. Good therapists in either camp probably manage to strike a balance between these two poles.

As sessions draw to a close, differences once more surface. CBT therapists by contrast see inter-session work as an essential counterpoint to therapy itself, devising homework tasks, 'experiments' in which the client tests more positive assumptions about themselves, and 'bibliotherapy' in the form of handouts and reading assignments.

Psychoanalysts feel under no pressure to produce a well-rounded ending: 'let's come back to that next week', or simply 'it's time to stop now' might be their rubric. It is hoped that the mutative aspects of therapy, including but not exclusively reliant on, accurate interpretation, have penetrated defences into the unconscious life of the client; this in turn leading to a more positive view of the self, acceptance of pain and loss, empowerment and efficacy, and, armed with new-found skills of mentalizing (Holmes, 2010), to interpersonal relationships more deftly handled. Psychoanalysis takes the inherently para-doxical nature of the unconscious and its workings into account: the more one tries directly to change things, the more resistance this may elicit: change may occur when one least expects it, in moments of mutual discovery, brought forth by the intimacy of one mind trying to understand another. CBT tends towards a more common-sense attempt to find 'solutions' to 'problems'.

Apart from the 'non-specific factors' of an attachment relationship and meaning-making in both therapies, recent developments suggest another area of partial convergence. Mindfulness-based CBT (MBCBT) (see Kuyken et al., 2005) was devised in the light of the finding that, despite the short-lived help-fulness of conventional CBT, both chronicity and relapse in severe depression are common. In MBCBT clients are encouraged, with the help of 'mindfulness' methods derived from Buddhism, to detach themselves from their depressive thoughts, to achieve affect regulation through breathing and quiet concentra-tion, and to see negative ideations, not as real but as 'just thoughts'. In a parallel development, conventional psychoanalysis has been shown to be rela-tively ineffective in severe BPD (Fonagy and Bateman, 2006). Bateman and Fonagy's (2004) modified psychoanalysis, mentalization-based therapy (MBT), addresses the difficulty that such clients have in differentiating their thoughts about the world from the world as it is. This is especially so when people are highly aroused (as people with BPD tend easily to become when stressed); their psychoanalytically informed 'partial hospitalization' therapy package treatment includes exercises not unlike those used in MBCBT.

This illustrates theoretical overlap at a much more therapy-near level. MBT, psychoanalytically derived, uses here-and-now transferential events in relation to the therapist and fellow group members as exemplars in which new learning takes place; skill acquisition arises in the course of 'living-learning'. CBT, less opportunistic, and more protocol-driven, teaches its clients to follow a meditation routine. Nevertheless, the connections are clear, and probably merit further collaborative work.

Evidence of evidence

The success of CBT as the first choice therapy for a wide range of disorders rests on its having from its inception in the mid-1970s successfully assimilated into talking therapies the blinded randomized controlled trial (RCT), the stan-dard medical yardstick for effective treatments. Psychoanalysis has belatedly picked up the challenge and is beginning to show that it too can compete on equal terms in the world of evidence-based therapies (e.g. Leischsenring and Rayburg, 2008).

It is beyond the scope of this chapter, and the competence of its author, to summarize and evaluate 30 years of complex and often contradictory psychotherapy research findings. Indeed, arguably the field still awaits an individual with the magisterial authority and Olympian detachment needed to do so. I shall instead briefly summarize the claims made on CBT's behalf as the definitive psychological therapy for most psychiatric disorders, and then present some of the arguments used in rebuttal of these claims by psychoanalysts, and in support of their own position.

A good starting point is the recent 'meta-meta analysis' offered in their 2006 article by Chapman et al. (Butler et al., 2006). This review summarizes the current literature on treatment outcomes of CBT for a wide range of psychiatric disorders. Based on '16 methodologically rigorous meta-analyses', they found large effect sizes for CBT in unipolar depression, generalized anxiety disorder, panic disorder with or without agoraphobia, social phobia, post-traumatic stress disorder (PTSD), and childhood depressive and anxiety disorders. Effect sizes for marital distress, anger, childhood somatic disorders and chronic pain were in the moderate range. CBT was somewhat superior to antidepressants in the treatment of adult depression, and showed, they claim, large but uncontrolled effect sizes in bulimia nervosa and schizophrenia.

This sort of data is routinely cited when advancing the merits of CBT, whether clinically, or when applying for training and treatment funds. It has forced psychodynamically minded clinicians to rethink their position and find ways to defend their own shrinking corner.

There is in fact now a number of RCTs convincingly demonstrating psychoanalytic psychotherapy's effectiveness in a wide range of conditions. These include mild to moderate depression (Shapiro et al., 1994), personality disorders (Bateman and Fonagy, 2004, 2008; Abbass et al., 2008), panic disorder (Milrod et al., 2007), somatization disorders (Guthrie et al., 1991) and eating disorders (Dare et al., 2001). In addition, cost–benefit studies (Gabbard et al., 1997) show that psychoanalytic psychotherapy, despite being resource-intensive compared with pharmacotherapy and CBT, given 'cost off-setting' – less time spent in or visiting hospital, fewer medications consumed, reduced time spent on benefits, greater capacity for paid employment and therefore more tax revenue – more than pays for itself.

However, the evidence for psychoanalytic psychotherapy is thus far generally less impressive than for its rival: compared with CBT, smaller numbers of trials, based on fewer patients, less replicated. Psychoanalysts tend to respond to this (Gabbard, 2005) in various ways. First, psychoanalytic psychotherapy is inherently less easy to research than other forms of treatment. Psychoanalytic therapies tend to be long term, so generating adequate research funding is problematic. In addition, the aims of psychoanalytic psychotherapy go beyond symptom relief to structural changes in personality, a deeper project, which is inherently more complex, time-consuming and expensive to study (Milton, 2001).

The argument runs that, given sufficient time and resources, psycho-analytic psychotherapy can and will be shown to be as effective as CBT, if not more so, and that its unique indications are gradually emerging: absence of evidence does not equate to evidence of absence (Holmes, 2001). Leischsenring and Rabung's (2008) meta-analysis of long-term (defined as more than one year) psychoanalytic psychotherapy, (LTPP), supports this. Compared with short-term psychoanalytic psychotherapy (STPP) – in which relapse post-therapy is common in all modalities of therapy (Parry et al., 2005) – LTPP patients showed effect sizes of around 1.8 (a very respectable figure, higher than the average antidepressant) for target problems, overall effectiveness and personality functioning. Although only around 10 studies met their stringent criteria, they estimate that more than 350 studies showing contrary findings would be needed for their conclusions to have arisen by chance alone. An example included in their analysis is the Bateman and Fonagy (2004, 2008) BPD project, an intensive programme that shows impressive reductions in suicidality, use of medical services and psychiatric consultation rates up to five years post-therapy. These findings are especially important given the pos-sibility that standard therapies (including STPT) with this diagnostic group may actually make patients worse, and the failure of cognitive approaches to show maintenance of gains once therapy comes to an end (Levy, 2008).

Another defence of psychoanalytic psychotherapy revives the famous 'dodo-bird verdict' of equal outcomes irrespective of therapy modality. Head-to head studies show few major differences in outcome for psychoanalytic psychotherapy compared with CBT, although those differences that do arise tend to marginally favour CBT. The argument here is that when it comes to 'parcelling out' the contributions of various factors affecting outcome, the role of 'common factors' such as the therapeutic alliance and remoralization, and the severity of the client's condition itself, far outweigh the technical contri-butions of specific therapies (Wampold, 2001). This aspect is played down by CBT enthusiasts, who are wont to cite the 15 comparisons in which CBT out-performed other modalities, and omit to mention the 2985 studies that failed to show any significant differences (Mollon, 2009).

Futher, there is a case to be made that the real-world clinical impact of CBT is far less dramatically effective than those responsible for health care funding (usually non-clinicians) have been led to believe. Outcome indicators in research studies do not always equate to clinically significant improvement. In clinical practice many, if not most, cases treated by psychotherapists show complexity and comorbidity, where the results for all forms of therapy including CBT tend to be less impressive. Also, as mentioned, long-term follow-up suggests that relapse is the norm for short-term therapies, which is where most of the outcome evidence favouring CBT is clustered.

The disingenuousness underpinning CBT's pitch to funders and managers of mental health services has recently been exposed in a rigorous meta-analysis looking at the impact of CBT on major mental illnesses (Lynch et al., 2009). They start from the premise that allegiance effects are widespread confounders in psychotherapy research. Researchers are reluctant to publish the results of studies that fail to support the particular therapeutic modality they espouse. Indeed, this could be adduced as an argument for a psychoanalytic perspective acknowledging the role of unconscious bias – these presumably being manifestations of unconscious wishes rather than deliberate deception – although this stricture applies no less to psychoanalytic researchers than to their CBT counterparts.

Lynch et al.'s (2009) meta-analysis only looked at studies that (a) took allegiance into account and (b) provided robust controls such as a weekly 'support group' without CBT content, since given the huge impact of placebo effects especially in psychotherapy, 'no therapy/treatment as usual' is no longer acceptable for comparison. Confining themselves to studies of CBT that met these stringent criteria, they found that in the major mental illness with which most psychiatric services are concerned; that is, schizophrenia and bipolar disorder, *CBT has no demonstrable effect beyond what occurs with non-CBT controls, while its impact in depression was relatively minor.* It seems that the emperor is, at best, very scantily clad!

A final argument, ironically closest to the heart of psychoanalytic psychotherapy yet perhaps least likely to cut ice in the public arena, is that the project of outcome evaluation is fundamentally misguided and contrary to the spirit of psychoanalysis, which is concerned with idiographic individual life stories, not nomothetic, instrumentalist 'best buys'. This applies particularly to 'full' psychoanalysis (e.g. five times a week for five years), which has never been, and perhaps never will be, subject to an RCT, although various methodological modifications can be used to evaluate its outcome, and which, on the whole, tend to be strongly favourable (see Sandell et al., 2000). While appearing at first sight to be an untenable 'back-woods' defence, there are growing hints of a wider dissatisfaction with over-technologized and compartmentalized health care, and an emerging interest in qualitative methodology and narrative-based medicine (e.g. Avdi, 2008), with which psychoanalysts following this tack might usefully ally themselves.

The politics of therapy

The CBT/psychoanalysis debate, especially on the CBT side, tends to present itself as a disinterested 'scientific' dispute about the effectiveness of various forms of therapy. But while the scientific method may be neutral, the uses to which science is put arise in a particular historical context. Behind the CBT/ psychoanalysis conflict loom sociological and political realities: the need to contain health care costs and to search for cheaper forms of therapy; an assault on the hegemony of the professions, and to move towards demonstrable competences rather than professional titles; instrumentalism and pragmatism and the 'end of ideology'; the search for quick, simple, 'solution-focused' answers in the face of increasing complexity; the rise of clinical psychology (allied with CBT) and the decline of psychiatry (associated with psychoanalysis); and the need to limit the costs of training therapists.

In all these arenas, the zeitgeist seems to favour CBT. This in turn is reflected in the UK government's National Centre for Clinical Excellence (NICE) guidelines for psychotherapies in major mental disorders, which almost exclusively advocate CBT (NICE, 2009). Cries of anguish from psychoanalysis go unheard; there is a real danger of it becoming an endangered species, especially in the public sector. 'Dodo-bird'-type arguments carry little weight, for if outcomes between different therapies are equivalent, why not invest in those that are cheapest and require least intensive training?

In psychoanalysis' favour there is the argument that 'on a rising tide all ships float'. In other words, psychoanalysis need have little to fear from the rise and rise of CBT, since at least psychological therapies, as opposed to pharmacotherapy, are gaining their rightful place in the treatment of mental illness, and in the long run its niche will emerge. While acknowledging that this argument has overtones of a sop designed to dampen envy, psychoanalysis does need seriously to consider what its niche might be.

In my view, psychoanalysis' contemporary role is fourfold. First, buttressed by attachment theory, it has an indispensable contribution to make to the science of intimate relations, whether parental, spousal or therapeutic (Fonagy et al., 2002; Holmes, 2010). Second, it is likely that psychoanalytic treatment will find its place among the psychotherapies as a first-line treatment for people with long-term complex illnesses and personality disorders. Third, derivative and modified forms of psychoanalysis, such as Balint groups, will increasingly be needed to underpin short-term approaches, especially in supporting front-line mental health staff. Finally, as a cultural presence, psychoanalysis need have no fear of extinction, albeit one mainly confined to 'high culture'. Like opera, nuclear physics and avant-garde architecture, psychoanalysis is an essential ingredient in the intellectual and aesthetic mix of modernity.

To return, finally, to the scenario with which we started: the CBT project of providing functional help for the mental miseries of the poor exemplifies a social democratic project that has driven the politics of the Western world for over a century, and is to be welcomed as such. But the limits of that project are beginning to be acknowledged. Despite progressive government policies, most

Western democracies remain riven with social inequity and widely discrepant health outcomes between rich and poor (Wilkinson, 2006). There is a need for a more nuanced, reflexive approach, taking into account unconscious as well as conscious factors, one that encompasses the 'helper' as well as the 'helped', and the interactions between them. In my view psychoanalysis has a unique contribution to make to that new beginning. But then, to paraphrase the immortal words of Mandy Rice-Davies, not a million miles from my post-office protagonists, thanks to the allegiance effect, 'I would claim that, wouldn't I?'.

References

Abbass, A., Sheldon, A., Gyra, J. and Kalpin, A. (2008) 'Intensive short-term dynamic psychotherapy for DSM-IV personality disorders: a randomized controlled trial', *Journal of Nervous and Mental Disease*, 196(3): 211–16.

Avdi, E. (2008) 'Analysing talk in the talking cure: conversation, discourse, and narrative analysis of psychoanalytic psychotherapy', *European Psychotherapy*, 8(1): 69–88.

Bateman, A. and Fonagy, P. (2004) *Psychotherapy for Borderline Personality Disorder: Mentalisation Based Treatment*, Oxford: Oxford University Press.

Bateman, A. and Fonagy, P. (2008) '8-year follow-up of patients treated for borderline personality disorder: mentalization-based treatment versus treatment as usual', *American Journal of Psychiatry*, 165: 631–8.

Bion, W. (1967) *Second Thoughts*, New York: Jason Aronson.

Brearley, M. (2007) 'What do psychoanalysts do?', in L. Braddock and M. Lacewing (eds), *The Academic Face of Psychoanalysis*, London: Routledge, pp. 20–32.

Butler, A., Chapman, J., Forman, E. and Beck A. (2006) 'The empirical status of CBT: a review of meta-analyses', *Clinical Psychology Review*, 26: 17–31.

Dare, C., Eisler, I., Russell, G., Treasure, J. and Dodge, L. (2001) 'Psychological therapies for adults with anorexia nervosa: randomised controlled trial of out-patient treatments', *British Journal of Psychiatry*, 178: 216–21.

Fonagy, P. (2006) 'The failure of practice to inform theory and the role of implicit theory in bridging the transmission gap', in J. Canestri (ed.), *Psychoanalysis from Practice to Theory*, Chichester: Wiley, pp. 69–86.

Fonagy, P. and Bateman, A. (2006) 'Progress in the treatment of borderline personality disorder', *British Journal of Psychiatry*, 188: 1–3.

Fonagy, P., Gergely, G., Jurist, E. and Target, M. (2002) *Affect Regulation, Mentalisation, and the Development of the Self*, New York: Other Press.

Gabbard, G. (2004) *Long-term Psychoanalytic Psychotherapy: A Basic Text*, Arlington VA: APPI, pp. 3–14.

Gabbard, G. (2005) 'Major modalities of psychotherapy: psychodynamic', in G. Gabbard, J. Beck and J. Holmes (eds), *Oxford Textbook of Psychotherapy*, Oxford: Oxford University Press.

Gabbard, G., Lazar, S., Horngerger, J. and Spiegel, D. (1997) 'The economic impact of psychotherapy: a review', *American Journal of Psychiatry*, 154: 147–55.

Guthrie, E., Creed, F., Dawson, D. and Tomenson, B. (1991) 'A RCT of psychotherapy in patients with refractory irritable bowel syndrome', *Gastroenterology*, 100: 450–7.

Hoglend, P., Kjell-Petter, B., Svein, A. et al. (2008) 'Transference interpretations in psychoanalytic psychotherapy: do they yield sustained effects?' *American Journal of Psychiatry*, 165: 763–84.

Holmes, J. (2001) 'All you need is CBT', *British Medical Journal*, 324: 288–94.

Holmes, J. (2010) *Exploring in Security: Towards an Attachment-informed Psychoanalytic Psychotherapy*, London: Routledge.

Imber, S., Pilkonis, P., Sotsky, S. et al. (1990) 'Mode-specific effects among three treatments for depression', *Journal of Consulting and Clinical Psychology*, 58: 352–9.

Kächele, H., Schachter, J. and Thomä, H. (2008) *From Psychoanalytic Narratives to Empirical Style Case Research: Implications for Psychoanalytic Practice*, Hove: Taylor & Francis.

Kuyken, W., Watkins, E. and Beck, A. (2005) 'CBT for mood disorders', in G. Gabbard, J. Beck and J. Holmes (eds), *Oxford Textbook of Psychotherapy*, Oxford: OUP, pp. 111–26.

Leichsenring, F. and Rabung, S. (2008) 'Effectiveness of long-term psychodynamic psychotherapy: a meta-analysis', *Journal of the American Medical Association*, 300: 1551–65.

Levy, K. (2008) 'Psychotherapies and lasting change', *American Journal of Psychiatry*, 165: 556–9.

Linehan, M. (1993) *Cognitive Behavioural Treatment of Borderline Personality Disorder*, New York: Guilford Press.

Lynch., D., Laws, K. and McKenna, P. (2009) 'CBT for major psychiatric disorder: does it really work? A meta-analytical review of well-conducted trials', *Psychological Medicine*, 57: 1–16.

Matte-Blanco, I. (1975) *The Unconscious as Infinite Sets*, London: Routledge.

Milrod, B., Leon, A.C., Busch, F., Rudden, M., Schwalberg, M., Clarkin, J. et al. (2007) 'A randomized controlled clinical trial of psychoanalytic psychotherapy for panic disorder', *American Journal of Psychiatry*, 164: 265–72.

Milton, J. (2001) 'Psychoanalysis and CBT – rival paradigms or common ground?', *International Journal of Psychoanalysis*, 82: 431–47.

Mollon, P. (2009) 'The NICE guidelines are misleading, unscientific, and potentially impede good psychological care and help', *Psychodynamic Practice*, 15: 9–24.

NICE (2009) *Depression in Adults (Update): Draft NICE Guideline for Consultation*, available online at www.nice.org.uk.

Parry, G., Roth, A. and Kerr, I. (2005) 'Brief and time-limited therapy' in G. Gabbard, J. Beck and J. Holmes (eds), *Oxford Textbook of Psychotherapy*, Oxford: Oxford University Press, pp. 507–22.

Piper, W.E., Ogrodniczuk, J.S., Joyce, A.S., McCallum, M., Rosie, J.S., O'Kelly, J.G. et al. (1999) 'Prediction of dropping out in time-limited, interpretive individual psychotherapy', *Psychotherapy*, 36: 114–22.

Power, M. (2002) 'Integrative therapy from a cognitive-behavioural perspective', in J. Holmes and A. Bateman (eds), *Integration in Psychotherapy*, Oxford: Oxford University Press, pp. 27–48.

Roth, A. and Lemma, A. (2008) *The Competences Required to Deliver Effective Psycho-analytic/psychodynamic Psychotherapy*, London: Department of Health. Available online at www.ucl.ac.uk/clinical psychology/CORE/Psychodynamic_ Competences/Background_Paper.pdf (accessed 12 December 2009).

Safran, J. and Muran, J. (2000) *Negotiating the Therapeutic Alliance: A Relational Treatment Guide*, New York: Guilford Press.

Samuels, A. and Veale, D. (2009) 'Improving access to psychological therapies: for and against', *Psychodynamic Practice*, 15: 41–56.

Sandell, R., Blomberg, J., Lazar, A., Carlsson, J., Broberg, J. and Rand, H. (2000) 'Varieties of long-term outcome among patients in psychoanalysis and long-term psychotherapy: a review of findings in the STOPP', *International Journal of Psychoanalysis*, 81: 921–42.

Sandler, J. (1976) 'Countertransference and role responsiveness', *International Journal of Psychoanalysis*, 3: 43–7.

Shapiro, D., Barkham, M., Rees, A., Hardy, G.E., Reynolds, S. and Startup, M. (1994) 'Effects of treatment duration and severity of depression on the effectiveness of cognitive/behavioural and psychodynamic/interpersonal psychotherapy', *Journal of Consulting and Clinical Psychology*, 63: 211–36.

Wampold, B. (2001) *The Great Psychotherapy Debate*, New York: Lawrence Erlbaum Associates.

Westen, D. (2005) 'Implications of research in cognitive neuroscience for psycho-dynamic psychotherapy', in G. Gabbard, J. Beck and J. Holmes (eds), *Oxford Textbook of Psychotherapy*, Oxford: OUP, pp. 443–8.

Wilkinson R. (2006) *Unhealthy Societies: The Afflictions of Inequality*, London: Routledge.

Young, J. (1994) *Cognitive Therapy for Personality Disorders: A Schema-focused Approach*. Sarasota, FI: Professional Resource Press.

3 Critically engaging CBT
The view from CAT

Anthony Ryle

Background: the development of the cognitive analytic therapy (CAT) model

CAT emerged from many years of my own practice and research and it has continued to develop over the last 25 years through a process of constant revision and extension and with increasing contributions from others. In order to understand the present theory, practice and values this history needs to be briefly described.

Because I worked largely on my own for many years, the basic beliefs, practices and values – the 'world view' – of the model reflect my background and values. One influence was my experience as a GP and the epidemiological research I carried out in that context, which demonstrated the high incidence of untreated psychological disorders. Another was my support for the principles expressed in the founding of the National Health Service (NHS) that reflected my wish for a more egalitarian society. A third influence could be attributed to my impatient or oppositional temperament.

Evolving ideas

As I became increasingly involved in psychotherapy, I was struck by the extraordinary confusion of ideas and methods and became interested in working towards an integration of some sort. This was made easier by the fact that I had followed an unconventional training that did not involve a commitment to any one approach. But I was never interested in an integration based on the denial of difference. Therapy models reflect various human assumptions and social values and call on different kinds of evidence to support their practices. These differences need to be debated.

Many of my ideas were generated from my increasing irritation with the main existing schools and my attempt to offer detailed alternative explanations and practices. My irritation with the psychoanalysts stemmed from their complacency, their unclear concepts and language, their failure to evaluate their effectiveness, the irrelevance of lengthy analyses to the widespread unmet needs in the population and from the power axis implied in the claim to interpret. With the behaviourists, it stemmed from the narrowness of their model of humans and from the way in which evidence derived from the treatment of simple problems was inflated to form the basis of arrogant assertions of general relevance and scientific rectitude.

Cognitive behaviour therapy (CBT) often evokes a similar, critical response from me, and in comparing and contrasting the models in this chapter I am an advocate, not an impartial judge.

Translation and integration

My aim of integration was initially pursued by restating the important extensive understandings buried in the assertions and disputes within psychoanalysis by attempting to translate its key ideas into a more direct language based on cognitive theory. The confusing use of the same terms within totally different theoretical contexts pointed to the need for an emerging integrative model to distinguish its own terms and concepts from those of the models it was derived from.

Differentiation and consolidation

Detailed alternative conceptualizations of a number of psychoanalytic case histories were published in the 1990s and the differences between CAT and personal construct and cognitive approaches were summarized in Ryle (2001). Theory was enriched by describing the development of personality through interpersonal and wider cultural influences in ways drawing on Vygotsky and Bakhtin and by noting the evidence from observational studies of infants. In this way CAT came to provide a serious developmental model, something lacking in CBT, and transformed psychoanalytic object relations theories by ruling out unverifiable constructions of unconscious mental events and emphasizing the important influence of the infant's actual experience.

CAT: the current theory and practice and comparisons with CBT

Psychotherapy, like teaching and parenting, is concerned with people. While all these activities may involve the exercise of defined skills, such skills are practised in the context of human relationships and convey wider meanings; therapy must therefore be based on an understanding of the whole person. It is of course true that some patients have problems confined to one or two areas that do not radically affect their view of themselves or their relationships with others. Such patients respond well to the acceptance and positive regard provided by therapists from most therapy models and may be helped by the specific techniques developed in CBT. But for the more numerous patients who have combinations of mood, behavioural and symptomatic disturbances and who are unhappy because of problems of living therapists need more than techniques, and CAT aims to meet that need.

Case formulation and reformulation

CAT emerged from research seeking to define the aims of brief psychodynamic therapy. Involving patients in discussing how their aims might be articulated at the start of therapy led to the practice of early joint reformulation that meant creating descriptions of the problems as described by the patient and in terms of the underlying patterns of acting and thinking proposed by the therapist. Over time this developed into a more complex procedure involving the joint construction by therapists and patients of a written summary of key historical and current issues (a narrative reconstruction) and a sequential diagram demonstrating the recurrent dysfunctional patterns of thought and behaviour serving to maintain the patient's problems (a paradigmatic reformulation). The early description of target problems resembled CBT practice but the creation of descriptions of the hitherto unrecognized patterns of thought and action that therapy would seek to modify, expressed as 'target problem procedures', was a feature of CAT.

The social and dialogic basis of personality

The introduction of ideas derived from Vygotsky and Bakhtin offered a more radical challenge to both psychoanalytic and cognitivist assumptions (Leiman, 1992). Influenced by these, the understanding of human psychological development and therapeutic change moved from the traditional focus, characteristic of CBT, on individual, 'in the head' processes to a radically social view in which, on the basis of universal and personal biological features, individual personality is seen to be formed and maintained through a web of relationships and dialogue with external and internalized others (Ryle and Kerr, 2002).

Practical methods

In practice, generalized descriptions of past and present relationship patterns are developed jointly with patients and are recorded (1) in a reformulation letter, offering a narrative account of the evident sources and nature of their difficulty, and (2) in sequential diagrams tracing their recurrent, damaging interpersonal and intrapersonal patterns. Involving patients in the joint construction of these verbal and diagrammatic descriptions of what needs to be changed establishes a cooperative relationship, sets the agenda of therapy, enlarges patients' psychological awareness and supports their development of a greater sense of responsibility and agency. It allows therapists to anticipate dysfunctional patterns that may be mobilized in the therapy relationship. The work of reformulation is itself powerfully therapeutic and many symptoms and problematic behaviours fade without being directly addressed.

The central claim made for CAT is that it seeks to offer a comprehensive understanding of human psychology and involves therapists in forming real, clearly defined and therapeutically powerful relationships with their patients. In this respect it is a 'psychodynamic' theory and is clearly differentiated from CBT.

Early development

Understanding the immense complexity of human psychological processes needs to be based on an understanding of their development. CBT provides a model of learning but takes little account of early development and its effects on psychological structures. CAT, in contrast, revised object relations theories in ways that sought to eliminate unverifiable assertions about 'the unconscious' and were consistent with observational studies of early development.

The current CAT model of personality emphasizes that human infants are genetically predisposed to be socially formed to a far greater degree than any other animal. They show active emotional engagement with others from birth, communicating through behaviour, expressive sounds, gestures, rhythms and imitation (Trevarthen, 2001). Over the first few years they increasingly demonstrate the highly developed human capacity to make and use symbols.

A child's unique inherited temperamental characteristics will influence its interaction with others, notably with those in its particular family. The repetition over time of early patterns of interaction are seen to initiate a unique repertoire of reciprocal role procedures (RRPs). RRPs are reiterated sequences of perception, thinking, affects and action linked to the expected or elicited responses of others. Their enactments are accompanied by communication that increasingly involves pre-linguistic signs and, eventually, by language. Self-processes and the self-conscious 'I' are derived from the internalization of these reciprocal interactions and communications. Conscious thought is essentially internal dialogue derived from sign-mediated exchanges with others. The intrapersonal procedures involved in self-care, self-control and self-judgement are derived from the internalization of the interpersonal patterns characterizing early relationships and the two remain permeable to each other. In this way CAT offers an adequately complex but accessible model of self-processes whereas in CBT the self is more often referred to than defined.

The stability of role procedures

The stability of role procedures is maintained by eliciting reinforcing reciprocations from others, and this is true of both normal, functional reciprocal role patterns and those that are harmful or restrictive. Revision occurs when others withhold the expected reciprocations or offer more functional ones or enlarge the person's awareness of them, so that conscious control may become possible. This understanding underlines the need for therapists to provide both non-reciprocation and clear descriptions of their patients' dysfunctional RRPs.

Personality structure

The most significant patterns acquired in early life are concerned with issues of care or neglect in relation to need and overcontrol or cruelty in relation to submission. 'The self' is normally multiple as individuals acquire a repertoire of RRPs; different ones being mobilized in ways appropriate to the context. 'Normal' multiplicity may include the manifestation at different times of contradictory patterns but in general links between patterns and awareness of the range is established. However, this is not the case where adversity and predisposition result in a structural dissociation of the individual's repertoire of role procedures. In such cases the sense of self is fragmented and discontinuous. In borderline personality disorder (BPD), which is the most frequently encountered type in clinical practice, patients commonly show abrupt switches between states and may have little recollection between them. This is confusing to the patient and to those around them, including clinicians, who as a result may feel 'deskilled' and may become rejecting.

In these patients therapists and other clinical staff need to support integration of the dissociated reciprocal patterns. This can be aided by verbal and especially by diagrammatic descriptions of the repertoire of RRPs that demonstrate their dissociation into separate self-states and trace the switches and links between them. Self-state sequential diagrams support the consistent, non-collusive attentive engagement of clinicians. They also have a direct therapeutic role in helping patients recognize their states and state switches and so gain more control over them. These are the essential elements of the multiple self-states model (MSSM) of BPD as described in Ryle (1997).

Many borderline patients are prone to switch into states of uncontrolled anger. Rather than relying on anger management, the CAT response would be to trace the dysfunctional RRPs that precede the switches into anger with the aim of establishing more adaptive modes. These prior dysfunctional modes usually represent long-term strategies evolved in response to deprivation and are attempts to avoid anger. They typically involve patterns of resentful compliance, emotional distancing or the avoidance of vulnerable need, all of which maintain a sense of deprivation and pain from which switches to rage states may be triggered. These states, whether expressed in hurting self or others, are liable to provoke rejection and hence perpetuate deprivation. CAT would seek to modify these preceding patterns as well as developing recognition and control of the switches.

Wider theoretical implications

While these structural understandings are crucial to psychotherapists, they have wider implications, for example, in clinical management and in education, where collusive responses to dysfunctional RRPs are often elicited. The CAT model of self-processes challenges the individualistic Cartesian assumptions of much contemporary psychology by emphasizing the essential role of interpersonal activity and communication in the formation and maintenance of individual self-processes and the sense of self. More generally, the CAT model, by pointing to the social formation of individuals, demonstrates the way in which cultural beliefs and practices are transmitted from generation to generation and challenges the fashionable overextension of Darwinian biological evolutionary theory into areas best considered in terms of cultural evolution.

Relative advantages of CAT and CBT

The scope and assumptions of CAT and CBT models are too disparate for direct comparisons to be of value. CAT offers a broad understanding of the development of personality through relationships, consistent with the observational studies of early development of recent years, and it offers a model of self and interpersonal functions that supports the use of the therapy relationship to assist change. These understandings guide the application of a wide range of techniques, some specific, others derived or modified from other models. From CBT, for example, came the use of patient self-monitoring to identify the events associated with symptoms. This technique was extended in CAT by focusing self-monitoring on the recognition of interpersonal and self-management reciprocal role procedures. Recognizing RRPs as they occur or are reported in therapy sessions allows the immediate discussion or initiation of alternative understandings and behaviours.

How does therapy support change?

In CBT theory the emphasis is placed on the description and challenging of the links between thinking, feeling and acting. When based on a skilful analysis of the sequences and sensitively carried out, this can clearly be an effective ingredient of therapy, but expressed through simple-minded analyses and schoolteacherly assertions of the patient's faulty thinking it can be experienced as critical or disrespectful. The therapist's positive responses to more effective behaviours may be reinforcing but in the case of persistent negative behaviours, especially when these undermine therapy, there is little theoretical understanding of what to do. In such cases CBT therapists rely on patient compliance with its technical procedures and the personal qualities of the practitioner to maintain the therapeutic work.

In CAT, creating an effective working relationship with patients is a main aim, but this must include skilful work with those whose destructive role procedures undermine the therapy. In CAT these are seen to represent the enactment of some part of the patient's dysfunctional repertoire; the patient brings into the therapy relationship the problems for which help is sought. Once identified and recognized with the help of the diagrammatic reformulation, these can be challenged rather than reinforced by reciprocation.

In understanding RRPs in the context of the therapy relationship, sensitivity to non-verbal affective communication is crucially important. Therapists need to be aware of the feelings induced by their patients. They may be induced by actions or words but often they can only be recognized by emotional resonance to the patient's expression, posture and other indirect messages. To recognize these, therapists need to be emotionally open and also aware of their own contributions to the patterns.

This aspect of CAT theory is a reconceptualization of the psychoanalytic understanding of transference–countertransference, understood as a particular example of the general way in which relationships depend on the meshing of reciprocal patterns. The CAT concept of RRPs is found accessible and useful by patients and by non-therapy staff, and provides a more adequate and comprehensive framework for therapists than CBT.

Objectivity, psychotherapy research and the nature of evidence

CAT seeks to offer a scientific basis for understanding human nature but insists that objectivity, in the sense of studying humans as objects, is inappropriate. We need to observe and record evidence in ways capable of being replicated by others but full evidence concerning human behaviour and experience can only be obtained by human beings and must include intersubjective understanding. We know each other through shared contexts and histories, speech, observation, expressive behaviours and also through incompletely understood, non-verbal communication: as Pascal said, 'The heart has its reasons of which reason knows nothing'.

In studies of infant development, it is recognized that infants' cognitive abilities are evident early and develop in observable ways but their parallel capacity to convey and respond directly to affective aspects of experience and behaviour – to 'feel other minds', to know others non-cognitively – are neglected or denied. The overemphasis on cognition and the need to explain affects as secondary derivatives of it is dominant in cognitive-behavioural approaches. Therapy practice and research needs to acknowledge and make use of such subjective-knowing and avoid the overvalorization of cognitive processes, a view that receives strong support from studies of early development focusing on how the child develops in relation to others (Reddy, 2008). Mirror cells and other yet to be discovered neurophysiology can throw some light on the neural pathways involved in our coming to know other minds feelingly but the fact that we do and how we do can be experienced and further studied without the neuroscience.

Cost effectiveness and the evidence base of CBT and CAT

The problems of demonstrating clinically useful effects for a psychotherapy model are formidable. Therapy is not comparable to the prescribing of a drug; it involves two people and what happens between them is only partly determined by the model. Trying to overcome this by delivering manualized therapy seems to me to be incompatible with a humanly respectful therapy and cannot eliminate the individual variations in therapists' work. The effects of factors common to any therapy delivered with reasonable tact and attention are difficult to distinguish from the effects of specific interventions. Change may occur during active therapy but may not endure, but adequately long follow-up is costly and rarely done. The aims pursued in different therapeutic models may differ, as they do between CBT and CAT, and standard measures are sensitive to only some types of change. In controlled trials the power of the model being researched may be inflated where the control intervention – often 'business as usual' – is clearly ineffective.

These problems have not been overcome in CBT research and the loud and persistent claims that it (almost alone among therapies) is evidence-based are increasingly criticized. David Richards (2007), a past president of the BABCP, attributes the growing criticisms of CBT to its selective use of evidence and to the 'naïve belief that the randomized control trial is the only weapon we now need' (pp 12–13). He observes how 'we ourselves write the research questions that now get funded; reviews have shown that RCTs can both exaggerate and under-estimate the likely real effect . . . most CBT trials are small and poorly executed; quality thresholds for RCTs in NICE guidelines are notoriously low, allowing the meta-analyses of small poor quality studies to direct policy; we pay no attention to qualitative evidence . . .' (pp 12–13). He points to the 'unproven contention that it is possible to take the results of experiments conducted by charismatic product champions in highly controlled environments and implement them in the widespread manner suggested by Layard' (pp 12–13).

CAT has different weaknesses and in particular is often criticized for its small research output; it has indeed been slow to accumulate evidence from large-scale RCTs. However, small-scale descriptive and controlled studies and evaluated case studies accompanied the development of the model, and research into process and aspects of theory and practice have continued to take place. This included work on BPD that for a long time had been neglected by psychiatrists and by dynamic and CBT therapists. CAT was shown to have an effect within a 24-session format (Ryle and Golynkina, 2000) and has been found to be particularly helpful by those who work with these patients and with other 'hard to help' (i.e. usually unhelped) patients, including abuse survivors, the elderly and offenders.

This research also contributed to an understanding of the importance of dissociation, a factor little attended to except in conditions directly attributed to trauma. It led to the development of the MSSM of BPD that emphasizes the alternating dominance of a range of dissociated self-states, each characterized by contrasting RRPs expressed in subjective symptoms and behaviours, some of which may be extreme. The MSSM is of importance in relation to diagnosis, case formulation, management and treatment. In work of particular relevance to mental health services, it has been shown that brief training and supervision enables staff with no formal psychotherapy training to use CAT reformulations to plan interventions and avoid collusive responses (Kerr et al., 2007).

Outcome research

A review of CAT research can be found in Appendix 1 of Ryle and Kerr (2002). Since then a well-designed RCT comparing the effect of the addition of either CAT or a humanistic cognitive intervention to a comprehensive treatment programme for late adolescent borderline patients has been reported by Chanen et al. (2008). This showed clinically relevant advantages from CAT. Other published outcome studies and those in progress are listed on the ACAT website (www.acat.ne.uk/).

Process research and the development of clinical and research tools

Studies of process providing detailed evidence of CAT practice include a single case experimental design study of the therapy of a case of dissociated identity disorder by Kellett (2005). This design is used in a current multi-centre trial of CAT for BPD carried out by skilled CAT therapists. This involves regular completion of questionnaires by patients and therapists through the course of therapy and the audiotaping of all sessions, allowing measures of therapist's skill in delivering therapy in general and in CAT-specific terms to be assessed by the use of the method of rating sessions developed by Bennett and Parry (2004). In an earlier study Bennett and Parry (1998) demonstrated the accuracy of the CAT reformulation of patients' problems.

In my view the findings of process research and the use of single case designs are more likely to influence therapy practice than are the large-scale RCTs on which CBT's claims to be evidence-based are based.

Other CAT research has been concerned with the development of instruments for clinical and research use. The eight-item personality structure questionaire (PSQ) (Pollock et al., 2001) was developed to assess the degree of dissociation and provides a reliable measure. High scores are characteristic of BPD; the mean scores of outpatients referred for psychological treatment are between those of normal subjects and those with BPD. Bedford et al. (2009) administered the PSQ to over 1000 outpatients; they confirmed the psychometric qualities of the PSQ and showed that scores fell in patients receiving a range of treatments while remaining stable in those not treated. The evidence suggests that the level of integration varies across the spectrum of psychological disorders.

Support for the MSSM of BPD has been provided by the use of the states description procedure (Ryle, 2007), a clinically useful method that contributes to the reformulation of borderline patients.

Therapeutic change

Therapeutic change, in the CAT understanding, involves, first, the revision, control or elimination of the dysfunctional RRPs, which are the source of patients' symptomatic and mood disturbance and their negative attitudes and behaviours towards self and others and, second, increasing the integration of markedly dissociated procedures. Some such changes follow the insight and control achieved during the reformulation process and the emotional impact of the therapist's concerned and accurate attention. This rapid early change may be stable but may result in idealization of the therapist that needs to be recognized and challenged, as does the predictable subsequent disillusion.

The therapist's role

Maintaining awareness of the shifting manifestations of problem RRPs and detecting them in the patient's accounts of daily life is a subtle and often difficult task; therapists are aided by the reformulation process and tools, and in the case of more disturbed patients may need a level of supervision that attends to the shifting transference and countertransference. A full and moving account of a difficult therapy is given by Kate Freshwater, then a clinical psychologist and CAT trainee, in Ryle and Kerr (2002: 189–97). This conveys the demands of working in this way and the value of the reformulation and supervision, and shows how, beyond ideas and techniques, therapy has an underlying ethical and existential dimension. Therapists often need to convey more faith in patients and in the possibility of a meaningful life than are within their present capacity. But the faith has to be genuine and realistic, not bland or sentimental.

CAT and the 'medical model'

Minds and bodies are not independent of each other and patients must be understood from both perspectives. Examples of the need for a combined perspective include: (1) symptoms due to purely physical disorders that vary in severity in response to psychological events; (2) somatic symptoms provoked by stress or personality features; (3) serious organic diseases where patients manage their treatments poorly. For example, CAT can help patients with inadequately controlled insulin-dependent diabetes, whose poor management, resulting in a range of serious medical complications, may be due to a variety of dysfunctional RRPs (Fosbury et al., 1997); and (4) mood disorders, whether in response to life events or resulting from genetic predisposition, are frequently accompanied by physical changes, and combined medication and psychotherapy may be indicated.

CAT understandings can make a useful contribution to medical and psychiatric treatment, the aim being not to make all psychiatrists or physicians into psychotherapists but to develop informed interpersonal sensitivity and avoid the development of collusive or hostile patterns.

Notions of happiness

Philosophers and writers have offered many different ways of considering whether 'happiness' is a desirable goal and if it is, how a person might pursue it. But therapists cannot contribute by prescribing the goal or explaining the meaning of life. For most people survival rather than happiness is the aim. I would argue that the belief that one is entitled to, or worse still should be able to purchase, happiness is a symptom of our individualistic consumer culture and may well contribute to unhappiness by ignoring the extent to which individuals need to be in a meaningful relationship with others and with their wider social context. Faced with the fact that our culture produces many hundreds of thousands of people needing relief from psychological/emotional distress and unhappiness, the proliferation of therapists, a response consistent with the Layard thesis, is like dealing with rising sea levels by issuing lots of buckets. Economic downturns, poverty, modern forms of colonialism and vast expenditure on weaponry are not natural phenomena like tsunamis; they are man-made and call for political action. Prescribing counselling or CBT for all serves to distract us from attending to the values and practices of the unhappy society in which we live.

If more resources are made available for psychotherapy and counselling, a first step might be to correct the underfunded and unevenly distributed services in the NHS. But prevention would be a more logical priority, achieved by increasing what might be called psychological literacy, centrally among those involved in parenting, education and management but also more generally. In that respect the CAT model is particularly suitable because of its focus on the relationship between individual psychological functioning and the social and relationship context.

Could CAT align itself with CBT?

Cognitive theory and to some extent cognitive behaviour therapy were among the early influences from which CAT was derived, along with behaviourism, personal construct theory and psychoanalytic object relations theory. Over time CAT diverged increasingly as the social and dialogic processes responsible for the formation and maintenance of personality functioning became the central theoretical concepts, replacing the individual 'in the head' focus of other theories such as CBT. CAT and CBT both attempt to provide therapy within modest time frames and share some techniques, but the two models are distinct and are likely to coexist for a long time, and the appropriate distribution of patients between them and how combined treatments might best be envisaged remains to be determined. They differ in scope and in their underlying assumptions about human psychology. Their common and distinct characteristics should be clearly defined in ways encouraging serious discussion of their social and philosophical implications. This, combined with clinically relevant research, would be of more use than the exercise of public relations skills.

References

Bedford, A., Davies, F. and Tibbles, J. (2009) 'The personality structure questionnaire (PSQ): a cross-validation with a large clinical sample', *Clinical Psychology and Psychotherapy*, 16(1) 77–81.

Bennett, D. and Parry, G. (1998) 'The accuracy of reformulation in cognitive analytic therapy: a validation study', *Psychotherapy Research*, 8: 84–103.

Bennett, D. and Parry, G. (2004) 'A measure of psychotherapeutic competence derived from cognitive analytic therapy (CCAT)', *Psychotherapy Research*, 14(2): 176–92.

Chanen, A.M., Jackson, H.J., McCutcheon, L.K. et al. (2008) 'Early intervention for adolescents with borderline personality disorder using cognitive analytic therapy: randomised controlled trial', *British Journal of Psychiatry*, 193: 477–84.

Fosbury, J.A., Bosley, C.M., Ryle, A., Sonksen, P.H. and Judd, S.L. (1997) 'A trial of cognitive analytic therapy in poorly controlled Type 1 patients', *Diabetes Care*, 20: 959–64.

Kellett, S. (2005) 'The treatment of dissociative identity disorder with cognitive analytic therapy: experimental evidence of sudden gains', *Journal of Trauma and Dissociation*, 6(3): 55–80.

Kerr, I.B., Dent-Brown, K. and Parry, G.D. (2007) 'Psychotherapy and mental health teams', *International Review of Psychiatry*, 19(1): 63–80.

Leiman, M. (1992) 'The concept of sign in the work of Vygotsky, Winnicott and Bakhtin: further integration of object relations theory and activity theory', *British Journal of Medical Psychology*, 65: 209–21.

Pollock, P.H., Broadbent, M., Clarke, S., Dorrian, A.J. and Ryle, A. (2001) 'The personality structure questionaire (PSQ): a measure of the multiple self-states model of identity disturbance in cognitive analytic therapy', *Clinical Psychology and Psychotherapy*, 8: 59–72.

Reddy, V. (2008) *How Infants Know Minds*, Cambridge, MA and London: Harvard University Press.

Richards, D. (2007) ' "Arrogant, inflexible, remote and imperious"; is this what is wrong with CBT?', *BABCP*, March.

Ryle, A. (1997) *Cognitive Analytic Therapy and Borderline Personality Disorder: The Model and the Method*, Chichester: Wiley.

Ryle, A. (2001) 'Cognitive analytic therapy', *Constructivism in the Human Sciences*, 6(1–2): 51–8.

Ryle, A. (2007) 'Investigating the phenomenology of borderline personality disorder with the states description procedure: clinical implications', *Clinical Psychology and Psychotherapy*, 14: 329–41.

Ryle, A. and Golynkina, K. (2000) 'Effectiveness of time-limited cognitive analytic therapy of borderline personality disorder: factors associated with outcome', *British Journal of Medical Psychology*, 73: 197–210.

Ryle, A. and Kerr, I.B. (2002) *Introducing Cognitive Analytic Therapy: Principles and Practice*, Chichester: Wiley.

Trevarthen, C. (2001) 'Intrinsic motives for companionship in understanding: their origin, development and significance for infant mental health', *Infant Mental Health Journal*, 22(1/2): 95–131.

4 Happiness and existential thought

John M. Heaton

I will attempt to keep to the broad framework of headings suggested by the editors. But I add a caveat. It is not at all clear to me what they mean by cognitive behaviour therapy (CBT). It is now a very broad brand of therapies. It includes traditional cognitive therapies; for example, Beck's cognitive therapy and Ellis's rational-emotive therapy (RET), problem-solving methods, mindfulness training based on an interpretation of the Satipatthana Sutra, to methods influenced by phenomenology and Heidegger such as discussed by Wheeler (2005). Some come close to existential and phenomenological therapy. So when I refer to CBT I mean the traditional forms of it that grew out of behaviour therapy. These assume that internal covert processes called 'cognition' occur, and these events may mediate behaviour change. These therapies tend to model themselves on artificial intelligence, assuming that human cognition is analogous to extraordinarily efficient computers. This is an interesting analogy or picture of human cognition but what it really illuminates is the *difference* between a computer and cognition.

1 The world view underpinning my approach.
   I do not have a world view that underpins my position. To have that would be the very opposite of existential thought that emphasizes the importance of choice, authenticity, of a subjectivity that is the mark of truth. What is basic is that we live *in* the world, seek to make sense of it as best we can, and so live in harmony with it: to live happily. We do not work with models of the person because a model, representation or theory of a person is not the same as the person. There is a world of difference between a representation of a person – a photograph, drawing, anatomical model of his body, a representation of processes in his mind – and that person as a living speaking being. We make representations in science for a purpose – to make predictions, to illustrate some particular point. A representation is a *selective likeness*. So there is no general valid inference from what the representation is like to what is represented.

It is confusing to say that a representation represents something. Strictly, it should be, 'X represents Y as F'. To represent something is to represent it as thus and so. Thus, the prime minister may be represented as a dictator, as a competent-looking man, as an idiot, as an ordinary man in a photograph, as the prime minister, and so on. We may represent the mind as a computer, and we may model neural networks that mimic known brain circuits for the purpose of simulating possible cognitive change. These representations may throw light on the nature of thought, but nevertheless a scientific representation is an artefact that has a role bestowed on it in a practice (a good contemporary account of scientific representation is in Van Frassen, 2008).

A model or representation is a metaphor. Suppose science gives us a model that putatively represents a human being and all its possible behaviour in full detail and we believe that it does so. Then still, before we can use that model, we must locate ourselves with regard to it. We need something *in addition* to what the model has given us. But what is that something more? It cannot be a new sort of fact that cannot be encoded on our model. As we have said, we have encoded all possible facts on our model. It is the indexical 'I' or 'we' that locates *ourselves* in relation to the model to use it. This point was made by Kant; Van Frassen (2008) elaborates on the inevitable indexicality of application from the point of view of modern science.

To give a simple illustration. Suppose I am lost in a strange city. I buy a map. Now a map will not have an arrow labelled 'You are here'. The extra information needed by the user of the map cannot be already encoded in *that* map. Only when I do have that information can I express it by pointing to a spot on the map and saying 'I am here'. Of course, that information could be included in a bigger map with the label 'Location of "X" map reading at time t'. But then to use this new map I still need a self-ascription of location with regard to it. Any attempt to replace or eliminate these self-ascriptions leads to an infinite regress. It is the uniqueness of the indexical 'I', of choice, the reader of the map, which is central to existential thought. As Kierkegaard, Sartre and others have emphasized, it is an energetic and unconditional choice, as the guarantor of the connection between the subject in time and eternity, which localizes the subject in the element of truth. Choice is decisive for the personality. It is through choice that the personality penetrates into what has been chosen; if it does not choose, it withers. The absolute, as choice, is precisely freedom itself.

It is freedom, choice, truthfulness that concern existential therapists. They converse with people trying not to get caught up in manipulating them according to a model. They act so as to free their clients from the models they have of themselves that confine them. For example, 'I am a failure', 'I must be guilty' and 'My mother was a perpetual worrier so I am too'. Truthfulness, authenticity, between therapist and client is central. So we are not concerned with objective evidence of change, in the sense of looking on the events of therapy from 'above' as if there is a non-perspectival, 'objective' view of therapy. People are not objects. It is they who have evidence if there is therapeutic change or not; but of course they may pretend for one reason or another and the therapist would challenge them on that. As Wittgenstein put it:

> Is there such a thing as 'expert judgement' about the genuineness of expressions of feeling? – Even here, there are those whose judgement is 'better' and those whose judgement is 'worse'. . . .
> Can one learn this knowledge? Yes, some can. Not, however, by taking a course in it, but through '<u>experience</u>'. – Can someone else be a man's teacher in this? Certainly. From time to time he gives him the right <u>tip</u>. This is what 'learning' and 'teaching' are like here. – What one acquires here is not a technique; one learns to judge correctly. There are also rules, but they do not form a system, and only experienced people can apply them right. Unlike calculating rules.
>
> (Wittgenstein, 2001: 193)

As we are concerned with freedom, we question the place of determinism in human life and so we differ profoundly from much CBT and psychoanalysis. Thus, Sulloway in his book on Freud wrote: 'Freud's entire life's work in science was characterised by an abiding faith in the notion that all vital phenomena, including psychical ones, are rigidly and lawfully determined by the law of cause and effect' (Sulloway, 1992: 94). It is essential to both the theory and practice of psychoanalysis that all mental processes are determined.

CBT is a much more complicated school of thought than psychoanalytic psychotherapy for it has many different approaches. Certainly, any form of CBT that is deterministic, that believes happiness can be produced with certainty by using certain technical procedures, would be alien to the existential understanding of human experience and happiness. It is noticeable that in mathematics, where algorithms play an essential part, ambiguity, contradiction, paradox, uncertainty and chaos play a fundamental role in its development. In fact, the very attempt to describe human activity as algorithmic and rule-based leads to paradoxes. Mathematics, in contrast to psychoanalysis and some CBT, is not deterministic.

Let us look briefly at the concept of chance and randomness – very important concepts in modern mathematics and science. Thus, it is a basic feature of quantum mechanics, the theory of evolution, and the mathematics of chaotic systems. What is randomness? It is the opposite of determinism. This reflects our ordinary sense that much in life is too complicated to admit of any explanation. Randomness is the absence of a pattern. The quintessential random event is the toss of a coin; the outcome of a single flip is not predictable. But in the long term, 'at infinity', it is completely predictable. Heads and tails are equally distributed – their ratio tends to 1. There is a paradox here; there is absence of order and yet in the long run it is present.

'Chaos' is the term now used to indicate that simple functions when iterated produce complex and even random behaviour. Chaos theory has reintroduced the random as the unavoidable feature of everyday physical systems; it implies that any system has an 'event horizon', a time beyond which it is impossible to predict the state of the system. Here again there is both order and disorder. Interesting phenomena in both physical and biological systems occur on the boundary of chaos; this is the place where one sees the emergence of regularities that were not obviously predictable from a knowledge of the underlying transformation rules. A world without randomness would be boring; a world of complete randomness would be unliveable. Contingency seems to be built into the world and our lives. Order and disorder are both inevitable parts of any description of reality. The boundary of chaos is where we live and where we need to stay if we are to be creative.

The random can reveal the existence of a world outside our everyday picture of things. We easily become fixated on a pattern or plan. Psychoanalysis and much CBT are examples of this tendency. Mathematics has sometimes been defined as the study of patterns and natural science studies the laws of nature that involves finding patterns. Randomness, chaos, is the absence of a pattern. Yet the paradox is that mathematics studies randomness and yet finds patterns in situations characterized by the lack of pattern. Randomness is impossible and yet fundamental to mathematics and modern science. And to happiness?

The attraction of algorithmic, rule-based thinking is enormous: psychoanalysis with its mental mechanisms; and CBT with its roots in information-processing are examples. They succumb to the dream that everything will eventually be under human control; that there is unlimited potential for algorithmic thought. In a sense this is right. Both the natural and the real numbers are infinite in extent; there is no limit to which they can be manipulated. If the whole universe became a computer, it could go on churning out results for ever. If we define intelligence as a kind of algorithmic rationality, such as may be found in a mathematical proof or a computer algorithm, then computers are intelligent and we have a metaphor for human thought. But this all-pervasive metaphor can become its own reality. Computers do what they do according to the algorithms that program them. Computers can generate correct mathematical proofs. But what stands behind the formal proof? Why should it be of interest? For the computer the domain of interest and understanding does not exist. But we humans are interested in discerning and understanding patterns in our world. A chaotic world would be impossible for us to live in; it would not be a world. We seek patterns but need reminding that this seeking rests on chaos.

The question as to where existentialism sits on the materialism/transpersonal continuum should be clear. We do not recognize a continuum between the two. A continuum implies algorithmic thought, but existential thought emphasizes the sudden, the moment, paradox, ambiguity and the other. Many existentialist thinkers are atheistic in the sense that they do not recognize the existence of spiritual entities like a god. But they are certainly not materialists in the sense that everything can be reduced to matter.

2 The advantages and disadvantages of this understanding of human life compared to CBT.

It is not clear what the criteria are for an advantage or disadvantage. Does it mean for the government, or the patient, or the professions of medicine and psychology? I think most existential thinkers would say they think and act in the way they do as it is more true to human life than CBT. Whether it is more popular is neither here nor there except for people who want to be popular.

3 The question of cost-effectiveness is a matter of economics and politics.

There is not a specific technique of existential therapy that can be measured by its cost. Some people are quite happy with one or two interviews; others may require seeing 5 times a week for a number of years. It depends entirely on what they want, how much money is available to them and the skill of the particular therapist. The evidence for the efficacy of existential therapy depends more on the judgement of the particular patient and therapist involved than on some abstract decision made by a committee of people who have their own interests to serve and may have little interest in understanding the concerns of others. Of course, the evidence for the usefulness of any therapy is not merely an empirical matter; logical, ethical, aesthetic concerns are also involved.

4 The concepts of therapeutic change have been addressed above.
5 It is unclear what is meant by a medical model as there are many of them.

The importance of the 'moment' of decision was emphasized by Hippocrates and has formed part of medical tradition. Galen, in his writing on psychotherapy, emphasized the importance of free speech, *parrhesia*, speaking freely to someone you could trust, which was important in the treatment of emotional disorder. This also has been part of the medical tradition. However, the model of the mind as an organ, which can be sick, is rejected as being incoherent by most existential thinkers.

6 The notion of happiness and well-being is briefly as follows.

We use terms such as 'joy', 'pleasure', 'delight' and 'bliss' to describe happiness. The existential view is that these are not purely psychological terms; we have bodies as well as minds and humans are social animals.

Bliss and ecstasy mean we are extremely happy but tend, in their modern use, to imply it is temporary; thus, we have drugs that produce 'ecstasy'. Delight is also linked with happiness but is used in relation to doing something – 'he delighted in teasing her'; or in giving enjoyment to people – 'The pianist delighted the audience with her playing'. So again it is not the same as happiness that has a sense of permanence about it.

Joy and pleasure are more closely related to happiness. Pleasure is more time-related than joy. Thus, we can roughly measure the time that pleasure lasts. Chocolate gives me pleasure; give me a bit of chocolate and I could signal when the pleasure begins and ends. Many pleasures are like this; for example, sexual pleasure. Also pleasure can be ordered; for example, a good meal, a play, sex. This, however, is not always so. A depressed person, who usually likes a good meal, will not get pleasure from one when depressed. We like pleasure but not continually – few of us would like sex continually day in day out!

Pleasure is often understood as a sensation; it is connected to the body as is its apparent opposite pain. Pleasure is essentially expressive, so it is not just a sensation. Thus, we can see a baby express pleasure long before it can describe itself as being pleased. We may express pleasure on our faces – a smile of pleasure, and then later we learn to feign pleasure, perhaps with a smile, which an infant cannot do. If we are pleased then it is usually senseless for someone else to contradict us for we do not judge whether we are feeling pleasure or not but we express it. Pleasure is not a mental state that we observe in our minds to see if we feel it or not.

The relationship between pleasure and its expression is not just causal. As I have said, a person may get pleasure from eating chocolate, but not if they are depressed. Pleasure is not just a sensation for it depends on the context for its meaning. Pleasure and its expression hang together in the way the parts of a sentence do. They are part of our life. But if we are to judge if someone else is pleased or not, then we may have to ask them and judge whether they are lying. Often however we know they are pleased because of our own reactions to their expressions of pleasure, and these expressions may not be verbal. It may be that a large part of our responses to the expressive behaviour of our fellow human beings is inherent from birth. Just watch an ordinary mother responding to her baby.

Babies do not wonder what its smiles and frowns mean, but respond to other people's smiles and frowns. These shared tendencies between people are basic and part of our animal nature. Mammals, especially monkeys and apes, make complicated gestures to one another and respond to them.

A smile, as an expression of pleasure, is a natural form of human expression. Thus:

> a facial expression not susceptible of gradual and subtle alterations; but which had, say, just five positions; when it changed it would snap

> straight from one to another. Would this fixed smile really be a smile? And why not – I might not be able to react as I do to a smile. Maybe it would not make me smile myself.
>
> A facial expression that was completely fixed couldn't be a friendly one. Variability and irregularity are essential to a friendly expression. Irregularity is part of its physiognomy.
>
> (Wittgenstein, 1980b: 614–5)

A face with a fixed smile or one that snapped from one position to another would not be alive with the smile. Expressions of pleasure are not fixed patterns. A smile holds the potential of laughter. If someone produced a laughter-like sound and facial expression, which was preceded by and followed by a straight face, we would be puzzled as to what to make of it.

Are smiles merely conventional, constituting discrete units of meaning? A celebrated case is that of the Japanese servant smiling as he tells his master his child has just died. Do Japanese then smile to express grief? Is the convention just different? This is not so. The servant smiles as it is unseemly in his tradition for him to burden his master with his own grief; he hides his feelings under an expression of well-being. His smile is a smile like ours. What is different is the convention that the servant must take care not to burden his master with his grief.

Joy is different from pleasure although the words can sometimes be substituted. 'I enjoyed my holiday' and 'The holiday gave me lots of pleasure' are very similar in meaning. But joy cannot be measured over time in the way pleasure can. If someone says they enjoyed their holiday we cannot sensibly ask for how long the joy lasted. We could enjoy a holiday but have felt pain at times, been bored, and so on.

Joy is not so closely bound to the body as is pleasure. Wittgenstein asks:

> How does one realize that the expression of joy is not the expression of some bodily pain? (An <u>important</u> question.)
>
> How does one know that the expression of enjoyment is not the expression of a sensation?
>
> (Wittgenstein, 1980a: 858–9)

Elsewhere he gives a tentative analysis of joy.

> 'I feel great joy' – Where? – that sounds like nonsense. And yet one does say 'I feel a joyful agitation in my breast'. – But why is joy not localised? Is it because it is distributed over the whole body? Even where the feeling that arouses joy is localised, joy is not: if for example we rejoice in the smell of a flower. – Joy is manifested in facial expression, in behaviour (but we do not say that we are joyful in our faces).

'But I do have a real <u>feeling</u> of joy!' Yes, when you are glad you really are glad. And of course joy is not joyful behaviour, nor yet a feeling round the corners of the mouth and the eyes.

'But "joy" surely designates an inward thing'. No. 'Joy' designates nothing at all. Neither any inward nor any outward thing.

(Wittgenstein, 1981: 486–7)

Joy, happiness and many other feelings and moods can be expressed by sense impressions. Think of the many feelings and moods that can be expressed in music.

One connection between moods and sense impressions is that we use mood-concepts to describe sense impressions and images. We say of a theme, a landscape, that it is sad, glad etc. But much more important, of course, is our using all mood concepts to describe human faces, actions, behaviours.

(Wittgenstein, 1981: 505)

We talk of friendly faces and eyes, of people looking happy. The friendly eyes and mouth, the wagging of a dog's tail, are among the primary symbols of friendliness; they are parts of the phenomena that are called friendliness. The characteristic mark of most feelings is that there is an expression of them – such as a facial expression or gestures. We give signs of delight, sadness and remorse. We cannot say that they are about physical sensations or psychological states (Wittgenstein, 1981: 506–27)

Yet still we mustn't forget that joy goes along with physical well-being, and sadness, or at least depression, often with being physically out of sorts. – If I go for a walk and take pleasure in everything, then it is surely true that this would not happen if I were feeling unwell. But I now express my joy, saying, e.g. 'How marvellous all of this is!' – did I mean to say that all of these things were producing pleasant feelings in me?

In the very case where I'd express my joy like this: 'The tree and the sky and the birds make me feel good all over' – still what's in question here is not causation, nor empirical concomitance, etc. etc.

(Wittgenstein, 1980b: 322)

There is a connection between happiness and a good life; authenticity, which is an ethical term, is vital to happiness. Wittgenstein (1961a: 6.43) wrote: The world of the happy man is a different one from that of the unhappy man.

An important point is the question of reward. Pleasure is an essential part of life; it is difficult to conceive of human life without it, although some fanatics have tried to get rid of all pleasure by practising various austerities such as starving themselves, shutting themselves away from all human contact, and so on. This is the result of a muddle. Authentic action is an activity that involves pleasure. But we are often tempted to seek 'pleasure' in itself, as if it were a sensation that we can possess outside of any activity. But this does not necessarily make us happy. Chocolate gives me pleasure but not to eat it all day. It is possible to give women prolonged orgasms with an instrument but it has been found that most women prefer sex with a man, although men are no rival to instruments. Ascetics who try to get rid of all pleasure are reacting against those who seek pleasure in itself; some people try to 'have' it, others try to get rid of it.

A vital point is that life involves uncertainty. Not only is this part of most people's experience but mathematicians and natural scientists have shown that chaos, randomness and contingency are part of the natural world and we are part of this. So there is a paradox. We seek happiness; we try to have it under control by the use of drugs, CBT, various other therapies, religious practices, scientific discovery, and so on. Yet life involves uncertainty; it cannot be completely controlled. If we could completely control happiness, would we be happy?

Many people have discussed this problem. I will keep to Wittgenstein who was an existential thinker. In his notebooks, mostly written when he was a soldier in the trenches in the First World War, Wittgenstein wrote: 'In order to live happily I must be in agreement with the world. And that is what "being happy" means' (1961b: 75).

A few lines later he wrote:

> Fear in face of death is the best sign of a false, i.e. a bad, life.
> When my conscience upsets my equilibrium, then I am not in agreement with something. But what is this? Is it <u>the world</u>? (p. 75).

Then a little later he wrote:

> Live happy (lebe glücklich).
>
> (Wittgenstein, 1961b: 75)

It is clear that a hedonistic interpretation of these remarks is way off the mark; it is not pleasurable to face bombs, bullets and other machines of war. Harmonizing with the world is not something that can be described by telling a person what to do because the world is contingent; we sometimes have to face bullets but at other times sunshine, music and love. We are not in a situation that can be identified with a particular set of facts in the world. *Live happy* implies that being happy is not something over and above our actions, nor can it be equated with any particular action. It implies that we should abandon all craving that is directed at something particular in the world. It seems that all we can say is that the world of the happy is a happy world. There is no objective mark of it that can be described.

But this leaves we therapists stymied. To tell our patients 'Live happy' would not be of much help. Yet to give them a set of rules or to imagine that we should use a particular set of techniques that will make them happy are equally false, if we see the importance and creativity of uncertainty and chaos in life.

Every description of things *in* the world consists of meaningful sentences. These sentences are contingent, depicting contingent situations; as everything in the world is contingent, they could be otherwise. So we have a paradox here. The only true thing to say about happiness is 'Live happy' but this is senseless as any meaningful sentence is contingent. What are we to say to our patients?

Wittgenstein wrote: 'There is indeed the inexpressible in speech. This shows itself; it is the mystical (1961a: 6.522 Ogden trans. modified).

Wittgenstein is not claiming that there are ineffable truths that can be known by mystics, 'spiritual' people, transpersonal psychologists, Wittgensteinians, and so on and that these truths are the solution to the problems of life. There is a vast literature on these 'truths' and various religions and sects fight over who really possesses them. Rather, he is showing that language itself will reveal how it functions if we attend to it closely. The inexpressible cannot be possessed by any group.

Wittgenstein (1975) is engaged in an activity of laying bare what language itself reveals. Thus: 'I cannot use language to get outside of language' (para 6). The attempt to do this is, however, very deep. We search high and low as we try to solve the problems of life. We feel compelled to do this but it is ultimately futile. 'The solution of the problem of life is seen in the vanishing of the problem' (1961a: 6.521).

7 The 'Layard thesis' that there are many hundreds of thousands of people in our society who seek relief from distress and unhappiness is of course true.

I would remind people of Aristotle. He thought that the prime need is to create a society that values *human* flourishing. A society like ours, which values therapy but does not seriously examine the society that helps to create this unhappiness, is corrupt.

I have much sympathy with Furedi's book (Furedi, 2004). He points out that that there is very little evidence that the enormous influence of the therapy culture in the last 100 years has done much to increase human happiness. It has enabled therapists to flourish but not much else.

People for many centuries have been searching for an algorithm for happiness. There is no reason to suppose that they will cease to do so. Happiness pills, therapies that guarantee happiness, are on the horizon. They will no doubt have enormous success, bringing much pleasure to some and pain and disappointment to others: followed by doubt and more searching. A pattern that has a long history.

A linguist from the Massachusetts Institute of Technology (MIT) studied the Pirahã for 15 years; they are a tribe living in the Amazonian jungle. He wrote: 'I have never heard a Pirahã say that he or she is worried ... psychologists from MIT Brain and Cognitive Science Departments, commented that the Pirahãs appear to be the happiest people they had ever seen ...'. They suggested that to measure happiness they would 'measure the time that the average Pirahã spends smiling and laughing and then to compare this with the number of minutes members of other societies ... spend smiling and laughing. They suggested that the Pirahãs would win hands down' (Everett, 2008: 278).

The Pirahãs have no psychologists, counsellors or medical doctors; few live beyond 50 years.

8 I fail to see any point in every therapy aligning itself with CBT. This merely seems to be a power move by CBT therapists.

References

Everett, D. (2008) *Don't Sleep, there are Snakes*, London: Profile Books.

Furedi, F. (2004) *Therapy Culture*, London: Routledge.

Sulloway, F.J. (1992) *Freud, Biologist of the Mind: Beyond the Psychoanalytic Legend*, 2nd edn, Cambridge, MA: Harvard University Press.

Van Fraassen, B.C. (2008) *Scientific Representation*, Oxford: Clarendon Press.

Wheeler, M. (2005) *Reconstructing the Cognitive World*, Cambridge, MA: The MIT Press.

Wittgenstein, L. (1961a) *Tractatus Logico-Philosophicus*, trans. D.F. Pears and B.F. McGuiness. London: Routledge & Kegan Paul.

Wittgenstein, L. (1961b) *Notebooks 1914–1916*, 2nd edn, trans. G.E.M. Anscombe. Chicago, IL: University of Chicago Press.

Wittgenstein, L. (1975) *Philosophical Remarks*, trans. R. Hargreaves & R. White. Oxford: Blackwell.

Wittgenstein, L. (1980a) *Remarks on the Philosophy of Psychology*, Vol. 1, trans. G.E.M. Anscombe. Oxford: Blackwell.

Wittgenstein, L. (1980b) *Remarks on the Philosophy of Psychology*, Vol. 2, trans. C.G. Luckhardt and M.A.E. Aue. Oxford: Blackwell.

Wittgenstein, L. (1981) *Zettel*, 2nd edn, trans. G.E.M. Anscombe. Oxford: Blackwell.

Wittgenstein, L. (2001) *Philosophical Investigations*, 3rd edn, trans. E. Anscombe. Oxford: Blackwell.

5 Systemic family and couples therapy

Peter Stratton

> No man is an island, entire of itself; every man is a piece of the continent, a part of the main . . .
>
> John Donne, Meditation XVII (1624) (women too, and children.)

The systemic paradigm was built first on the radical shift in thinking around the 1950s from energy to information. Engineers such as Norbert Wiener (1948) who had studied guided weapons systems during the Second World War started to apply the ideas of goal-seeking systems guided by feedback of information to aspects of human functioning. There may have been an element of hubris in choosing schizophrenia for their first attempts to understand psychopathology in these terms. But it led to the discovery that behaviour that had seemed bizarre and inexplicable when people were observed in isolation suddenly made much more sense when they were observed with their families. So the field developed its emphasis on meaning, communication and context, and was ready to welcome von Bertalanffy's (1968) general system theory as a core paradigm. The early development of the field from around 1950 onwards is well described in Chapter 2 of Dallos and Draper (2005). This text also offers an excellent overview of systemic family and couples therapy (SFCT) as does Carr (2006). While the role of systems theory has been challenged (e.g. Rivett and Street, 2003), and it is true that SFCT has not been good at incorporating the advances in systems science over the past 40 years, the basic concept still underpins the modality.

A note on naming. Although there are differing views in the field, I am taking the systemic approach not as a metaphor but as a fundamental position about psychological aetiology and treatment. In my view the systemic position is a core basis on which all other approaches to family and couples therapy are built. Where useful, the particular orientations of some of the major current models are considered in this chapter. But always within a framework of systemic thinking. As a label, I am using SFCT. Systemic psychotherapists work with individuals, couples, whole and part families, several families at once, and the systems of professionals from many disciplines that become involved with families. All this work is conducted within a systemic framework. I have explicitly included couples work because systemic therapy is widely used with couples in relationship and this way of working has good evidence based on an excellent manual (Jones and Asen, 2000). In the USA couples have been assumed to be married and the field has the label 'marital and family therapy' (MFT).

The world view underpinning SFCT

The systemic view is that when something is part of a powerful reciprocally influencing system, then its behaviour not only has to be understood in terms of the ways the system operates. Long-term change is more likely to be achieved by changing the way the system operates rather than changing the individual and hoping the system adapts. A psychology colleague, John Richards, in the 1970s, described individual psychotherapy as being 'like fishing a drowning man out of a river, teaching him to ride a bicycle, then throwing him back into the river'. Not entirely fair to all therapies, but very systemic.

SFCT attends to the ways that family and other close relationships form people's meanings. From conception onwards, each individual is sustained by the family relationships that surround them and their major formative adaptations are to and through these relationships. When we see a consistency in the way a person operates, whether conceptualized as a pathology, a personality or an unfortunate habit, we look to the family, past, present and future, for understanding. The understanding needs to be both cognitive and emotional, and different forms of the therapy will find a different balance between alternative understandings of the origin, and the seeking for alternative futures. But all will work with using the understandings in order to increase people's options. And, in general, the more different perspectives that can be brought into play the better, which naturally leads to finding that having several family members present makes the work much easier.

Model of the person

Systemic therapy has taken a keen interest in the ideas of philosophers such as Foucault and Derrida. It is therefore consistent with this way of thinking to move quickly to deconstruct meanings and identify dominant societal assumptions in what we encounter. Here we are offered a heading that bypasses the main thrust of systemic thinking. SFCT does not work primarily in terms of a model of the individual person. Furthermore, as a systemic therapist, I not only notice that every other chapter in this book is concerned only with therapy for the individual client; they are also only concerned with adults. But most adult clients are involved with children who are a major source of happiness and a non-trivial source of psychopathology. And children are also entitled to happiness. And they are fun to work with. How do other therapies get quickly to the point with a depressed mother without the benefit of a young child saying, 'Mummy gets cross with us when daddy comes home drunk'?

So this heading points up the difference between systemic and individual therapy. The currently dominant paradigm of social constructionism sees reality as what is constructed between people, but finds it unhelpful to think of the person as an independent entity. As Andersen put it:

> Language is a creative living force in the process of making meaning and the formulation of it. Since language also is a basic element in and indivisible from conversations, meanings are to a large extent created in the space between persons. This . . . says that; if a centre of a person exists, it exists between the person and other persons; in the language; in the conversations, in the relationships, in the culture.
>
> (Andersen, 1998: 75)

SFCT has been returning to ideas of Bahtin and Vygotsky (Seikkula, 2003) to develop a concept of therapy as collaborative dialogue (Anderson and Goolishian, 1988; Bertrando, 2007). Also in parallel with other modalities, SFCT has taken up the concept of positioning, drawing particularly on the formulations by Rom Harré (Harré and Moghaddam, 2003) Out of these developments has come an interest in the idea of the self as dialogically constructed in each encounter (Hermans, 2001). Valsiner (2002) stresses the dynamic functioning of the dialogical self as the way that people create meaning in their relationships. With this perspective, the self is not a fixed or laboriously changing entity, but is fluidly created in dialogue and thereby readily open to change as the therapist enters the web of relationships. However, there is a corresponding risk that changes achieved during therapy may be quickly lost once the client moves to a different context. But the special flavour of family therapy is that the therapist becomes a participant, perhaps with a referred client, in the operation of their family relationships. So the perturbations created by the therapeutic activity must be responded to in the session, and have the capacity to co-create an enthusiastic reconstruction of definitions of selves in relation.

Within all this, when working with a family, you are conversing with individual people. Entering the world of another person is a skill shared with all other therapies including CBT, and constructivism has been a substantial movement within systemic therapy. The radical constructivism of Maturana (Maturana and Varela, 1980) helped the field shift to a clear relativistic position with a recognition that each person is a system as well as a part of relational systems. In fact, Stratton (2003a) has argued for a positioning of SFCT with constructivism at the centre in order to be able to access in one direction the biology of emotions, neuropsychology and when useful, 'reality'; while in the other direction being able to readily make use of social constructionism and, when useful, postmodernism. Where SFCT has adopted something like this position, it can draw on aspects of many other therapies including CBT.

The possibility of objectivity?

A major shift in systemic thinking developed from a rejection of the idea of an 'observing system' in the second cybernetics and culminated from around 1980 with a rejection of the idea of the therapist as an expert on the problems of the client. The move was to a collaborative position in which understandings were cultivated for their capacity to improve relationships and the lives of individuals within the family. Anderson and Goolishian (1988) attempted a strong position of 'not knowing' in order to combat therapist assumptions of expert knowledge.

A position on objective reality from that time:

> when we perceive a complex reality, the meaning that emerges is not a property of the external object, and it is not something just inside us. It is created (we tend to say co-created) between us and the reality. Giving up the idea of perception as being a kind of picture, more or less accurate, of reality, enables us to recognise that there may be many alternative perceptions. Furthermore it is not the case that one is correct and the others are wrong. Now we can see that when our perceptions are not helping us, it may be possible to find an alternative perspective to lay alongside the view we already have. In this way we can enrich our understanding, and open up new possibilities for action. Although we reject the idea of one perspective being true and the others false, we do not see all perceptions as equally useful.
>
> (Stratton et al., 1990: 11)

As SFCT moved from observing to participating and with increasing value attributed to feminist and multicultural working, the power of therapist assumption became apparent. A powerful influence in helping therapists to recognize and control the effects of their assumptions was provided by Cecchin, et al. (1994) in what they called 'the cybernetics of prejudices'. SFCT has gone through a phase of strong postmodernism in which attempts were made to deny the existence of reality, but has now largely settled for focusing on the meanings created through dialogue as the most effective therapeutic strategy. Because we are dealing with major life issues, therapists will be confronted by situations where this stance has to be abandoned, and probably realities attended to. A solution has been the proposal by Lang et al. (1990) of working in different 'domains'. There will be times when a therapist needs to indicate to the family that they are moving out of the therapeutic domain and into a position of, for example, reporting to the police, or helping with housing.

Can we generalize about human experience on the basis of your approach?

Because SFCT is formulated on understanding family processes, the field has created a detailed understanding of family functioning. Since family life is a cornerstone of human experience, it is in an excellent position to offer its understandings in a wider context. For example, contributions by systemic family therapists have been an important part of recent conferences of the Family and Parenting Institute and, as discussed below, family therapists are meeting with politicians and government advisers to provide an understanding of family needs and how to address them. Within academic disciplines, Stratton (2003b) has reviewed for developmental psychology the range of contributions that systemic family therapy can make to an understanding of development within the family.

Does your approach have a distinctive view on 'evidence'?

Neither the objectives of SFCT nor the usual practice in the UK lend themselves to standard paradigms of evidence. Also, where randomized control trials (RCTs) have been carried out, they have generally used outcome measures designed for other purposes. For example, Leff et al. (2000) demonstrated substantial effects of systemic couples therapy using the Beck depression inventory that was specifically designed to be sensitive to the effects of CBT. There are four further issues that mean that SFCT requires a different approach to research:

1 In generic practice a clinic will see families with a wide variety of problems and so will find it difficult to amass a sample of clients with a specific diagnosis.
2 There are few manualized formulations of SFCT specific to diagnostic conditions.
3 The experience that in practice the referral diagnosis is a route into therapy but is frequently supplanted by the more fundamental problems of relationship in the family. So family therapists do not work

through diagnoses though they may engage in negotiations with the family about the nature of the problems, develop hypotheses that they can share with the family, and work in terms of formulations (Vetere and Dallos, 2003).

4 The focus is, as described below, on 'second-order change' in the family relationships as a way of maximizing the potential for therapeutic gains to be carried through into the future lives and new challenges of the family.

These issues are problematic because practitioners regard findings of efficacy from specialist research clinics uninformative about the effectiveness of everyday practice. One solution is to base studies on available data from ordinary practice. This approach has many advantages: the data are collected after the therapy is reported so there is much less scope for researcher bias to influence the results; and data sets can be far more substantial than is possible in experimental designs. The differences from randomized control trial methodology can be seen, according to choice, as limitations in research purity or as advantages in making the findings relevant to practice. For example, clients have gone through the usual processes of gaining access to a particular therapy rather than being randomly allocated; wider consequences of the therapy can be examined, not just the symptom reduction specified in the research; data are generated about normal practice, such as number of sessions, rather than having these specified by the needs of research; direct indicators of client satisfaction, especially dropouts, are not affected by the exceptional efforts made in most RCTs to ensure that people complete the treatment. One such series of studies by Russell Crane (2009) at Brigham Young University reports samples of up to 470 000 therapies. For example, Moore et al. (in press) conclude that MFT is effective and cost-effective, but needs to be delivered by properly trained therapists. It also has beneficial consequences for the whole family and can save the health system substantial amounts of money through the healthier functioning of all family members. A summary of the findings of this group has been published by Stratton (2009).

Despite a preference by constructionist therapists for qualitative research, the requirement for quantitative outcome measures will increase both from purchasers of therapy and clients. Also it is clear that NICE is determined to base guidance only on results from RCTs. As a response to these challenges, research teams have been creating new measures of change in family functioning during therapy to fit current practice. In the USA Pinsof et al. (2009) have produced a new measure: the systemic therapy inventory of change, which would need to be administered in the context of a research study. A team in the UK has created a brief indicator of therapeutic changes in family functioning for routine clinical use (Stratton et al., in press). Because it is a systemic measure but was modelled on the CORE, it is called the SCORE.

Does your approach have a view on, or approach to, 'intersubjectivity'?

SFCT is intrinsically intersubjective. but has not generally taken up the concept in these terms. One approach with a bearing is the theory of coordinated management of meaning (CMM) (Barge and Barnett Pearce, 2004). See also Stratton (2007a) for an example of a CMM analysis of a failure of intersubjectivity. Hoffman (2007: 5) discussed Gregory Bateson's ideas about metaphor rather than logic being the natural form of communication so that 'advice and expertise were not enough (for psychotherapy) – you had to reach for connection at levels that lay beyond the scope of words'. Hoffman also discusses the work of Shotter (2005) who replaces dialogical versus monological with 'withness and aboutness'.

A sophisticated analysis of the relationships between systemic, intersubjectivity and paradigms of science is provided by Vasconcellos:

> Thus, I consider that when we speak of constructivism/constructionism we are referring mainly to one of the epistemological assumptions of the new-paradigmatic science, that of intersubjectivity. But given the integration of the three dimensions of the new paradigm of the science, I assume that it is impossible to have a new-paradigmatic proposal if it does not accomplish an integrating advance on the three epistemological dimensions. Thus, when we are constructivist or social constructionist and adopt not only the assumption of intersubjectivity, but also those of complexity and instability, we continue to be systemic and frankly new-paradigmatic.
>
> (Vasconcellos, 1999: 31)

What are the advantages and disadvantages of your approach in relation to CBT?

Because SFCT has very wide application and therapists work with whatever a family brings, it is not restricted to the diagnoses offered in referrals. There is a possible disadvantage in that the openness to the family dialogue very often means that the referral problem comes to be recognized as subordinate to a wider family difficulty. So whereas CBT can simply concentrate on the diagnosed 'mental illness', SFCT has come to deal with the full gamut of problems faced by families. We have, for example, no specialism in treating arachnophobia but have developed wide-ranging expertise in being useful to clients with major life issues such as child abuse, chronic illness, family violence, cultural displacement and poverty (Vetere and Dallos, 2003; Minuchin et al., 2007). While we have no diagnostically driven RCTs to compare our effectiveness in such areas with other therapies, there is extensive research evidence of effectiveness in the range of problems that affect family members (Stratton et al., in press).

A CBT therapist may sometimes see a parent and child together but we would claim that the four-year intensive training for SFCT, its focus on working with multiple generations (and not just working with a child in the presence of his or her parent) and the widespread use of a therapeutic team make the work very different. There is a specific orientation that comes from a starting position of a systemic perspective, of multiple understandings provided by family members and, if available, a supportive team. We work from an understanding that any individual person's psychological difficulties are intrinsically bound up with the relationships within which they function. Working directly with these relationships offers possibilities that are just not available when the perspective is to relieve the symptoms of an individual.

What is your approach's view about the alleged 'cost-effectiveness' and evidence/research-based 'efficacy' of the CBT approach?

CBT has good evidence that it achieves its primary objectives for many conditions; that is, it can take a person with a clear diagnosis of a specific mental illness and relieve their symptoms. It has rarely been compared with high-quality alternative treatments that take a very different approach, such as SFCT, and so it is difficult to make claims for its cost-effectiveness. More fundamentally, the support that this research provides for CBT is limited by the framing of research questions (Stratton, 2007b). If you see psychotherapy as a matter of curing a patient of some condition, then you will inevitably adopt research methodologies that were designed for that purpose. And so CBT has come to be evaluated primarily with RCTs that were developed to examine the efficacy of medical treatments for physical illnesses. A consequence is that CBT can only be compared with therapies that fit the same model, or with regimes that do not provide a specific alternative. So CBT has been primarily compared with drug treatments 'treatment as usual' or no treatment. There has not been a well-supported process of developing a research methodology specifically to determine the efficacy and cost-effectiveness of other forms of psychotherapy. If such a methodology was available and agreed, CBT could be compared with other therapies in their own terms.

Conception of therapeutic change?

The general systemic position is that change comes through changed relationships. The move during the 1980s to second-order cybernetics (mentioned above) led to a specification of second-order change: this being a change in the 'rules of the family game' that would transform the way family members tackled their lives, including their difficulties. All approaches to family therapy aim to give the family (and the therapist) a position that stands more outside their usual total immersion in their life, so that they can see alternatives. Whether this is expressed as meta-perspective, envisaging different futures, or restorying, it always has the character of a different vantage point. It derives from Bateson's ([1972]1973) proposal that if you cannot solve a problem you go to the next logical level, where the problem can be seen in a wider context.

How this is achieved varies with the model of family therapy. For example, transgenerational approaches see the roots of problems as having built up over generations and will work with the families of origin of parents, uncovering the assumptions that have been passed down and which have formed the definitions of what it is to be a spouse, a mother or a father. Others are almost entirely oriented to the future and how understandings of the future are affecting the present.

One particular aspect of SFCT is the emphasis on reflexive practice, and a recognition that the aspect of the therapeutic system that therapists can change directly is themselves. So there is some emphasis on the family changing through seeing their effect on the therapist. A related move is attention to reflecting processes (Anderson and Jensen, 2007). This concept was introduced by Tom Andersen writing about bringing the therapeutic team into the room to describe the effects of observing the therapist and family. This practice has become widespread in the UK so that when a therapist is working with the team, regular and imaginative use is made of the presence of the team that previously would have been invisible to the family.

Progressively, the research into 'common factors' is influencing SFCT. Concepts such as the therapeutic alliance, allegiance to the model and cultivating hope all have their counterparts within systemic theories of change.

How well, if at all, does or can your approach cohere with medical-model thinking?

The medical model, especially as operated by CBT, sees problematic behaviour as a condition of the individual that should be treated by changing the individual. This is clearly very different from the view that psychological difficulties arise as people struggle to cope with their lives and relationships, and are best helped through direct involvement in those lives and relationships.

However, a strongly held value in SFCT is to respect and attempt to understand the cultural positions of those with whom we work. Families very often come for therapy with a medical-style belief system ('we thought it was the orange juice but we need to find out what it is in his diet that makes him behave like this'). The systemic skill is to create other perspectives without the need to contradict the existing story (see the quote under 'Objectivity' on p. 60). This applies to other professionals as much as to families and is essential if we are to fulfil the role we often take of coordinating the actions of several different professionals on behalf of a client family. With this perspective, a medical model is just one particular cultural perspective that works well for certain people. Systemic practitioners do not share it, but are fortunate that the whole framework of their thinking equips them to help those who feel constrained to operate within that model.

What are the notions of 'happiness' and well-being in your approach?

Systemic therapists know about happiness because we spend all of our time working with people who want their families to be happier. It is easy in the face of current statistics and dissatisfaction with changes in family structures, the behaviour of youth and maybe of our personal family experiences, to problematize the family. This can lead to an acceptance that people who are unhappy (which covers nearly all *Diagnostic and Statistical Manual of Mental Disorders (DSM)* classifications) should be taken out of their families to a different context, and cured. Research tells a different story about families; one that leads to forms of therapy that treat the family as the most powerful resource for positive change. The task of therapy then becomes one of mobilizing that resource especially in families that have somehow become stuck in unproductive cycles of functioning from which they are not managing to escape.

But SFCT has wider objectives. As will be clear from various parts of this chapter, the profession feels that our experience of working with families while being able to call on a variety of theoretical perspectives and research from several disciplines has put it in a position to make a major contribution to enhance the capacities of families to create happiness and well-being.

How could or might your approach respond to the 'Layard thesis' that many hundreds of thousands of people are needing relief from psychological/emotional distress and unhappiness?

We appear to be in agreement with Lord Layard: 'In every study, family relationships (and our close private life) are more important than any other single factor in affecting our happiness' (2005: 63).

In light of this statement it is surprising that Lord Layard has given his support to an approach of taking people out of their family context to cure them by correcting their negative thinking. At present it seems that between 25–40 per cent of people referred to the 'improving access to psychological therapies' (IAPT) programme gain some benefit from low-level CBT. This is a major achievement, especially if it is found that the benefit is sustained.

The field of SFCT also recognizes that if we had wanted to make family therapy available on this scale, it would have been necessary to expand the training exponentially over the past 20 years. But we are pursuing other solutions. One is to use the understandings and techniques that we have developed to enhance the capacities of other professionals to work in relation to families. The optimal model appears to be to cascade systemic competences throughout service provision. The second option is to take a longer view in making our understanding of family processes available to agencies that can use it to improve family life and support the abilities of families to dissolve their own problems.

The family is at the top of the political agenda and the connection between family and social well-being is increasingly recognized. But while politicians value the family, their thinking comes from a whole cultural orientation of individuality. Thus, parenting programmes are primarily about applications of (well-researched) operant conditioning plus some attachment concepts. There is good evidence for the effectiveness of these, especially at the mild-to-moderate problems of children's behaviour. But humans are learning organisms, and operant conditioning is only about learning at a very basic level – it is really about training performance. So these programmes are effective in convincing parents that they have got their parenting wrong and work by training both children and parents into more approved behaviours. This is very different from constructing a repertoire of functional selves through communication within relationships. The Association for Family Therapy and Systemic Practice (www.aft.org.uk) has engaged with government agencies and programmes such as 'Think Family' to make as full a contribution as we can to implement their objectives.

One of the frameworks used within SFCT to approach societal difficulties is the ecosystemic position of Urie Bronfenbrenner (2005). This is a 'Russian doll' image of nested systems of the family. He identifies five levels of system interaction, and for a family problem of any complexity, intervention will have to take account of all of them. Each system opens up a wider context and provides greater diversity of options and sources of growth. We may choose to focus on the microsystemic level of events within the family, but each of the other shells will be operating. We might be particularly interested in the chronosystem through which the transgenerational history of the household exerts its influences, or the community within which the family lives. Swick and Williams (2006) describe how Bronfenbrenner's successive systemic levels can be mobilized to empower stressed families. Stratton (2008) offered a summary of a systemic response to the widespread psychological distress that Layard has publicized:

> Giving ourselves and families messages of pathology and deficit is undermining, and encourages agencies to concentrate on professional

expertise. If we give messages of resilience and empowerment we potentiate the orientations we need in families, while encouraging agencies to work collaboratively. Interventions must be assessed in terms of their effectiveness in having parents elicit what they need from their children and their own parents, and their other relational systems, to know what to do. Systemic family therapy methods are informative, but can be used within a framework of ecosystems and transactional adaptation to help families that have moved away from the collaborative position and are having difficulty finding their way back.

To what extent, if at all, would it be possible for your approach to align itself with, or even create a hybrid with, CBT?

When SFCT incorporates a constructivist position, it can make good use of CBT techniques. The more prescriptive CBT approaches sit uneasily with SFCT that has found collaborative dialogue to be a much more powerful source of change than expert instruction.

Some current models that have to some extent developed away from a systemic position appear to have more in common with CBT. In solution-focused therapy (Dallos and Draper, 2005; Trepper et al., 2006: chapter 3), the therapist might resolutely work to prevent the client talking about problems and focus only on things that have made the problem, even if only slightly, better. Then to build a plan for the future that builds on what the solutions say about the client's strengths and resources. Although solution-focused therapy grew out of systemic work, it is sometimes presented now as not requiring a systemic understanding. A similar process applied to narrative therapy (White, 2007). SFCT has eagerly taken up many of the techniques and imaginative ideas of both solution-focused and narrative therapies but it is interesting that during their development these approaches came to work primarily with individual clients. With their clear intention that the therapist should bring about change in the individual, they are closer to CBT than the systemic therapies that work by creating space for relationships to change in ways that make the problems of individual family members unnecessary or at least manageable.

Behaviour therapists have worked with families though usually only with the subsystem directly involved with the referring problem. As Nichols and Schwartz (2007: 196) say, 'unfortunately, failure to include – or even consider – the entire family in treatment may be disastrous' but they propose that the weaknesses could be corrected by broadening the perspective to include families as systems.

Some specific attempts have been made to create systemic CBT. Dummett (2006) has developed a systemic CBT approach largely based on attachment theory; Rhodes and Jakes (2009) have recently published an account of narrative CBT for psychosis. Janet Treasure and co-workers have reported on 'working with the families with eating disorders: a systemic approach' (see Treasure et al., 2008).

Given how SFCT welcomes diversity and has detailed structures for putting alternative world views alongside each other, there should be further scope for the two approaches to benefit from each other. Even when CBT takes account of a client's relationships, its practitioners may do well to adopt the theoretical positions and skills that SFCT has developed to work equally strongly for the benefit of all the people in that relationship.

References

Andersen, T. (1998) 'One sentence of five lines about creating meaning: in perspective of relationship, prejudice and bewitchment', *Human Systems*, 9: 73–80.

Anderson, H. and Goolishian, H. (1988) 'A view of human systems as linguistic systems: some preliminary and evolving ideas about the implications for clinical theory', *Family Process*, 27: 371–93.

Anderson, H. and Jensen, P. (2007) *Innovations in the Reflecting Process*, London: Karnac Books.

Barge, J.K. and Barnett Pearce, W. (2004) 'A reconnaissance of CMM research', *Human Systems*, 15: 13–32.

Bateson, G. ([1972]1973) *Steps to an Ecology of Mind*. Boulder, CO: Chandler Publishing Co. and Paladin Books.

Bertalanffy, L. von (1968) *General System Theory*, New York: Braziller.

Bertrando, P. (2007) *The Dialogical Therapist: Dialogue in Systemic Practice*, London: Karnac Books.

Bronfenbrenner, U. (2005) *Making Human Beings Human: Bioecological Perspectives on Human Development*, Thousand Oaks, CA: Sage Publications.

Carr, A. (2006) *Family Therapy: Concepts, Process and Practice*, 2nd edn, Chichester: Wiley.

Cecchin, G., Lane, G. and Ray, W.A. (1994) *The Cybernetics of Prejudices in the Practice of Psychotherapy*, London: Karnac Books.

Dallos, R. and Draper, R. (2005) *An Introduction to Family Therapy*, 2nd edn, Maidenhead: Oxford University Press.

Dummett, N. (2006) 'Processes for systemic cognitive-behavioural therapy with children, young people and families', *Behavioural and Cognitive Psychotherapy*, 34: 179–89.

Harré, R. and Moghaddam, F. (2003) *The Self and Others: Positioning Individuals and Groups in Personal, Political, and Cultural Contexts*, London: Praeger.

Hermans H.J.M. (2001) 'The dialogical self: toward a theory of personal and cultural positioning', *Culture & Psychology*, 7(3): 243–81.

Hoffman, L. (2007) 'Practising "withness": a human art', in H. Anderson and P. Jensen (eds), *Innovations in the Reflecting Process*, London: Karnac Books, pp. 3–15.

Jones, E. and Asen, E. (2000) *Systemic Couple Therapy and Depression*, London: Karnac Books.

Lang, P., Little, M. and Cronen, V. (1990) 'The systemic professional: domains of action and the question of neutrality', *Human Systems: The Journal of Systemic Consultation and Management*, 2: 39–56.

Layard, R. (2005) *Happiness: Lessons from a New Science*, London: Penguin Books.

Leff, J., Vearnals, S., Brewin, C.R., Wolff, G., Alexander, B., Asen, E., Dayson, D., Jones, E., Chisholm, D. and Everitt, B. (2000) 'The London depression intervention trial: randomised controlled trial of antidepressants v. couple therapy in the treatment and maintenance of people with depression living with a partner: clinical outcome and costs', *British Journal of Psychiatry*, 177: 95–100.

Maturana, H.R. and Varela, F.J. (1980) *Autopoeisis and Cognition*, Dordrecht: D. Riedel.

Minuchin, P., Colpatino, J. and Minuchin, S. (2007) *Working with Families of the Poor*, 2nd edn, New York: Guilford Press.

Moore, A.M., Hamilton, S., Crane, D. Russell and Fawcett, D. (in press) 'The influence of professional license type on the outcome of family therapy', *American Journal of Family Therapy*.

Nichols, M. and Schwartz, R. (2007) *Family Therapy: Concepts and Methods*, 6th edn, Boston, MA: Allyn & Bacon.

Pinsof, W.M. et al. (2009) 'Laying the foundations for progress research in family, couple, and individual therapy: the development and psychometric features of the initial systemic inventory of change', *Psychotherapy Research*, 19: 143–56.

Rhodes, J. and Jakes, S. (2009) *Narrative CBT for Psychosis*, Hove: Routledge.

Rivett, M. and Street, E. (2003) *Family Therapy in Focus*, London: Sage Publications.

Seikkula, J. (2003) 'Dialogue is the change: understanding psychotherapy as a semiotic process of Bakhtin, Voloshinov, and Vygotsky', *Human Systems*, 14: 75–86.

Shotter, J. (2005) 'Inside processes: transitory understandings, action guiding anticipations, and withness thinking', *International Journal of Action Research*, 1(1): 157–89.

Stratton, P. (2003a) 'How families and therapists construct meaning through anticipatory schemas', *Human Systems*, 14: 119–30.

Stratton, P. (2003b) 'Contemporary families as contexts for development: contributions from systemic family therapy', in J. Valsiner and A.K. Connolly (eds) *Handbook of Developmental Psychology*, New York: Sage Publications, pp. 333–57.

Stratton, P. (2007a) 'Systemic perspectives on how simultaneous dialogical relationships create the self of the therapist', *European Journal of School Psychology*, 4(2): 417–24.

Stratton, P. (2007b) 'Formulating research questions that are relevant to psychotherapy', *Mental Health and Learning Disabilities Research and Practice*, 4: 83–97.

Stratton, P. (2008) 'Parenting is a family process: a story from research'. Keynote address to the Family and Parenting Institute Conference 2008 'Getting it Right for Families?' Available online at www.psyc.leeds.ac.uk/staff/p.m.stratton/ (accessed 3 September 2009).

Stratton, P. (2009) 'Amazing research by Russell Crane and colleagues', *Context*, 104: 40–1.

Stratton, P., Preston-Shoot, M. and Hanks, H. (1990) *Family Therapy: Training and Practice*, Birmingham: Venture Press.

Stratton, P., Bland, J., Janes, E. and Lask, J. (in press) 'Developing a practicable outcome measure for systemic family therapy: The SCORE', submitted to *Journal of Family Therapy*.

Swick, K.J. and Williams, R.D. (2006) 'An analysis of Bronfenbrenner's bio-ecological perspective for early childhood educators: implications for working with families experiencing stress', *Early Childhood Education Journal*, 33(5): 371–8.

Treasure, J., Schmidt, U. and MacDonald, P. (2008) *The Clinician's Guide to Collaborative Caring in Eating Disorders*, London: Routledge.

Trepper, T.S., Dolan, Y. and McCollum, E.E. (2006) 'Steve De Shazer and the future of solution-focused therapy', *Journal of Marital and Family Therapy*, 32: 133–9.

Valsiner, J. (2002) 'Forms of dialogical relations and semiotic autoregulation within the self', *Theory and Psychology*, 12(2): 251–65.

Vasconcellos, M.J.E. de (1999) 'Setting constructivist/social constructionist proposals in the context of the new-paradigmatic science', *Human Systems*, 10: 25–34.

Vetere, A. and Dallos, R. (2003) *Working Systemically with Families*, London: Karnac Books.

White, M. (2007) *Maps of Narrative Practice*, New York: W.W. Norton.

Wiener, N. (1948) *Cybernetics: Or Control and Communication in the Animal and the Machine*, Cambridge, MA: The MIT Press.

6 Lacanian psychoanalysis and CBT

Gaps

Ian Parker

One way of taking a distance from cognitive-behaviour therapy (CBT), opening up a gap between the pervasively influential CBT in mental health service provision and our own practice, is to locate that particular form of therapy as a cultural form; a construction peculiar to a particular point in history. Layard (2005) in his book *Happiness: Lessons from a New Science* claims that there is congruence between positive psychological approaches like CBT and Buddhism; a rather strange claim given that Buddhism 'accepts suffering as a regular part of the emotional flux of living and dying' (Pilgrim, 2008: 253). Such congruence only pertains to modern forms of Buddhism that have adapted to contemporary capitalism, perhaps only to one Japanese sect felicitously called the 'Institute for Research in Human Happiness' that has its own temples with the slogan 'Happy Science' inscribed over the entrance. In that approach 'The past only provides material for contemplation now, and the future is unknown. Each and every person, without exception, is living in the single day of "now" ' (Okawa, 2002: 1).

Happy Science has an interesting take on one of Lacan's favourite Chinese philosophers, Chuang-Tzu, who puzzled about the relationship between dreaming and reality, who showed that we open our eyes so we can carry on dreaming, that reality is suffused with fantasy and so that this reality must be differentiated from the 'real'. For Lacan (1973) a key defining characteristic of waking consciousness is that we are always in the gaze of the other, present to them as a function of being a human subject. According to happy scientists, Chuang-Tzu was a reincarnation of Eros, and he later enjoyed another life as René Descartes and later still, in a curious twist that is uncannily resonant with the dualist pretensions of cognitive-behaviour therapists, as Franz Kafka (Okawa, 2002: 98).

World views and models

Unlike CBT, Lacanian psychoanalysis does not present a 'model' of the person, and so we are immediately at odds with the idea that we should step back into what we pretend is an 'objective' position from which we can assay the evidence for and against different approaches. Different approaches function well in different cultural contexts, and what we face today is a therapeutic approach that is suited to the kind of common sense at work in the administered world that Kafka described. Let us first take a distance from this world view, a collection of 'common sense statements' (Miller, 2005: 129), a common discourse 'infested with CBT' in which even children reveal 'how evaluation haunts their dreams, transforming them into nightmares' (Mariage, 2007: 111).

The problems with CBT pertain not so much to the therapeutic approach itself as to the normative system that it embeds itself in, underlying assumptions that it mirrors and moral goals that it endorses. Each of those particular aspects can be attended to using the concepts of the symbolic, imaginary and real (Lacan, 2006), and then it is possible to see that the way those aspects are threaded together poses problems for psychoanalytic practice.

A normative system

First, we can grasp this normative system as a particular organization of what we call the *symbolic*. Now what should be noticed about this symbolic is that it is composed not only of spoken and written language – the instructions and training manuals of a CBT programme, for example – but also the material institutional practices that enclose and define those who are being trained as therapists and assistants. The symbolic encompasses all the signifying elements through which practitioners and their clients come to understand their relation to each other and possibilities for change, and so it includes the process of diagnosis by which the complexity of distress is rendered into something that is given a psychiatric label, the procedure by which it is turned into a psychological phenomenon and the relationship through which the assistant seems to be providing therapy.

CBT became popular in clinical psychology, but 'it is essentially a form of psychiatric treatment, the roots of which are not in cognitive science' (Pilgrim, 2008: 252). One only has to look at the history of the *Diagnostic and Statistical Manual of Mental Disorders (DSM)* to see how 'the standardization and transformation of qualitative categories into quantitative scales' then managed 'to eliminate the psychiatrist's subjectivity' (Guégen, 2005: 133), a first step to eliminating the subjectivity of the patient. It is a normative system insofar as it targets certain categories of subject, primarily those on incapacity benefit who live in deprived areas of London or the north of England, the site of the first two improving access to psychological therapies (IAPT) pilot studies, and it turns CBT as such into an apparatus governed by a certain economic agenda.

Lacanians work in and with the symbolic, of course, but we facilitate the emergence of something for the analysand as subject of the symbolic that is quite distinctive, even therapeutic. The symbolic system operates as a normative series of prescriptions in CBT, for it stipulates how the subject should and should not understand reality. For Lacanians, in contrast, this symbolic is a space of movement in relation to which the subject may take different positions as they combine signifying elements of the system in their own distinctive way. The analyst does not pretend to know how this system should be put together, and a gap is opened up between what the symbolic is as the treasury of signifiers and how it functions as something 'other' to the subject, an audience and point of reference for them. The 'otherness' of the symbolic, a realm into which an individual speaks but which is not entirely within their grip, is destroyed in CBT in the name of prediction and control, the subject is encouraged to predict and control how they will think and behave, but within strictly circumscribed limits, limits defined by what the CBT practitioner thinks the problem is and how the manual indicates it should be tackled.

Underlying assumptions

Second, what are therefore brought into play are underlying assumptions that mirror the system in which it operates; in the case of CBT in the context of an IAPT programme, this often pits the incapable or work-shy client against the poorly paid and newly trained assistant. This set of underlying assumptions that mirror the system itself sets in place a mirror relation between client and therapist that invites rivalry and identification, and this phenomenon Lacanians conceptualize as *imaginary*. At the one moment the client is positioned as 'other' to the therapist, but along a dimension, as an opposition between the two players in which therapist as expert draws on the knowledge they have been socialized into during their training to understand the client as someone who is treatable, but only treatable insofar as they fit into available categories and insofar as they follow certain procedures (House, 2003).

There is an educational component to the CBT process, but the potential identification between client and therapist is stalled by the fact that it would be very unusual for the therapist to have undergone CBT themselves. The imaginary dimension through which two subjects communicate with each other and think they are able to understand exactly what the other thinks and feels is an unavoidable and necessary illusion. CBT operates on a particular theory of language, a theory of description of external objects and internal states; in this approach it is assumed that 'language is unambiguous . . . may easily be used in an unequivocal fashion and that it can be explicit' (Miller, 2005: 130).

The supposed site of pure communication, the fantasy that there is such a thing as 'intersubjectivity', shared meaning in which there is supposed to be agreement about what the problem is and what the outcome should be, is then infused with hostility; 'the patient's subjectivity is annulled either because the explicit demand of the individual is answered immediately, or it is ignored and combated with a treatment that reforms and forbids by attempting to block thoughts' (Guégen, 2005: 133). There is therefore an allocation of positions in which the best that the client can hope for is that they will end up thinking in the way the therapist thinks that thinking should be. In this there is a connection between Lacanian and 'post-existentialist' perspectives in which 'we will never know what the other person thinks, and it is only through allowing a gap, with all its associated anxieties, that desire will emerge' (Loewenthal, 2008: 152).

Lacanians work with this imaginary dimension, even also inside it, but in order to give the subject a space to speak to them as other, a symbolic function that provides one of the formulae for transference as the 'subject supposed to know', that the analysand supposes that there is a subject who knows. The Lacanian psychoanalyst does not insist that they should understand exactly what the analysand means to communicate to them, and this is also why, in contrast to other psychoanalytic traditions, Lacanians do not as a rule interpret the transference. Such interpretation would lead them to imagine that they really were a subject who knew and it would convey to the analysand that someone else knew what they thought and even, as is the case in CBT, how they should think. This is why Lacanian psychoanalysis 'is not a psychological treatment in the sense of something done to the analysand by the analyst'; instead, it is 'the suspension of any pre-defined knowledge on the side of the analyst that allows the patient the opportunity to discover something about the particular forms of desire at stake in their suffering' (Litton, 2007: 186).

Moral goals

Third, the moral goals that CBT endorses operate not only at a symbolic and imaginary level but seal over what Lacanians call the dimension of the *real*, which in the clinic is the dimension of the subject that escapes from and confronts taken-for-granted reality with something unpredictable and wilful. This real is something disturbing and traumatic that a CBT programme must do its very best to avoid, but it is that dimension of the subject that the Lacanian psychoanalyst directs the treatment in order to open up, or to open up the possibility for. The real names a number of different phenomena, and Lacan conceptualizes it slightly differently at different points in his work.

At one point it is what is not susceptible to representation and as such has a traumatic quality, striking the subject as something completely out of their control, even at the level of chance (Lacan, 1973). At another point this real is conceptualized as if it is a kind of fold in the symbolic, a contradiction, an impossible site of antagonism internal to representation, and so to speak of something as real is to mark it as something that breaks from our definition of reality (Lacan, 1998). Objects produced under capitalism are 'constructed, deduced, calculated' and also produce a certain kind of relation of the subject to them; 'this is a new form of real that appeared with the industrial revolution, a real that is the product of measurement and figures' (Miller, 2007: 30).

What should be noted about CBT is that there are symbolic and imaginary dimensions to it as a practice that are organized in such a way as to preclude the real, for the therapist schooled in that tradition is only able to grasp phenomena insofar as they operate inside the system of reality that they think they understand and into which they are attempting to induct the client. In other words, there are aspects to the symbolic, imaginary and real that Lacanians can use to conceptualize what CBT is and what the problems boil down to, and the biggest problem is the way in which those three dimensions are locked together.

It should be said that Lacanian psychoanalysis does not operate as a world view, and does not aim to cure the world by taking everyone into analysis. By the same token, it has no reason to object to the range of weird and wonderful therapeutic modalities that are available today, including CBT. CBT is a useful and sometimes quite sufficient approach, and there is no reason why individuals should not engage in it to question their conception of the world and think through alternatives. The problem is that CBT is locked together into a world view and is given institutional power to define what therapy is within the National Health Service (NHS). It threatens to supplant other approaches and it threatens to redefine how those other approaches should understand themselves. It is this that Lacanians object to most.

Characteristics of Lacanian psychoanalysis

By bringing the notions of symbolic, imaginary and real to bear on this problem we face now – CBT embedded in a model of service provision that then threatens the existence of alternatives in the NHS – we are thereby able to highlight the distinctive Lacanian revolution in psychoanalysis that transforms psychoanalytic practice from being a helpmeet of psychiatry and the other psy sciences into a radical alternative. It is in this sense that Lacanian psychoanalysis pits itself against the medical model that is still powerful inside psychiatry and which casts its shadow over much contemporary psychology and psychotherapy. Instead, this radical alternative approach to the human subject and the way the subject comes to terms with its biologically grounded natural capacities and limits and its cultural–historical 'second nature' circles around a gap and how each of us tries to fill it (Haraway, 1989).

This gap that confronts the subject as an impossible chasm at the heart of their being at times of crisis, and which is most of the time sealed over by formations of the unconscious that we call symptoms, takes a number of different forms that we have specific terminology for. At one moment the gap operates as a lack, lack of satisfaction and lack of an object that would we think provide satisfaction; it is a lack that drives the movement from one thing to another, a movement that we sometimes refer to as the metonymy of desire. At another moment the gap configures yearning for connection with others and disappointment that it is not so easy or comfortable to fuse with the desire of another as we might have wished, and this we may refer to as the lack or impossibility of a sexual relation (Lacan, 1998).

Clinical work homes in on the forms of object that are conjured into being; forms of object that are sometimes given semblance in conscious representation in speech in analysis, but which function at another level of the subject tantalizingly ungraspable and unnameable as such. If there is one concept that Lacan (1973) could claim to have 'invented', and it should be remembered that he claimed that Freud 'invented' the unconscious rather than discovered it as if it was always already there, it is this ungraspable and unnameable object around which we trace ourselves in fantasy and in the reality that we try to make correspond with fantasy, the '*object a*'.

The singularity of the subject and the organization of their desire is therefore defined by the specific relation they have to what they have constructed as their object a, and so the specific orbit they trace around the specific representations they have of it as it sustains representations of others in the world. Lacanian psychoanalysis does not aim to correct faulty representations of the self or others but opens a space for the subject to speak something of the truth of their own particular relation to their objects, a space within which other positions may be taken towards the symbolic, imaginary and real aspects through which those objects are apprehended through modes of anxiety and enjoyment. This is why Lacanians argue that their practice stands in stark contrast to CBT, and that what is at stake is 'the possibility of transforming oneself through analysis on the basis of the work that operates as the care of the self' (Le Blanc, 2007: 85).

Evidence, efficacy and adaptation

The singularity of the subject is what we work with in psychoanalysis and it means that a standard treatment and routine implementation of it would betray not only the ethical stance of the analyst but invite each analysand to betray themselves. The desire that takes form as the subject journeys from one position to another as they track their way around their own objects is a desire that calls for an ethics of the gap, ethics that is crushed by the cognitive-behavioural grid through which treatment turns into adaptation. CBT is now embedded in a series of signifiers that name this adaptation as 'employment' and 'happiness', for instance, and that series of signifiers which is reduced to the rule of a 'master-signifier' then indicates that as a symbolic constellation into which the subject should be inducted there are ideological stakes to the success of IAPT.

For Lacanians it is this reduction that defines our age of happiness: 'Becoming a countable and comparable unit is the effective translation of the contemporary domination of the master-signifier in its purest, most stupid form: the number 1' (Miller, 2007: 9). This is above and beyond the cynical calculations that might be made about economic investment, in the pro-gramme paying for itself as it blocks access to incapacity benefit for those who have been rendered willing and able, cognitively and behaviourally prepared, for work. The assumption is that 'a symptom will respond to CBT to the satis-faction of the evaluation systems and return to productive happiness' (Evans, 2007: 145).

Lacanian objections to IAPT should indeed connect with arguments against this crude exploitative agenda, against the pretence that patching over distress leads to meaningful employment, but there are some deeper reasons why we do not buy into this agenda, reasons that are again rooted in our conception of the subject as subject of the symbolic, imaginary and real. Adap-tation is antithetical to Lacanian clinical practice not simply because we are against the adaptation of the subject to capitalist economic imperatives, production geared to profit that entails relentless exploitation of human and natural resources, but because there is a problem with adaptation as such. The problem of adaptation as such is particularly pertinent today, for 'The dis-course that supports the necessity of CBT is that of a generalised adaptation, of adaptation as the only value' (Le Blanc, 2007: 80). The attempt to adapt the subject itself runs against the 'second nature' that defines us as human beings and in which there is a difference between the kind of 'adaptation' that we might see governing animal behaviour and the 'disadaptation' that character-izes those beings for whom instinct has been derailed when it has turned into fantasy, beings who speak and who then also inhabit a symbolic universe that they must navigate but will fail to master.

CBT seems to sidestep the question of a biological bedrock to the 'cogni-tive' and 'behavioural' aspects of distress that it focuses on, but it surrepti-tiously reintroduces biological motifs, and in this way 'adaptation' is chained to a conception of our second nature that treats it as directly correlative to what an original and still operative first nature is supposed to be like. Adapta-tion as a potent ideological fantasy – one that circulates among IAPT adminis-trators and CBT trainees and so as institutionally normative, that is itself as such adapted and interpellates those who participate as adapting themselves and their clients to it – operates here in two ways, at two levels.

First, it operates in such a way as to close the gap between first and second nature that defines the disadapted human subject, and then it makes perfect sense that the human being could and should be happy. That the subject could be dissatisfied, discontent and unproductive – conditions of the subject as such for the psychoanalytic tradition that is born from a more restless, redemptive, romantic vision of humanity – is unthinkable for CBT or is treated as something faulty into which the individual should have insight so that it could be repaired. Adaptation thus serves as one of the avatars of 'nature', and an accumulating knowledge of what that nature is supposed to be like recruits each individual and their happy labour into a conservative version of positivist nostrums concerning order and progress.

Second, the motif of adaptation warrants a fusion of horizons of CBT with the worst of old psychoanalysis, with the very psychoanalysis from which it emerged in the first place, but now with something even worse added in for good measure. As has been noted, unlike behaviourism, cognitive psychotherapy 'developed outside of the academy, and not in response to academic psychology, but to American practices in psychoanalysis' (Svolos, 2005: 140); CBT 'is a kind of horrible side-product of psychoanalysis itself' (Miller, 2005: 129), and so it is 'a form of return to Ego Psychology (as predicted by Lacan in 1966) that reduces the psychoanalytical discourse to normative psychology' (Guégen, 2005: 135).

Not only is there a concern with 'reality' as it is understood by the analyst, underpinned by an assumption that someone will know what forms of reality are correct and incorrect so that the real of the subject can be made to conform to it, but now there is also an attempt to define that reality in terms of human nature. This image of nature is saturated with descriptions of 'attachment' that govern how a mother relates to the child and then how the analyst relates to the analysand. This attachment is one of the names of adaptation today, and it is claimed to be visible using a scientific apparatus: functional magnetic resonance image (MRI) scanners reveal failures of attachment in teenage mothers, and may discover who will and will not benefit from therapy (Fonagy, 2004). The pragmatic and limited ambitions of a CBT practitioner are in this way enclosed within a dangerous hygienist account of pathology and of the kinds of behaviour and cognition that need to be detected and wiped out so that adaptation to what is taken to be normal may be accomplished.

Conceptions of therapeutic and social change

What should be noticed about the Lacanian psychoanalytic gap is that it speaks at one and the same time of an interconnection between the world of the subject and the world they inhabit, and of a separation between the two. This interconnection and separation gives to human activity a dynamic quality through which each is pulled towards the other but resists the impulse to merge with them. It reproduces as a developmental and actual phenomenon 'alienation', but this alienation of the subject at the level of what we might call 'first nature' is intensified and twisted into the alienation of the subject under capitalism whereby the extraction of surplus value produces a 'second nature' in which powerlessness, hopelessness and inevitability, or other such signifiers, are installed in the subject. These signifiers are installed in their self-conception at the level of the ego where they may be available to conscious rumination in an obsessional circuit, or outside the ego where they take on a life of their own in repetitive self-sabotage that appears in the clinic as the unconscious.

In this way, then, Lacan gives us a new take on psychoanalysis that brings it as close as possible, the closest that a theory of subjectivity has come, to what Marx (1845), drawing on a Hegelian tradition that was itself a crucial conceptual resource for Lacan, specified in the argument that the human being is an 'ensemble of social relations'. This proximity of Lacan to Marx is also crucial to the way we should understand the place of CBT as a therapeutic modality in contemporary neoliberal capitalism, but it necessitates, at the same time, an appreciation of the force of 'negativity' in the subject that Hegel emphasized and that is still alive in our psychoanalysis. Negativity, which is conceptually reduced to the death drive or infantile aggression in some forms of psychoanalysis, now assumes its proper place as the 'drive', hysterical refusal and, perhaps, 'act' of the subject. Here we encounter the side of 'separation' in what can be conceived of as the dialectical interconnection between the subject and others; a dialectical interconnection that comes alive in the clinic as transference.

Lacanian psychoanalysis then intersects, as a necessary and inescapable function of its clinical work, with political change, but the connection is not immediate or seamless. It is a connection forged through a dialectical relationship that is structured by negativity, contradiction and disjunction between the two realms of personal and political change. But Lacanian work does not pretend to arrive at a synthesis between the two realms, either as that assumed by deterministic approaches or as that aimed at in humanist therapy. Still less does it promise a synthesis that is bureaucratically engineered by those seeking to bring about equivalence between 'cognition' conceived of as transparent auditable procedures and as individual mental processes, an equivalence that would amount to 'an extension of the ideology of management and control into the psyche itself' (Svolos, 2005: 141).

Conclusion

So, as we have seen, Lacanian psychoanalysis answers the questions posed in this book in a particular way. There is no one agreed standard version of Lacanian psychoanalysis, and the account I have given here is grounded in a historical argument about the development of psychological treatments. Psychiatry and psychoanalysis operate alongside psychology and psycho-therapy in a cluster of practices that are most of the time normative but in which there are possibilities for change. There have been many attempts to recuperate psychoanalysis, to combine it with conservative prescriptions for how an individual should behave and how they should think. It is all the more important now to argue against any such collusion with the state, the state as a system of 'material practices and cognitive categories' (Bratsis, 2006: 120).

Here I have stressed the particular role of Lacanian psychoanalysis in opening a space for revolutions in subjectivity (Parker, forthcoming). Yes, some practitioners are doing their best to shift CBT from a 'monological' to a more 'dialogical' engagement with problems (Strong et al., 2008), but it has been pointed out that the power gradient is such that even in such a dialogue 'clients take over the therapist's role and become surveyors and regulators of their own thoughts' (Proctor, 2008: 243). This argument made from within a humanist perspective draws attention to the importance of grasping the prob-lem from a variety of different theoretical perspectives (Le Blanc, 2007), but it also means that any alignment with CBT, or temptation to construct hybrid forms of Lacanian psychoanalysis and CBT, should be refused.

Lacanians avoid a 'model of the person' and we do not generalize about human experience on the basis of our approach. We respect the singularity of the subject, and refuse the lure of 'objectivity' and 'evidence'. Lacan did early on in his writing claim that there was 'intersubjectivity' in psychoanalysis, but later came to see this as problematic, as a lure into illusory 'understanding' of the internal world of the patient, a slippery slope into 'objectivity' and 'evi-dence' once more. Lacanian psychoanalysis is materialistic, but it is a form of materialism that takes seriously the materiality of language, and so it is 'trans-personal' in the respect that language transcends each particular individual.

Our refusal to fit our work within the prevailing 'objective' standards that CBT informs and conforms to should itself be seen as an advantage of our approach, and so we have nothing but contempt for 'cost-effectiveness' and evidence/research-based 'efficacy' as a measure of therapeutic work.

Our conception of therapeutic change is of it as being a 'side-effect' of the analysis, and antithetical to the medical-model thinking because we are aiming at truth, which is not necessarily the same as 'happiness'. In our view, the claim that people should be made happy, and should undergo therapy to lead them to happiness and well-being, is a dangerous fraud.

The 'Layard thesis' that – which many hundreds of thousands of people are needing relief from psychological/emotional distress and unhappiness – may be well-meaning, but in practice it is a cynical attempt to get those 'hundreds of thousands' of people back to work and to encourage them to tell administrators that they are happy.

For these reasons it is not possible for our approach to align itself with, or even worse, to create a hybrid with, CBT.

The connection between Lacanian psychoanalysis and revolutionary Marxism that was touched on in the course of this chapter also indicates that we should adopt a dialectical materialist response to the fake materialism of CBT that simply smuggles in through the back door some very dubious idealism – that is, ideological – notions about human nature. Yes, it is true that countless numbers of people suffer by virtue of being human and many more suffer needlessly under capitalism. The attempt by Layard (2005) to make them happy with a dose of CBT and put them back to work is well-meaning but mistaken. In this respect Lacanians will agree with those from other therapeutic orientations who point out that 'thought modification' is not an adequate solution to poverty (Strong et al., 2008: 216). One might say that CBT fills a much-needed gap in mental health service provision, and that it is Lacanian psychoanalysis that keeps the gap in mind, and keeps in mind the importance of a space for the subject to come to terms with what 'happiness' is and what it could be, what it could be for them.

References

Bratsis, P. (2006) *Everyday Life and the State*, Boulder, CO: Paradigm Publishers.

Evans, J. (2007) 'Wellbeing and happiness as used by the UK Government', *Psychoanalytical Notebooks*, 16: 143–54.

Fonagy, P. (2004) 'Psychotherapy meets neuroscience: a more focused future for psychotherapy research', *Psychiatric Bulletin*, 28(10): 357–9.

Guégen, P.-G. (2005) 'The battle of psychoanalysis in the twenty-first century', *Psychoanalytical Notebooks*, 14: 132–6.

Haraway, D.J. (1989) *Primate Visions: Gender, Race, and Nature in the World of Modern Science*, London and New York: Routledge.

House, R. (2003) *Therapy Beyond Modernity: Deconstructing and Transcending Profession-centred Therapy*, London: Karnac Books.

Lacan, J. (1973) *The Four Fundamental Concepts of Psycho-analysis (The Seminar of Jacques Lacan, Book XI, 1964)*, Trans. A. Sheridan, Harmondsworth: Penguin.

Lacan, J. (1998) *On Feminine Sexuality, The Limits of Love and Knowledge, 1972–1973: Encore (The Seminar of Jacques Lacan, Book XX)*, Trans. B. Fink, New York: W.W. Norton.

Lacan, J. (2006) *Écrits: The First Complete Edition in English*, Trans B. Fink in collaboration with Héloïse Fink and Russell Grigg, New York: W.W. Norton.

Layard, R. (2005) *Happiness: Lessons from a New Science*, Harmondsworth: Penguin.

Le Blanc, G. (2007) 'The unevaluable: the timeliness of Canguilhem', *Psychoanalytical Notebooks*, 16: 77–87.

Litton, R. (2007) 'Letter to the Department of Health from ALP', *Psychoanalytical Notebooks*, 16: 183–7.

Loewenthal, D. (2008) 'Post-existentialism as a reaction to CBT?' in R. House and D. Loewenthal (eds), *Against and For CBT: Towards A Constructive Dialogue?*, Ross-on-Wye: PCCS Books, pp. 146–55.

Mariage, V. (2007) 'CBT's hold over children's speech', *Psychoanalytical Notebooks*, 16: 110–12.

Marx, K. (1845) 'Theses on Feuerbach', available online at www.marxists.org/archive/marx/works/1845/theses/theses.htm (accessed 16 July 2009).

Miller, J.-A. (2005) 'The response of psychoanalysis to cognitive-behavioural therapy', *Psychoanalytical Notebooks*, 14: 126–31.

Miller, J.-A. (2007) 'The era of the man without qualities', *Psychoanalytical Notebooks*, 16: 7–42.

Okawa, R. (2002) *The Golden Laws: History through the Eyes of the Eternal Buddha*, New York: Lantern Books.

Parker, I. (forthcoming) *Lacanian Psychoanalysis: Revolutions in Subjectivity*, London and New York: Routledge.

Pilgrim, D. (2008) 'Reading "happiness": CBT and the Layard thesis', *European Journal of Psychotherapy and Counselling*, 10(3): 247–60.

Proctor, G. (2008) 'CBT: the obscuring of power in the name of science', *European Journal of Psychotherapy and Counselling*, 10(3): 231–45.

Strong, T., Lysack, M. and Sutherland, O. (2008) 'Considering the dialogic potentials of cognitive therapy', *European Journal of Psychotherapy and Counselling*, 10(3): 207–19.

Svolos, T. (2005) ' "The American plague" ', *Psychoanalytical Notebooks*, 14: 138–42.

7 Being in process, being in context

A person-centred perspective on happiness[1]

Keith Tudor

> The object of government in peace and in war is not the glory of rulers or of races, but the happiness of the common man.
>
> (Beveridge, 1942)

> The goal [of psychotherapy] must be nothing less than a shift from radical individualism to a notion of citizenship based on a more complex understanding of individual and social happiness.
>
> (Bellah et al., 1981)

These two epigrams represent a difference – and a shift – in thinking and in social policy and purpose about happiness. Viewed by some as simply an emotion involving feeling and thought, by others as a goal or state, the concept, subject and pursuit of happiness has exercised human beings, since time – or, at least, the species – began. Philosophers, theologians and spiritual leaders, politicians, psychologists and, more recently, economists, have all contributed to our understanding of this complex subject.

This chapter approaches the subject of happiness or being happy from a person-centred perspective. The first part of the chapter introduces and summarizes key philosophical ideas about happiness that provide a background to person-centred and other perspectives that inform – and, perhaps, do not sufficiently inform – current responses to and debates about the subject. The second part discusses and develops a person-centred perspective on happiness as a process with particular reference to Rogers' concepts of the good life ([1957]1967) and the fully functioning person (1959, [1960]1967). Building on this material, the third part addresses the themes of the book and offers

[1] My thanks to Rihi Te Nana and Saul Tudor for their comments on and discussion of earlier drafts of this chapter.

a critique of several aspects of what has come to be known as 'the Layard agenda'.

Happiness – a philosophical background

Buddhism – Gautama Buddha (c. 563–483 BCE)

Happiness forms a central theme of Buddhist teachings in which it is proposed that ultimate happiness is only achieved by overcoming craving in all forms. Buddhism also encourages the generation of loving kindness and compassion: the desire for the happiness and welfare of all beings. According to the Buddha (in the second verse of the *Dhammapada*): 'All [mental] states have mind as their forerunner, mind is their chief, and they are mind-made. If one speaks and acts with a pure mind, happiness follows like one's own shadow'. This emphasis on the mind has been developed in recent times by the practice of mindfulness (e.g. Kabat-Zinn, 2003; Neff, 2004) which, in turn, has been adopted by some cognitive-behavioural therapists (see Lau and McMain, 2005).

Greek philosophy – Aristotle (384–322 BCE)

In his book *Nicomachean Ethics* Aristotle argues that happiness is the only emotion that humans desire for its own sake, although he viewed happiness as an activity rather than an emotion or state and a characteristic of 'the good life', a concept that has been taken up by others, including Rogers ([1957]1967) (see below). For Aristotle, perfect happiness is only to be found in intellectual contemplation. In this sense, philosophy, or the love of wisdom (*philo* = love + *sophia* = wisdom), is the supreme intellectual virtue. He developed the concept of *eudaemonia* (*eu* = good + *daimōn* = spirit) meaning happiness in the sense of well-being or flourishing, a concept about which Keyes (2003, 2007) has undertaken extensive research, as a result of which he has identified a number of dimensions of well-being including those that are *eudaimonic*; that is, to do with self-fulfilment and positive functioning, including positive *social* well-being. In proposing this view, Aristotle in effect focused on happiness in the long term or happiness as way of being in life or, indeed, living life itself. As happiness is a characteristic of a life in which a person fulfils human nature in an excellent way, the happy person is a virtuous person: happiness is 'the virtuous activity of the soul in accordance with reason' (Aristotle, [1925]1980: §13). These concepts represent a virtue ethics that focus on character as distinct from consequentialist ethics which has been developed by other philosophers, notably the utilitarians (see below).

Greek philosophy – Epicurus (341–270 BCE)

Epicurus thought that all good and bad things come from sensations; thus, as all pleasure is good, and all pain is bad, in order to achieve happiness, we should try to maximize the amount of pleasure we experience. Nevertheless, Epicurus warned against overindulgence in the pursuit of pleasure and happiness as he thought it often led to negative consequences. Epicurus also talked about desires and the nature of desire. In order to increase pleasure we can either strive to fulfil desire, or seek to eliminate desire as a source of pain. Others since have taken up this distinction:

> Vronsky, meanwhile, notwithstanding the complete fulfilment of what he had so long desired, was not entirely happy. He soon began to feel that the realization of his desires brought him no more than a grain of sand out of the mountain of bliss he had expected. It showed him the eternal error men make in imagining that happiness consists in the realization of their desires.
>
> (Tolstoy [1878]1954: 490)

At the heart of Epicurean philosophy, then, is the practice of eliminating as many desires as possible so that remaining wants (natural or unnatural, necessary or unnecessary) are easy or easier to satisfy with the result that the person attains a state of tranquillity. This view of happiness as moderation, even happiness in moderation, offers an antidote to more modernist conceptions of happiness as fulfilment (a filling full), goal or outcome.

Māori world view

There are, in addition to Buddhism, many wisdom traditions outside the hegemonic 'Western' (and Northern) intellectual traditions. In Aotearoa – New Zealand – māori have, for some eight centuries, had and embodied a holistic approach to health and 'happiness', which, according to Turia (2009), is underpinned by a philosophy of well-being that involves and includes: ronga māori – traditional māori healing, and the capacity of the environment to sustain this; the importance of ritenga – custom, and karakia – incantations; and the embodiment of wairuatanga – spirituality (ibid.) 'as a vital component of nurturing our physical, mental and social health'. The māori word koa describes a holistic sense of *being* joyful or contented, as distinct from a state of happiness, a point also made by Rogers ([1957]1967) and by Shlien ([1989]2003) (see below). While holism may have been 'discovered' in the last century, notably by Smuts ([1926]1987), and taken up by some psychotherapeutic approaches, in particular gestalt and person-centred psychologies, many wisdom traditions, including māori tradition have been suppressed. The

Tohunga Suppression Act 1907, for example, outlawed traditional healers and practice in Aotearoa – New Zealand – and was only repealed in 1964. As Durie (2001: 51) comments: 'By outlawing traditional healers, the Act also opposed Māori methodologies and the legitimacy of Māori knowledge in respect of healing'. In this sense how 'happy' people are and can be depends on how they experience themselves which, in turn, depends on how free they are to experience themselves within their frame of reference, beliefs and values, that is, with regard to relationships, identity and health. As Shlien ([1989]2003: 70) observes: 'Happiness is a poor substitute for health' (see also Tudor, 2008a). How we understand, conceptualize and promote happiness or being content, and health has been – and continues to be – not only the subject of some debate, but of great and sometimes bitter dispute, of suppression and oppression.

Empiricism – John Locke (1634–1704)

The classical statement of empiricism and of empiricist epistemology is Locke's *An Essay Concerning Human Understanding* (1690) in which he advanced the view that the genuine business of human life is the unalterable pursuit of happiness, and argued that 'The necessity of pursuing happiness [is] the foundation of liberty'. The pursuit of happiness or 'satisfying living' is also embedded in US culture. It was written into the *American Declaration of Independence* by Thomas Jefferson who was influenced by the Greek and Roman philosophical traditions in which happiness was understood in the context of civic virtues of courage, moderation and justice, by Epicurus, and by Locke. Jefferson viewed this pursuit, along with life and liberty, as an inalienable right of man and a self-evident truth. Despite this provenance, however, the US pursuit of happiness is framed in a constitution that extols the individual, individual rights, individualism and, in both political and psychological senses, autonomy – which is a common and almost universal value in psychotherapy. It is, however, not without its critics. As Miller (2001: 31) puts it (echoing an Epicurean view): 'Foolish to found a country for the pursuit of happiness. People just got into a panic when they hadn't got it'. By contrast, the Canadian constitution refers to 'the common good', a sentiment that reflects a trend to homonomy (Angyal, 1941) or a sense of belonging (see below, and for an elaboration of which see Tudor, 2008b).

Romanticism

This refers to an artistic, literary and intellectual movement that originated in the second half of the eighteenth century in Western Europe. It combined a revolt against aristocratic and social norms of the Age of Enlightenment, and a reaction to the scientific rationalization of nature, with an emphasis on strong emotion as a source of aesthetic experience. Broadly, Romanticism, expressed

in music, writing and art, viewed happiness in terms of freedom and, in particular, freedom from constraint, a perspective that informs much current
thinking about happiness. Citing Rogers' metaphysical belief 'that the inborn
capacities for self-reflection and creative agency are reflections of a formative
tendency in the universe', O'Hara (1995: 64) refers to him as a Romantic.
Romanticism favoured and promoted emotion and intuition, but, as Pessoa
([1998]2002: 52) points out: 'The fundamental error of Romanticism is to con-
fuse what we need with what we desire. We all need certain basic things for
life's preservation and continuance; we all desire a more perfect life, complete
happiness, the fulfilment of our dreams'.

Utilitarianism

This tradition – represented notably by Jeremy Bentham (1748–1832) and
John Stuart Mill (1806–1873) and, contemporarily, by Peter Singer (b. 1946) –
was founded on the idea that the moral worth of an action is determined by its
contribution to overall utility; that is, its contribution to happiness. Bentham
suggested that an ethical act is one that increases utility; that is, it increases
happiness or reduces pain. Utilitarianism advocates 'the greatest good for the
greatest number', a perspective that is known as 'the greatest happiness principle'. In terms of ethical traditions, it is a form of instrumentalism or con-
sequentialism in which the moral worth of an action is determined by its
outcome, and is thus distinct from deontological ethics, which hold that acts
are inherently good or bad (and are therefore concerned with duty or obliga-
tion), and virtue ethics that focus on character. Although what is now referred
to as 'philosophical utilitarianism' is much broader than the original form
of utilitarianism, there is a distinctly utilitarian flavour to the arguments
presented by Layard ([2005] 2006) with regard to happiness and to depression,
and to the UK government's obsession with promoting brief (time-limited)
cognitive-behaviour therapy (CBT) to the greatest number for what it thinks is
the greatest good; that is, individual 'happiness', measured in social/political/
economic terms by the reduction in people receiving invalidity benefit.

Happiness as a process

Although Rogers did not write about happiness or well-being as such, he
did discuss 'the good life' ([1957]1967), and develop the concept of 'the fully
functioning person' ([1957]1967, [1960]1967).

The good life

Rogers ([1957]1967: 185–6) first describes this in terms of what it is not:

> It seems to me that the good life is not any fixed state. It is not, in my estimation, a state of virtue, or contentment, or nirvana, or happiness. It is not a condition in which the individual is adjusted, fulfilled or actualized. To use psychological terms, it is not a state of drive-reduction, or tension-reduction or homeostasis.

Rogers ([1957]1967) states clearly that he does not view these states, including happiness, as the goal of the process of living; rather (p. 186): 'The good life is a *process*, not a state of being. It is a direction, not a destination' – and this direction (pp. 186–7, author's emphasis): 'is that which is selected by the total organism, when there is psychological freedom to move in *any* direction'. Rogers goes to comment ([1957]1967: 187):

1   that organismic direction has certain 'discernable general qualities' – in other words, that they are generalizable; and
2   that 'the general qualities of this selected direction appear to have a certain universality' – in other words, they are applicable to all human beings – with the proviso that, from an organismic/environmental perspective, we cannot understand or claim to understand any individual, family, couple, group, or tribe outside her, his, or its environment. Rogers' theory and perspectives are, thus, relational, contextual and systemic (see Kriz, [2006]2008; Tudor and Worrall, 2006).

Shlien ([1989]2003: 71, author's emphasis) also comments about direction in terms of therapy:

> I would say that the primary objective of [client-centred therapy] is freedom, informed choice, responsible choice, self-determination – whether or not that includes happiness ... Therapy does not *make* happiness. The client may *create* it, as a secondary effect.

Clearly, then, from a person-centred perspective, the good life is not about happiness or even about necessarily being happy; it is more about being. Moreover, Shlien and other person-centred practitioners and theorists are sceptical about goals, especially ones imposed or determined by external authorities and loci of control and evaluation.

For Rogers, the good life is one based on the concept of the human organism, inextricably linked with its environment. Rogers' use of the term 'organism' signifies both a unified concept of human motivation (see Rogers, 1963), and emphasizes the holistic and experiential nature of humans, of life, and of the integration of the person and personality. As Rogers ([1953]1967: 80) puts it:

> one of the fundamental directions taken by the process of therapy is the free experiencing of the actual sensory and visceral reactions of the organism . . . The end point of this process is that the client discovers that he can be his experience, with all of its variety and surface contradiction; [and] that he can formulate himself out of his experience.

So, the good life is the experiential life, but not one lived selfishly. It is a life lived with others in an environmental/social context, according to values that are assessed by the organism, again in the context of its environment. As formulated in his theory of personality and behaviour, Rogers (1951: 487) asserts that the human species, as with other species, has one basic tendency and striving: 'to actualize, maintain, and enhance the experiencing organism'. However, Angyal (1941), a Hungarian psychologist on whose ideas Rogers drew, sees the organism as having two related tendencies: one towards increased *autonomy*, and one towards *homonomy*. Angyal defines the organism (p. 23) as autonomous in the sense that it is 'to a large extent, a *self-governing* entity', and homonomous (p. 172) in the sense that it longs 'to be in harmony with superindividual units, the social group, nature, God, ethical world order, or whatever the person's formulation of it may be'. Angyal's contribution to psychology as well as his influence on Rogers' thinking emphasizes the relational, social, contextual, *eudaemonic* view of the good life and of happiness as a social concept – or, more accurately, of being happy as a social construct.

The fully functioning person

Rogers' concept of the fully functioning person represents a person in process living the good life that Rogers describes (1959: 234) as: 'the ultimate in the actualization of the human organism'. The fully functioning person, then, is synonymous with optimal psychological adjustment, complete congruence and extensionality, and is characterized, according to Rogers ([1957]1967), by having: an increasing openness to experience; the ability to live fully in each moment; and an increasing trust in her or his organism (p. 189) 'as a means of arriving at the most satisfying behavior in each existential situation'. In later work Rogers developed other concepts of the person: the emerging person, and the political person (Rogers, 1978), and the person of tomorrow (Rogers, 1980) – which he describes as having a number of qualities, including: having an openness, a desire for authenticity and for wholeness, and the wish for intimacy, an authority within, and a yearning for the spiritual, as well as a scepticism regarding science and technology (in the sense that it is used to conquer nature and control people), and an antipathy for highly structured, inflexible, bureaucratic institutions; being caring and of help to others, 'process persons' aware that life is change; and feeling a closeness to and care for elemental nature.

There are, of course, some important implications of this view of life and of the person. Rogers ([1957]1967) identifies them as entailing:

- that the person is free to be and become her or himself;
- that the person is creative – and not necessarily adjusted to her or his culture in the sense of being conformist;
- that the person is trustworthy;
- that (p. 195) 'this process of living in the good life involves a wider range, a greater richness, than the constricted living in which most of us find ourselves'.

One of the problems with the concept of 'fully functioning' is that it sounds more complete and fixed than the theory or Rogers intends, more akin to Maslow's (1954) notion of the self-actualized person than a person in process, although, interestingly, Rogers' description of the person of tomorrow relies on verbs – 'being', 'having' and 'feeling' – rather than nouns (or substantives). The implication of this grammatical point has been made by Shlien ([1989]2003) when he refers to a client who, as a result of successful therapy, is or is seen to be 'a much happier person'. Shlien suggests (p. 69): 'That sounds true, but also incomplete and therefore superficial. It does not necessarily extend from adjective, "happier", into noun, "happiness" '. Moreover, it raises for Shlien a (rhetorical) question: 'Is happiness the description of a constant and permanent condition?' Rogers ([1957]1967) comments that adjectives such as happy, contented, blissful, enjoyable, and so on are not sufficiently accurate enough reflections of the state or process he is describing; he prefers to use adjectives such as enriching, rewarding, challenging and meaningful. This vision of being in process allows for life in all its variety: suffering as well as pleasure; the 'downs' as well as the 'ups'. As the singer Adele puts it (Silverman et al., 2007): 'who wants to be as right as rain/It's better when something is wrong/I get excitement in my bones/Even though everything's a strain'.

It is in the philosophical and psychological context discussed in these first two parts that the final part of this chapter takes up the challenge offered by and in this book by addressing a number of themes with regard to happiness, the 'Layard thesis' and the 'Layard agenda', and the impact of the rise of CBT.

The age of 'happiness': the age of CBT

The 'Layard thesis'

What has come to be known as the 'Layard thesis' (Layard [2005] 2006) is well known, as increasingly, are its critics (see, for example, House and Loewenthal,

2008; Leader, 2008). While it is undoubtedly true that many hundreds of thousands, even millions of people suffer from psychological/emotional distress and unhappiness, it is debatable whether they would, could – or should – be helped by one form of therapy (CBT) applied by mental health professionals trained (briefly) to deliver a manualized treatment in a short (brief) number of sessions. Layard's thesis is problematic on four main counts:

1. It conflates economic and psychological arguments. Layard's work on happiness advances an economic argument based on a political agenda to reduce the number of people in the UK who are in receipt of invalidity benefit. It does not advance a valid psychological argument for this agenda.

2. It determines and restricts choice. Layard's ([2005] 2006) book on *Happiness* does not offer a systematic or even a comparative review of effective therapies; it simply presents and extols CBT as *the* solution to people's unhappiness and distress. This, together with the UK government's initiative (National Health Service NHS, 2007), is actually *decreasing* clients' access to a range of psychological therapies (see Tudor, 2008a).

3. It individualizes people's unhappiness and distress. With his emphasis on the achievement of individual happiness, Layard is following in the footsteps of Beveridge and, in a sense, advocating that the UK's National Health Service (NHS) become a provider of individual happiness – but a 'happiness' defined by the government, not a functioning or a process defined by the client. This therapy is, in effect, 'government-based therapy'.

4. It medicalizes unhappiness, depression and distress. Layard's agenda for 10 000 mental health professionals to be trained as CBT 'therapists' operating within the NHS to the exclusion of other therapists, theoretical orientations and models privileges CBT within a medical context and model (for a critique of which see Sanders, 2006).

The Layard thesis and agenda needs to be seen in the light of a series of policy initiatives that the UK government has taken which, in effect, have reduced patient access to a variety of psychological therapies and, therefore, client choice (see Holmes, 2002; Tudor, 2008a), and are an expression of the current Labour party and government to exert more and more social control over patients and consumers of the NHS.

The medical model

There are many models of understanding health and illness, ease and disease, psychosanology and psychopathology (see, for example, Siegler and Osmond,

1976). The medical model (of diagnosis → treatment → cure) is only one model of understanding these aspects of human life and human nature, although in many societies it is the dominant – and funded – one. While we may need to understand the medical model, those of us in other professions and other traditions should not introject it or accept its hegemony. Person-centred psychology is a case in point: it is a growth model, not a medical model (see Rogers and Russell, 2002); its conceptualization of the person is a holistic and integrated one, not an atomistic and compartmentalized one; its conceptualization of change is one based on growth enhanced by certain relational conditions centred on and experienced by the client, not one based on an analysis of deficit and dependent on repair by an external expert. In this sense the person-centred approach does not – and does or should not seek to – cohere with medical-model thinking. Medicine and person-centred psychology can sit alongside each other but only if there is mutual understanding and respect. While there are other therapeutic approaches that may align more closely to the medical model, not all medicine or all therapy is about 'cure'. As Shlien ([1989]2003: 69) puts it: 'If you had asked, "Does therapy bring sweet dreams?" I could answer with considerable confidence, "No – it brings more lucid dreams" '. Indeed, to extend the metaphor, therapy may facilitate a client to have nightmares or, in other words, to be more in touch with their unhappiness. Growth does not ensure happiness. Other views of the purpose and end goal/s of therapy include consciousness-raising (see Agel, 1971); social action (e.g. Holland, 1990); and active, engaged, participatory citizenship (see Tudor and Hargaden, 2002).

The question of evidence

CBT is often presented as being 'evidence-based'. However, there are three principal problems with this commonplace assertion:

1 There is a conceptual and methodological bias towards CBT based on the medical model and particular views of what constitutes – or is accepted as constituting – 'scientific' 'evidence' (for a summary of critiques of which see Tudor, 2008a). This bias marginalizes the evidence and thus the therapy of other therapeutic orientations, such as person-centred therapy and many other humanistic and psychodynamic therapies, the evidence base for which often includes case reports, and involves qualitative methodologies.

2 There are a number of studies that have questioned the different claims made for CBT with regard to it being 'empirically validated', and beneficial over time and, therefore, cost-effective (see, for example, Western and Morrison, 2001; Elkins, 2007).

3 That, despite its obsession with 'evidence', when faced with the

results from meta-analyses and comparative studies over 20 years (see Stiles et al., 1986), which show CBT to be no more effective than other forms of therapy; that is, which demonstrate 'psychotherapeutic equivalence', governments and regulatory bodies simply do not acknowledge this evidence, a response that suggests that politics and again, economics, are more important than so-called 'objective' 'science'.

Cognition and behaviour in person-centred therapy

Finally, there is a fundamental if somewhat obvious flaw in the argument that prioritizes CBT as the therapy of choice (at least for governments) on the basis that it helps to change people's cognition (thinking) and behaviour (actions). The implication is that other therapies do not do this when, of course, they do. In the current climate, the challenge is for other therapeutic approaches to reclaim how they work with these aspects of whole human experience (for a discussion of the behavioural and cognitive aspects of person-centred therapy see Tudor, 2008a). Moreover, in what is a profession comprising theoretical diversity, it is important: (a) to make serious and informed comparisons between approaches as, for instance, does Nye (1999), and (b) to take up opportunities for critical engagement between approaches (for a course on which see www.temenos.ac.uk).

Conclusion

We do not live in an age of happiness, nor should we seek to do so. Many societies, particularly those in the West and North, promote and promise happiness, and, as Shlien ([1989]2003) observes, the entertainment and drug industries are devoted to manufacturing and indulging the desire for happiness as outcome. From a person-centred perspective, the issue is to develop and support ways of being happy/healthy/in process, and to have a virtue ethics that supports this or, as Shlien ([1989]2003) puts it, 'to lead an honourable life'.

References

Agel, J. (ed.) (1971) *The Radical Therapist*, New York: Ballantyne Books.

Angyal, A. (1941) *Foundations for a Science of Personality*, New York: Commonwealth Fund.

Aristotle, [1925](1980) *The Nichomachean Ethics*, trans. D. Ross, Oxford: Oxford University Press.

Bellah, R.N., Madsen, R., Sullivan, W.M., Swidler, A. and Tipton, S.M. (1981) *The Good Society*, New York: A.A. Knopf.

Beveridge, W. (1942) *Social Insurance and Allied Services*. London: HMSO.

Durie, M. (2001) *Mauri Ora: The Dynamics of* Māori *Health*, Auckland: Oxford University Press.

Elkins, D. (2007) 'Empirically supported treatments: the deconstruction of a myth', *Journal of Humanistic Psychology*, 47(4): 474–500.

Holland, S. (1990) 'Psychology, oppression and social action: gender, race and class in black women's depression', in R. Perelberg and A. Miller (eds), *Gender and Power in Families*. London: Routledge, pp. 256–97.

Holmes, J. (2002) 'All you need is cognitive behaviour therapy', *British Medical Journal*, 324: 288–94.

House, R. and Loewenthal, D. (eds), (2008) *Against and For CBT: Towards a Constructive Dialogue?*, Ross-on-Wye: PCCS Books.

Kabat-Zinn, J. (2003) 'Mindfulness-based interventions in context: past, present, and future', *Clinical Psychology: Science and Practice*, 10(2): 144–56.

Keyes, C.L.M. (2003) 'Complete mental health: an agenda for the 21st century' in C.L.M. Keyes and J. Haidt (eds), *Flourishing: Positive Psychology and the Life Well-lived*, Washington, D.C.: American Psychological Association Press, pp. 293–312.

Keyes, C.L.M. (2007) 'Promoting and protecting mental health as flourishing: a complementary strategy for improving national mental health', *American Psychologist*, 62(2): 95–108.

Kriz, J. ([2006]2008) *Self-actualization: Person-centred Approach and Systems Theory*, Ross-on-Wye: PCCS Books.

Lau, M.A. and McMain, S.F. (2005) 'Integrating mindfulness meditation with cognitive and behavioural therapies: the challenge of combining acceptance- and change-based strategies', *Canadian Journal of Psychiatry*, 50: 863–9.

Layard, R. ([2005]2006) *Happiness: Lessons from a New Science*, London: Penguin Books.

Leader, D. (2008) *The New Black: Mourning, Melancholia and Depression*, London: Hamish Hamilton.

Locke, J. (1690) *An Essay Concerning Human Understanding*.

Maslow, A.H. (1954) *Motivation and Personality*, New York: Harper & Row.

Miller, A. (2001) *Oxygen*, London: Sceptre.

National Health Service (2007) *Commissioning a Brighter Future: Increasing Access to Psychological Therapies*, London: NHS.

Neff, K. (2004) 'Self-compassion and psychological well-being', *Constructivism in the Human Sciences*, 9(2): 27–37.

Nye, R.D. (1999) *Three Psychologies: Perspectives from Freud, Skinner, and Rogers*, 6th edn, Pacific Grove, CA: Brookes/Cole.

O'Hara, M. (1995) 'Streams: on becoming a postmodern person', in M.M. Suhd (ed.), *Positive Regard: Carl Rogers and Other Notables He Influenced*, Palo Alto, CA: Science and Behavior Books, pp. 105–55.

Pessoa, F. ([1998]2002) 'A factless autobiography' in *The Book of Disquiet*, trans. R. Zenith, London: Penguin Books, pp. 1–392.

Rogers, C.R. (1951) *Client-centered Therapy*, London: Constable.

Rogers, C.R. (1959) 'A theory of therapy, personality and interpersonal relationships, as developed in the client-centred framework', in S. Koch (ed.), *Psychology: A Study of a Science. Vol. 3: Formulation of the Person and the Social Context*, New York: McGraw-Hill, pp. 184–256.

Rogers, C.R. (1963) 'The actualizing tendency in relation to "motive" and to consciousness', in M. Jones (ed.), *Nebraska Symposium on Motivation 1963*, Lincoln, NE: University of Nebraska Press, pp. 1–24.

Rogers, C.R. ([1953]1967) 'Some of the directions evident in therapy', in C.R. Rogers (ed.), *On Becoming a Person*, London: Constable, pp. 73–106.

Rogers, C.R. ([1957]1967) 'A therapist's view of the good life: the fully functioning person', in C.R. Rogers (ed.), *On Becoming a Person*, London: Constable, pp. 183–96.

Rogers, C.R. ([1960]1967) ' "To be that self which one truly is": a therapist's view of personal goals', in C.R. Rogers (ed.), *On Becoming a Person*, London: Constable, pp. 163–82.

Rogers, C.R. (1978) *Carl Rogers on Personal Power*, London: Constable.

Rogers, C.R. (1980) 'The world of tomorrow, and the person of tomorrow', in C.R. Rogers (ed.), *A Way of Being*, Boston, MA: Houghton Mifflin, pp. 339–56.

Rogers, C.R. and Russell, D.E. (2002) *Carl Rogers the Quiet Revolutionary: An Oral History*, Roseville, CA: Penmarin Books.

Sanders, P. (2006) 'Why person-centred therapists must reject the medicalisation of distress', *Self and Society*, 34(3): 32–9.

Shlien, J.M. ([1989]2003) 'Macht therapie glucklich?' [Can therapy make you happy?], in P. Sanders (ed.), *To Lead an Honorable Life: Invitations to Think About Client-centered Therapy and the Person-centered Approach*, Ross-on-Wye: PCCS Books, pp. 69–78.

Siegler, M. and Osmond, H. (1976) *Models of Madness, Models of Medicine*, New York: Macmillan.

Silverman, J., Adkins, A.L.B., Holley, C., Movshon, N. and Michels, L. (2007) *Right as Rain*, Santa Monica, CA: Universal Music.

Smuts, J. ([1926]1987) *Holism and Evolution*, New York: Macmillan.

Stiles, W.B., Shapiro, D.A. and Elliot, R. (1986) 'Are all psychotherapies equivalent?', *American Psychologist*, 41(2): 165–80.

Tolstoy, L. ([1878]1954) *Anna Karenina*, trans. R. Edmonds, Harmondsworth: Penguin.

Tudor, K. (2008a) 'Person-centred therapy, a cognitive behavioural therapy', in R. House and D. Loewenthal (eds), *Against and For CBT: Towards a Constructive Dialogue?* Ross-on-Wye: PCCS Books, pp. 118–36.

Tudor, K. (2008b) 'Psychological health: autonomy and homonomy' in B. Levitt (ed.), *Reflections on Human Potential: Bridging the Person-centered Approach and Positive Psychology*, Ross-on-Wye: PCCS Books, pp. 161–74.

Tudor, K. and Hargaden, H. (2002) 'The couch and the ballot box: the contribution and potential of psychotherapy in enhancing citizenship', in C. Feltham (ed.), *What's the Good of Counselling and Psychotherapy?: The Benefits Explained*, London: Sage Publications, pp. 156–78.

Tudor, K. and Worrall, M. (2006) *Person-centred Therapy: A Clinical Philosophy*, London: Routledge.

Turia, T. (2009) *'Rongoa Maori and integrative care'*. Speech at Conference on Working Alongside Health Organizations, Taupo, New Zealand, 11 May.

Western D. and Morrison K. (2001) 'A multinational meta-analysis of treatment for depression, panic and generalized anxiety disorder: an empirical examination of the status of empirically supported therapies', *Journal of Consulting and Clinical Psychology*, 69: 875–99.

8 A dialogic between analytical psychology and CBT

Ann Casement

We should not try to 'get rid' of a neurosis, but rather to experience what it means, what it has to teach us, what its purpose is. We should even learn to be thankful for it, otherwise we . . . miss the opportunity of getting to know ourselves as we really are . . . We do not cure it – it cures us.

(Jung, 1992: 361)

Introduction

Jungian analytical therapy or *analytical psychology* as it was initially named by its founder, the Swiss psychiatrist and psychoanalyst, Carl Gustav Jung (1875–1961), is a psychodynamic approach to treating the psyche. He renamed it 'complex psychology' in the 1930s after his theory of complexes; the latter described as psychic fragments that have been split off owing to traumatic experiences that '. . . lead a life of their own so long as they are not made conscious and integrated with the life of the personality' (Jung, 1960: 121). The new term was not widely adopted as it was never taken up in the English-speaking world, which became the most influential sphere for developments in the Jungian field post-Second World War.

Jung was a gifted psychiatrist who worked at the Burghölzli Hospital in Zürich from 1900 to 1909, which was the foremost psychiatric hospital in the world at that time. Through his work there he became convinced that the psychoses were amenable to treatment by psychotherapy as they were psychic in origin. At this time, he also became interested in psychoanalysis after reading Freud's *The Interpretation of Dreams* and increasingly linked the thought formations produced by schizophrenics with dream formations to be found in Freud's book.

The two pioneers, Freud and Jung, collaborated closely from their first meeting in 1907 in Vienna until their contentious parting in 1913. In the course of those years, Jung was elected the first President of the International Psychoanalytical Association when it was founded in 1910, and was thought of as the heir apparent to Freud in taking forward 'the cause' of psychoanalysis. Interestingly enough, it was towards the end of their collaboration, which had collapsed into mutual diagnosis, that Jung put forward the proposal that analysts had to have training analysis as part of their formation. 'It was with the adoption of the practice of training analysis that psychoanalysis differentiated itself from rival forms of psychotherapy, and ultimately ensured its continuance' (Shamdasani, 2003: 54).

A great deal has been written about the impact Freud and Jung had on each other though the formation of both their approaches derived extensively from other sources. In Jung's case, these were from the following disciplines and thinkers among others: philosophy, in particular, Plato, Kant, Schopenhauer and Nietzsche; mystical thinkers such as Meister Eckhart and St John of the Cross, as well as gnosticism and kabbala; psychologists like Wilhelm Wundt, Théodore Flournoy and William James; and, later in his work, alchemy. These sources were important to Jung partly because they gave philosophical and historical legitimacy to his theories; for example, Kant's 'thing-in-itself' was linked by Jung to his theory of archetypes; and alchemy provided a historical underwriting to his analytical work conceived of by him as analyst and analysand contained in the metaphorical alchemical vessel of the analysis.

The Red Book: Liber Novus: C.G. Jung that was published by W.W. Norton in the Philemon Series of the Philemon Foundation and Edited and introduced by Sonu Shamdasani, was launched at the Rubin Museum in New York on the 7 October 2009. This is a previously unpublished work by Jung who spent 16 years of his life working on it from 1914 to 1930 setting out his private cosmology. Prior to working on this text, Jung had formulated his structural theory including complexes, non-sexual libido, the unconscious, archetypes, the compensatory nature of dreams, two types of thinking and typology. What *Liber Novus* represents is Jung's controntation with the unconscious that results in the individuating process and the discovery of the self. Professor Shamdasani claims that Jung's *Collected Works* will need to be re-evaluated in the light of the contents of *Liber Novus* – the bedrock of his public works.

Model of the individual

The model of the individual in the Jungian approach can best be addressed through Jung's work with *alchemy* that he discovered in the 1920s. During that time, Jung came to see the parallels between alchemy and in-depth psychoanalysis and from then on alchemy became central to his thinking evidenced by the fact that out of the 20 volumes of Jung's Collected Works, three are devoted to alchemy: *Psychology and Alchemy* (1953a), *Alchemical Studies* (1967), and *Mysterium Coniunctionis* (1963). Alchemy features in many of the other volumes and, most importantly, in a late paper 'The psychology of the transference' in *The Practice of Psychotherapy* (Jung, 1954c). When the English translation of the Collected Works was being worked on, Jung insisted that *Psychology and Alchemy* be the first one to be brought out (personal communication Gerhard Adler).

According to Jung, the individual's mental life is governed by *psychic reality* that incorporates the centrality of the *collective unconscious* (the realm of *archetypes*), *individuation*, the *self* as a superordinate structure, and the religious nature of psychic life 'all developed and/or deepened through his engagement with alchemy' (Marlan, 2006: 288; see also Neumann, [1949]1954). Through his study of alchemy, Jung came to an understanding of the unconscious as a process whereby a dialectical interaction between opposites, for instance, the ego and the unconscious, leads to the transformation of both. This in turn leads to the central concept in Jung's psychology, the process of individuation, as well as a stablized sense of wholeness represented as the self, or in alchemy as the philosopher's stone, which comes into being through the transforming of what is termed in alchemy the *prima materia*, the chaotic elements in an analysis. The sublimation that is a key feature of the alchemical process leads to the creation of the *transcendent function* 'in which thesis and antithesis both play their part . . . in the shaping of which the opposites are united (in) the living symbol' (Jung, 1971: 480).

For Jung, the systems *Cs. 22 Uncs.* were not in a state of conflict but of cooperative opposition mediated by the transcendent function leading to individuating. Alchemy became the metaphor for the work done by the analyst and analysand in the analytical container when the alchemical opus 'becomes an analogy of the natural process by means of which instinctive energy is transformed, in part at least, into symbolical activity' (Jung, 1954a: 250). The mutuality implied in this model is a central feature of Jungian psychoanalysis requiring the emotional involvement of the analyst for any significant shift to occur in both participants. The alchemical process in which analyst and analysand are immersed in the slow cooking of an in-depth analysis is a metaphor for this approach.

The union of opposites is the goal of Jungian psychoanalysis through the constellation of the *coniunctio* or higher marriage and the birth of the *divine child*; namely, the process of individuation, the psychological gold distilled through the metaphorical alchemical process of analysis. In 'positing a prospective or future orientated function of the unconscious, he (Jung) claimed that this led to a process of individual development which broadly took typical forms' (Shamdasani, 2003: 153). Dreams were taken as furnishing the main evidence for the existence of such a process and were Jung's 'principal psychoscope' (ibid). What individuating is *not*, but is at times mistaken for, is narcissism or self-indulgence. It is, instead:

> An act of high courage flung in the face of life, the absolute affirm-
> ation of all that constitutes the individual, the most successful
> adaptation to the universal conditions of existence coupled with the
> greatest possible freedom for self-determination.
>
> (Jung, 1954b: 171)

The Jungian emphasis on the value of the individual and her or his unique
individuation process can be seen to contrast quite starkly with the kind of
normalizing ontology that sometimes prevails within CBT praxis. Michael
Guilfoyle, writing from a deconstructionist, post-structuralist perspective, has
also recently written of 'CBT's integration into societal networks of power'
whereby therapists risk 'becoming inadvertent agents of "social control",
a position that we should surely resist' (quoted in House and Loewenthal,
2008: 16). A Jungian perspective would certainly fundamentally eschew any
pretensions towards a therapeutic approach that was used in any way as a
mechanism of social control or social engineering.

The materialism/transpersonal continuum: generalizing and objectivity about human experience on the basis of the Jungian approach

Jung's theory of the *collective unconscious* grew out of his understanding and
acceptance of the generality of human psychology. This psychic reality
underwrites all human experience at the archetypal level and 'As the sun
shines upon the just and the unjust . . . so we also are part and parcel of this
amazing nature . . .' (Jung, 1954b: 172). Interestingly, Jung referred to himself
as an 'empirical scientist' as, in his view, psychology as a science was a means
of corroborating the data of inner experiences to help them achieve general
validity, and this might suggest, at least initially, some semblance of commonality with the scientific pretensions of CBT. Yet, as pointed out by Davies
(2009: 197), for Jung, 'it is the physician's personality, rather than his heavy
bag of tools, or his "mastery" of so-called "clinical competences", which best
facilitates the healing potential of the therapeutic relationship'; and for Jung,
moreover, whenever rules, guidelines and 'competences' became too rigid or
rigidly enforced, they were as likely to asphyxiate the personality as would the
absence of any guidelines leave it dangerously uncontained (Davies, 2009:
197). For Davies, then, the creative tension that necessarily exists between
honouring 'techniques', on the one hand, and 'responsibly contravening
them in the light of one's own creative cadences' (p. 197), on the other, is one
that psychotherapists must continually and creatively strive to balance. Jung
was strongly against the 'routinization' of practice; that is, the process in
which 'clinical creativity becomes ever more subject to a bureaucratic control

which standardizes behaviour across the board and resists creative idio-syncrasy and initiative' (p. 197).

So the pursual of so-called 'clinical competences', with their predefined, manualized set of clinical procedures and guidelines in the name of 'improving practice', which typifies much of current CBT praxis, is anathema to a Jungian approach. On this view, then, such standardization arguably contravenes many if not most of the basic principles underpinning clinical work, with clinical creativity being a major casualty (Davies, 2009: 197).

In the course of the lectures Jung gave at the Tavistock Clinic in 1935, he touched on what he called 'psycho-physical parallelisms', stating that they are only separated by our minds but not in reality. 'We see them as two on account of the utter incapacity of our mind to think them together' (Jung, 1968: 72). With the advent of neuroscience, in particular, the specialized branch of neuropsychoanalysis, there is increasing evidence that mind and body, psychology and biology, are interdependent. Through what Shamdasani calls 'psychification' (2003: 254), instincts become psychological factors determining human behaviour that lead to them losing their compulsiveness. An example of this is hunger that may be seen as unequivocal whereas its psychic consequences are variable. As Jung stated, 'psychic forms ... like instincts are common to all mankind' (1960: 122). He noted that the archetypes formed such close analogies to the instincts so that 'the archetypes are the unconscious portrayals of the instincts themselves; in other words they represent the *fundamental patterns of instinctual behaviour*' (Jung, 1959: 44, original italics). Usage of the term 'instinct' gradually disappeared from psychology but reappeared in the work of ethologists like Konrad Lorenz and Nikolaas Tinbergen, who argued that the appearance of patterns of behaviour could not be explained by learning alone but was due to the existence of innate releasing mechanisms. Lorenz often related his concept of instinct to Jung's theory of archetypes.

To summarize, the importance of the *collective unconscious* rests on its being psychic reality or the *objective psyche*; the realm from which all symbolic activity and religious systems arise common to all humanity.

The generality of the *collective unconscious* had its counterpart for Jung in the diversity to be found in consciousness, one aspect of which he termed *collective consciousness*, a term he borrowed from Durkheim, which denotes the beliefs and assumptions collectively held by individuals embedded in a particular socio-cultural environment that they unconsciously accept. This hypothesis of Jung's allows for generalizing about human behaviour within specific spatial and temporal loci.

Collective consciousness might appear to offer a bridge from the Jungian approach to CBT as expressed by the practitioner, Warren Mansell, who states that CBT proposes that the most effective method of facilitating change is 'to help them (clients) to become aware of their conscious experience of meaning-making' (quoted in House and Loewenthal, 2008: 11). However, the analytical psychologist Andrew Samuels writes that:

> . . . there is what I perceive to be the silence of CBT around questions of meaning and purpose that are central to the contemporary clinical project of psychotherapy. I do not think the situation is changed much when an attempt is made to bolt on a bit of meaning in the case of mindfulness-based cognitive therapy.
>
> (Samuels, in House and Loewenthal, 2008: iv)

A distinctive view on 'evidence' of the Jungian approach

In the course of his work as a psychiatrist, Jung was aware of the importance of evidence to support his findings and there is a growing body of work that underpins the efficacy of Jungian psychoanalysis and psychotherapy such as the Berlin Jungian Study replicated below. This Study was financed by independent funding from the Bosch Family Foundation. All members of the German Society for Analytical Psychology (Deutsche Gesellschaft für Analytische Psychologie – DGAP), the umbrella organization of Jungian psychoanalysts in Germany, were asked to participate in this retrospective study. Over 78 per cent responded to this request and 24.6 per cent participated.

There were three objectives for this study:

1   To prove the effectiveness of long-term analyses (more than 100 sessions) in routine treatment practice and to examine the stability of treatment results by a follow-up study six years after the end of therapy.
2   To evaluate some aspects of cost-effectiveness.
3   To implement research strategies in the area of outpatient psychotherapeutic care for quality assurance purposes.

(Keller et al., 1998: 110)

Self-assessment of the patients at follow-up showed that compared with their state before therapy, six years after the termination of treatment 70–94 per cent of the former patients reported good to very good improvements with regard to physical or psychological distress, general well-being, life satisfaction, job performance and partner and family relations as well as social functioning (see Table 8.1).

Table 8.2 gives a comparison of the Jungian follow-up sample (N = 111) with a one-year follow-up sample of inpatient cognitive behavioural treatment (N = 142).

On the basis of their clinical notes, participating therapists in private

Table 8.1 ICD-10 classification of patients prior to treatment

Affective disorders	Neurotic and somatoform disorders	Behavioural disturbance with physical symptoms	Personality disorders
Bipolar affective disorder	Phobic disorder	Eating disorder	Specific personality disorder
Depressive episode	Anxiety disorder	Sexual dysfunction	Complex or other personality disorder
Recurrent depressive episode	Compulsion disorder		Abnormal habits
Cyclothymia	Stress reaction		
	Somatoform disorder		

Table 8.2

Jungian sample (N = 111)	CBT sample (N = 142)
Positive change: N 78. 70.3%	N 105. 73.9%
Moderate change: N 31. 27.9%	N 34. 24.0%
Negative change: N 2. 1.8%	N 3. 2.1%

practice documented all their cases (including dropouts) that terminated in 1987 and 1988. They completed a basic questionnaire regarding clinical and sociodemographic data and setting characteristics at the outset of therapy and give a retrospective global assessment of their patients' state at the end of therapy. In 1994, 111 former patients, who had finished Jungian psycho-analysis or long-term psychotherapy in 1987 or 1988 and who agreed to take part in the study, were sent a follow-up questionnaire that included measures of life satisfaction, well-being, social functioning, personality traits, inter-personal problems, self-rated health care utilization and some psychometric tests. Thirty-three cases in the Berlin region had a follow-up interview carried out and actual health status was rated by two independent psychologists trained in Jungian psychoanalysis. Table 8.2 of the study carried out by Keller et al. (1998) shows the relationship of therapy success to treatment length, which indicate that the longer the treatment the better the treatment success six years after termination of psychotherapy. Long-term psychotherapy was more successful than short-term psychotherapy.

Health care utilization was looked at in various ways, for instance, psycho-tropic drug use significantly reduced over the course of the post-therapy period (Keller et al., 1998, Figure 5). Furthermore, an increased percentage of the treated patients no longer use psychotropic drugs compared to pre-psychotherapy and the proportion of those taking medication regularly reduced substantially.

Neurotic and personality disorder patients often use resources by present-ing at primary care with physical symptoms or for support. More than half of the patients reported a substantial reduction in the frequency of doctor visits compared with the frequency of visits before therapy. The most meaningful index of resource use is days lost from work due to illness and the cost of hospitalization. An examination of the data recorded by national insurers before and after treatment revealed a substantial reduction of working days lost to sickness (Keller et al., 1998, Figures 8 and 9).

The overall conclusion and evaluation carried out by the researchers of the study show that even after five years, the improvement in the patients' state of health resulted in a measurable reduction of health insurance claims (work days lost to sickness, hospitalization, doctors' visits and psychotropic drug intake) in a significant number of patients treated. This means that in spite of the limitations of the study, the data garnered by it provide convincing arguments for the effectiveness of Jungian psychoanalysis. This is a study that could readily be replicated on other patient populations. The comparison of the data in Table 8.2 between the Jungian and CBT results is worth noting.

While the kind of scientific research study just described is clearly open to the kind of post-positivistic critique referred to in House and Loewenthal's Chapter 1, it does show that relatively conventional research methodologies can be used to yield encouraging evidence about the efficacy of Jungian therapy.

The Jungian approach to intersubjectivity

Jung's approach to intersubjectivity is encapsulated in the following words from *The Practice of Psychotherapy* where he states:

> If I wish to treat another individual psychologically at all, I must for better or worse give up all pretensions to superior knowledge, all authority and desire to influence. I must perforce adopt a dialectical procedure consisting in a comparison of our mutual findings.
>
> (Jung, 1954c: 5)

The conjunction of this *dialectic* and *mutuality* is a central feature of Jungian analysis requiring the emotional involvement of the analyst as well as the analysand for any significant shift to occur in both participants. The relationship in which analyst and analysand are immersed in an in-depth analysis is portrayed by Jung as follows '. . . hence wholeness is the product of an intrapsychic process which depends essentially on the relation of one individual to another. Relationship paves the way for individuation and makes it possible . . .' (Jung, 1954a: 245).

Contemporary Jungian analysts have engaged critically with the work of intersubjectivists like Daniel Stern and Beatrice Beebe. In his chapter 'From moments of meeting to archetypal consciousness' the Jungian analyst, George Hogenson, points to recent work done by Daniel Stern on the critical instances of interaction called 'moments of meeting' in analysis. These replicate the dynamic pattern in the early developmental stage between infant and care and take place along a continuum of temporal interactions punctuated by 'now moments'. The latter 'are instances of close connection but not transformative connection' (Hogenson, 2007: 295). 'Now moments' occur when the structure of analysis temporarily breaks down and the participants 'meet as persons relatively unhidden by their usual therapeutic roles for that moment' (p. 296).

To illustrate a 'moment of meeting' a clinical example is offered wherein the analyst struggled with her reaction to the analysand's charged reaction to the observing position of the analyst. The tension here is fraught with danger because of the sexual implications of the exchange but it was only when the analyst realized she was caught between retreating to the superior position or submitting to the analysand that 'she suddenly felt free to be spontaneous and communicate to her analysand her actual experience' (p. 296) that the 'moment of meeting' was fulfilled. As Hogenson says: 'What matters is the depth and human reality of the analyst's encounter with the analysand' (p. 296). Admirable as this is, Stern et al. (1998) do not reach up to the next level that shows how analysis truly effects transformation in both analyst and analysand as Jung did with his appreciation of the infinity of archetypal symbolic experience; namely, 'the nature of the Self, as imaged in the form of God, rather than a well-grounded ego' (Hogenson, 2007: 311).

The psychotherapist, David Brazier, echoes this in his critical article on CBT in House and Loewenthal (2008), when he asks the key question – who is caring for our souls now, and how are they to do so? For Brazier, real healing is required of the gradual erosion of standards and mounting ruthlessness of our culture. For this to happen, there needs to be a 'higher-level integration' (p. 13) between psychoanalysis and CBT for them to be able to work together towards this vital goal.

Jean Knox (2009) has explored the relational aspects of analysis in a recent article in which she illustrates how Jung's understanding of the analytic rela-tionship anticipated many of the insights in the intersubjective approach. For instance, the emphasis on the importance of the infant and the adult patient's unconscious but active contribution to the interactive dynamic process of dis-ruption and repair on relations (Beebe and Lachman, 2002). The idea that the unconscious and the self contribute actively to psychic recovery originates with Jung who argued that 'the collaboration of the unconscious is intelligent and purposive, and even when it acts in opposition to consciousness its expression is still compensatory, in an intelligent way, as if it were trying to restore a lost balance' (Jung, 1939: 282).

Conception of therapeutic change

The conception of therapeutic change that results from the Jungian approach has already been signalled in the first part of this chapter, namely, individu-ation. The person who is on the individuating path will have found a way of living that gives equal value to the contents of the unconscious as to the conscious part of the psyche. Neurosis stems from being unbalanced and living too much according to conscious demands or in opposition to the unconscious. Creativity lies in the dialectic between the two in what Jung calls the 'coniunctio', the symbolic union that gives birth to the new life that results from the unifying of these opposites.

However, as Andrew Samuels has pointed out, there is in CBT 'a lack of any perspective on, or consideration of, the unconscious, especially the creative unconscious' (in House and Loewenthal, 2008: iv). Instead, 'a claim is made for the success of conscious and realistic control of "thought" at the very moment when the *Zeitgeist* is redolent with a ubiquitous sense of perpetual and unmanageable risk . . .' (p. iv).

In the 1970s, I conducted a brief transatlantic telephone interview with B.F. Skinner for an article I was doing for *The Economist*. The single most striking thing he said, which I have always remembered, was that he never doubted there is an unconscious but he had not found a way of accessing it in his psychology which, as a result, focused on phenomena that were observable. The time is overdue for CBT therapists to embark on filling this lacuna in their approach.

Jungian therapy's coherence, or otherwise, with medical-model thinking

As has been pointed out earlier in this chapter, Jung was a psychiatrist at the Burghölzli Hospital in Zurich during the years 1900–1909. In the course of that time, he conducted extensive research that underpinned his theory of 'feeling-toned complexes', defined as certain psychic situations that are strongly accentuated emotionally and which are autonomous. A simple example would be a negative mother complex which, in a clinical situation, would sooner or later present itself as a projection onto the therapist of either gender whereby the therapist would be experienced as a cold, overbearing, withholding or smothering mother. Complexes are ubiquitous and affect every individual's relationships, personal as well as professional, and have a profound impact on their associations. Jung (1973: 291) puts is as follows: 'Every psychogenic neurosis contains a complex that differs from normal complexes by unusually strong emotional charges, and for this reason has such a constellating power that it fetters the whole individual'.

Jung and his colleague at the Burghölzli, Franz Riklin, conducted experiments on 'normal' subjects using 400 different stimulus words grammatically classified as follows:

Nouns	231
Adjectives	69
Verbs	82
Adverbs and numerals	18

The first 200 reactions were measured with a stop-watch in order to establish a general idea of reaction times to various stimulus words. Jung and Riklin developed their experiments obtaining 12 400 associations in the process. In simple terms, a subject was told to answer as quickly as possible to stimulus words with the first word that occurred to them. The responses were timed so that a long delay or a value-laden response to a word (e.g. mother/bad) were noted. Likewise, changes in the subject's bodily functions were recorded; for instance, respiration, sweating, flushing, and so on.

In a lecture delivered to the Department of Psychology at Clark University, Worcester, Massachusetts in September 1909, Jung delivered a paper called 'The Association Method' in which he gave the case history of an educated Roman Catholic woman of 30 years of age, married for three years to a Protestant, who had been suffering from periodical states of agitation since her marriage. In the course of the *Word Association Experiment* (WAE), the stimulus words that produced the maximum disturbances were: *to pray, to marry, happiness, unfaithful, anxiety* and *contented*. The conclusion Jung drew from this was that she was not indifferent to the fact that her husband was a Protestant; that she was thinking again about prayer and felt there was something wrong with her marriage; that she was unhappy; that she was having fantasies about being unfaithful; that she suffered anxieties about her husband and her future. Jung concluded she had a *divorce complex*, which initially left her shaken and in denial but she eventually agreed it was the right diagnosis.

Recent research done on Jung's WAE was conducted by a team of Jungian analysts at the Psychiatric Clinic of Milan University. The Psychotherapy Unit there is a public service and provides short-term treatment for subjects who develop acute psychopathological symptoms who prove to be suitable for psychotherapy intervention. The team set out to test the clinical application of the WAE when they decided to use Jung's theory of complexes in the psychodiagnostic evaluation and treatment of patients applying to the Psychotherapy Outpatients Unit of the Clinic. In psychopathological situations, complexes with a particularly high emotional charge become autonomous and disturbing, inhibiting ego functioning. In this experimental study, the team's starting point was that psychotherapeutic work should lead to a progressive shift in the patient's initial complex set-up. Jung's WAE was administered during the first phase of clinical-diagnostic evaluation and after one year of treatment was evaluated to see if it revealed any changes occurring in the patients' set-up of complexes. The results after one year of treatment were that the ego complex was more differentiated from the maternal and paternal complexes and was strengthened. In a corresponding fashion, the maternal complex proved to be diminished, thus made less powerful and relocated outside the ego complex. One important element from the clinical point of view was that the paternal complex no longer overlapped the maternal complex. The limitations of space mean that this is a brief summary of the study done by the team in Milan but interested readers can locate it in full from the references at the end of this chapter.

Another aspect of Jung's work taken up by psychologists is the work Jung did on psychological types as a result of which his terms 'introversion' and 'extraversion' were taken up in common speech. The Myers-Briggs type indicator is the experimental and statistical derivative of Jung's work on psychological types and is the most widely used personality test in the USA today.

It is important to note that a whole volume of Jung's 20 volumes of the Collected Works is dedicated to psychological types; three volumes to his psychiatric work; and a further volume to the practice of psychotherapy. The brief examples given in this section are, in part, a response to the alleged 'cost-effectiveness' and evidence/research-based 'efficacy' of the CBT approach.

Jung on the evolution of human consciousness

In considering the Jungian approach to the evolution of consciousness (e.g. Neumann [1949]1954), a crucial point in relation to CBT and its therapeutic ontology is that 'the ego only plays one of the roles, since the consciousness of other archetypal components . . . is also an aim of the work' (ibid.). In the current era of late modernity, typified as it is by scientism, materialism and even narcissism (e.g. Levin, 1987), it can be argued that human consciousness has become substantially unbalanced in the direction of ego development; and it could further be argued that the therapeutic approach of CBT is merely reinforcing this profoundly anti-Jungian trend. Such an insight might explain why, at both individual experiential and cultural levels, we find it very difficult to contain psychotic experience and its accompanying loss of ego (in the process pathologizing and treating it as an 'illness' that needs to be extinguished), but more generally, perhaps those who do experience such (often deeply distressing) ego loss – for whatever reason and in whatever circumstances – might even be expressing a crucial species-wide evolutionary imperative from which we must be open to learning (cf. House, 2001).

Perhaps until 'ego' is prepared to reflect critically on its grandiose pre-eminence in the human psyche (as is now starting to happen in much 'new-scientific', postmodern and transpersonal thinking), then the unusual in human experience will likely continue to be 'psychopathologized', scientifically medicalized and subjected to a fear-driven bludgeon of objectification and normalization (House, 2001). It might be very challenging for those steeped in the ideology of modernity to accept the Jungian-type view that 'the ultimate development of the ego is its submission to, even immersion in, a field of wider psychic consciousness' (Hillman, in Krishna, 1971: 155).

Notions of 'happiness' and well-being in Jung's approach compared to Layard's approach

The Collected Works have a few references to happiness as follows: 'Happiness' . . . is such a noteworthy reality that there is nobody who does not long for it, and yet there is not a single objective criterion which would prove beyond all doubt that this condition necessarily exists' (Jung, 1953a: 148).

Jung goes on to say that the alchemical opus offers as its goal 'tranquillity of mind' (1967: 152), and that happiness results from purging the body of 'black, burnt-out blood' (p. 153) in uniting itself with the 'supracelestial coniunctio' (p. 153) as a remedy for melancholia.

He sounds similar to Richard Layard in giving as sources of unhappiness the fact that humans are driven to alcoholic excess 'or expend themselves in the rush of money-making, or in the frenzied performance of duties, or in perpetual overwork' (Jung, 1953b: 260). Nature has armed defenceless and weaponless humans with a vast store of energy in order to equip them for tremendous hardships and 'has placed a costly premium on the overcoming of them' (p. 259). In the same work, Jung quotes Schopenhauer in saying that happiness is merely the cessation of unhappiness.

Layard's thesis for bringing relief to many hundreds of thousand of people needing relief from psychological/emotional distress and unhappiness is a clear philosophy based on achieving the greatest happiness of all. 'If we really pursued that, we should be less selfish, and we should all be happier' (Layard, 2003: 20). This worthy goal could be taught by 'good moral education' (p. 19).

The two main branches of Jung's psychology are treatment and education on one side and theory on the other wherein he warns against identification with collective consciousness and the catastrophes this can inevitably lead to as evidenced by the twentieth century. For Jung, the only solution is the recognition of the existence of the collective unconscious and the importance of the archetypes as 'these latter are an effective defence against the might of social consciousness and the mass psyche corresponding with it' (Jung, 1960: 423).

Jung and Layard exemplify the former's typology in their approaches – the one, is an introvert, who places the greater value on inner reality, pointing to the inner path as the way to 'tranquillity of mind'; the other, is an extravert, who places the greater value on outer reality.

To what extent, if at all, could the Jungian approach align itself with, or even create a hybrid with, CBT?

The previous section has already pointed to the introverted orientation of the Jungian approach versus the extraverted one of CBT. These are complementary opposites that need to be synthesized so that they are not in conflict. Practitioners from both disciplines already utilize insights from each other in the course of their work as well as from neuroscience that will increasingly have an impact on therapies of every description. Jung was not a systemizer but, instead, saw psychology as an encyclopaedic enterprise that would include analytical psychology and cognitive-behavioural psychology. A unified approach on their part to the study of, say, complexes and phobias would represent a creative coniunctio of opposites.

There are indeed some interesting attempts in the literature to synthesize Jungian and CBT approaches. First, the founder of rational-emotive behaviour therapy (REBT), Albert Ellis himself, also writes about 'integrating REBT and CBT with Jungian methods' (Ellis, 2007). Ellis refers to Jung as 'a brilliant personality theorist' (p. 247), and he lists four ways in which what he calls 'Jungianism' can be integrated with REBT and CBT (p. 248; cf. Colman, 2009).

Also, recent developments in CBT for schizophrenia, for example, emphasize the need to move from a sole focus on challenging beliefs towards a more person-centred approach in which recognition of the vulnerability of the self guides the therapeutic process, and the content of therapy is perceived as personally meaningful by the patient. Silverstein (2007) has recently demonstrated how the Jungian technique of archetypal amplification can be modified and used within the structure of CBT treatment of a young man with schizophrenia with a religious delusion who refused to engage in standard CBT 'treatment'. What this case example demonstrates is that schizophrenia patients who initially refuse to question the validity of their delusional beliefs can nevertheless be successfully engaged in CBT when the focus promotes alternative understandings of the self and preserves self-esteem.

Finally, the Society for Psychology and Healing (nd) has recently developed a training course that attempts to integrate CBT with CAT and aspects of Jungian therapy. So it does seem that the message is a mixed one; for while there do seem to be a number of fundamental world-view incommensurabilities between CBT and a Jungian cosmology, as discussed earlier in this chapter, at least some practitioners seem to be finding ways in which the two approaches can respectfully work with one another in creative and productive ways.

And to end, finally, with a telling epigraph from Carl Jung, which again strongly suggests substantial divergences between CBT and Jung's world view: 'You must learn everything you are required to know, and then forget it once you enter the consulting room' (quoted in Davies, 2009: 196).

References

Beebe, B. and Lachman, F. (2002) *Infant Research and Adult Treatment: Co-constructing Interactions*, Hillsdale, NJ, and London: Analytic Press.

Colman, W. (2009) 'Response to Umberto Galimberti', *Journal of Analytical Psychology*, 54: 19–23.

Davies, J. (2009) 'Psychotherapy and the third wave of professionalization', *European Journal of Psychotherapy and Counselling*, 11(3): 191–202.

Ellis, A. (2007) *Overcoming Resistance: A Rational Emotive Behavior Therapy Integrated Approach*, 2nd edn, New York: Springer.

Hogenson, G. (2007) 'From moments of meeting to archetypal consciousness', in A. Casement (ed.), *Who Owns Jung?*, London: Karnac Books.

House, R. (2001) ' "Psychopathology", "psychosis" and the Kundalini: "post-modern" perspectives on unusual subjective experience', in I. Clarke (ed.), *Psychosis and Spirituality: Exploring the New Frontier*, London: Whurr, pp. 107–25.

House, R. and Loewenthal, D. (2008) *Against and For CBT: Towards a Constructive Dialogue?*, Ross-on-Wye: PCCS Books.

Jung, C.G. (1939) *Conscious, Unconscious and Individuation*. Collected Works 9i, London: Routledge & Kegan Paul.

Jung, C.G. (1953a) *Psychology and Alchemy*. Collected Works 12, London: Routledge & Kegan Paul.

Jung, C.G. (1953b) *Two Essays an Analytical Psychology*, New York: Bollingen Foundation, Inc.

Jung, C.G. (1954a) *The Psychology of the Transference*. Collected Works 12, London: Routledge & Kegan Paul.

Jung, C.G. (1954b) *The Development of Personality*. Collected Works 17, London: Routledge & Kegan Paul.

Jung, C.G. (1954c) 'The psychology of the transference', in C.G. Jung (ed.), *The Practice of Psychotherapy*, Vol. 16, London: Routledge & Kegan Paul.

Jung, C.G. (1959) *The Concept of the Collective Unconscious*. Collected Works 9i, London: Routledge & Kegan Paul.

Jung, C.G. (1960) *Psychological Factors in Human Behaviour*. Collected Works 8, London: Routledge & Kegan Paul.

Jung, C.G. (1963) *Mysterium Coniunctionis*, Vol. 14, London: Routledge.

Jung, C.G. (1967) *Alchemical* Studies, Vol. 13, London: Routledge & Kegan Paul Ltd.

Jung, C.G. (1968) *Analytical Psychology: Its Theory and Practice*, New York: Vintage Books/Random House.

Jung, C.G. (1971) *Definitions*. Collected Works 6, London: Routledge & Kegan Paul.

Jung, C.G. (1973) *Experimental Researches*. Collected Works 2, London: Routledge & Kegan Paul.

Jung, C.G. (1992) *Civilization in Transition*. Collected Works 10, Princeton, MA: Princeton University Press.

Jung, C.G. (2009) *The Red Book: Liber Novus*, Verona: W.W. Norton.

Keller, W., Westhoff, G., Dilg, R. and Rohner, H.H. (1998) 'Studt and the study group on empirical psychotherapy research in analytical psychology', Department of Psychosomatics and Psychotherapy, University Medical Center Benjamin Franklin, Free University of Berlin. In P. Fonagy (ed.), (2002) *Open Door Review*. Second revised edition, London: International Psychoanalytical Association.

Knox, J. (2009) 'The analytical relationship: integrating jungian, attachment theory and developmental perspectives', *British Journal of Psychotherapy*, 25(1): 5–23.

Krishna, G. (1971) *Kundalini: The Evolutionary Energy in Man*, Berkeley, CA: Shambhala.

Layard, R. (2003) 'What would make a happier society?' Lecture 3 delivered at the Lionel Robbins Memorial Lectures 2002/2003, London School of Economics, 3–5 March.

Levin, D.M. (ed.) (1987) *Pathologies of the Modern Self: Postmodern Studies on Narcissism, Schizophrenia, and Depression*, New York: New York University Press.

Marlan, S. (2006) 'Alchemy', in R. Papadopoulos (ed.), *The Handbook of Jungian Psychology: Theory, Practice and Applications*, Hove: Routledge, pp. 263–95.

Neumann, E. ([1949]1954) *The Origins and History of Consciousness*, New York: Pantheon Books.

Samuels, A. (2008) 'Foreword', in R. House, and D. Loewenthal (eds), *Against and For CBT: Towards a Constructive Dialogue?*, Ross-on-Wye: PCCS Books, pp. iii–iv.

Shamdasani, S. (2003) *Jung and the Making of Modern Psychology: The Dream of a Science*, Cambridge: Cambridge University Press.

Silverstein, S.M. (2007) 'Integrating Jungian and self-psychological perspectives within cognitive-behavior therapy for a young man with a fixed religious delusion', *Clinical Case Studies*, 6(3): 263–76.

Society for Psychology and Healing – Inst for Contemporary and Natural Medicine (nd) Post-graduate Certificate Course in Cognitive Behavioural, and Cognitive Analytical Therapy; available online at www.marian2000.org.uk/index. php?main_page=page&id=20 (accessed 4 September 2009).

Stern, D.N., Sandner, L.W., Nahun, J.P. et al. (1998) 'Non-interpretative mechanisms in psychoanalytic therapy: the "something more" than interpretation', *International Journal of Psychoanalysis*, 79: 903–21.

9   Critically engaging CBT
Psychosynthesis

Stacey Millichamp

Introduction

Cognitive behavioural therapy (CBT) is receiving a great deal of attention, support and funding in the current challenging economic climate. The government have assigned the Health Professions Council the task of drawing up proposals that may ultimately govern all forms of talking therapy. Can the government seriously be planning to produce a prescriptive code of skills and techniques to be applied to the thousands of complex and unique therapeutic relationships existing now and in the future around the country?

CBT with its rational approach, clearly defined structures and lack of prioritizing the therapeutic relationship lends itself well to this idea of prescriptive codes of working, and therefore is being seen as something of an ideal model by those seeking a centralized blueprint. However, these plans to generalize the conducting of what is, for many practitioners, an art, not a science, threatens to dilute the richness of diversity and the current right of every potential client to find a therapist tailored to their own specific needs, world views and preferences. These issues in the current climate seem to have political, economic and social, as well as therapeutic, implications. Questions of cost-effectiveness have profound implications for those who receive therapy, and likewise which therapists are considered 'useful', not just to the client, but ever increasingly to a centralized body that is motivated by far wider issues than simply therapeutic ones. In an age of increasing 'big brother' intervention, it seems that increasingly the public are having decisions made for them, including which therapeutic approaches should be made available to them.

Standards for good practice are currently held by the British Association for Counselling and Psychotherapy (BACP) and the United Kingdom Council for Psychotherapy (UKCP), so it is intriguing to wonder about the motivation of moving this highly specialized area into the auspices of a medically oriented establishment. As Hewerd Wilkinson writes in his article in *The Times* on 15 July 2008: 'to put it bluntly: therapists disagree about most things, but few would argue that only one form of treatment is "right" and must be imposed'.

There has been much debate and discussion consequently about the possibility of 'measuring' psychological interventions in order to prove their effectiveness, and there is a growing unease about government intervention, the authorization of a council whose main approach is a medical model, and concerns that diversity may be lost as psychotherapeutic schools become 'mainstreamed' and defined purely by their ability to produce measurable outcomes, with an eye on a good economic return in relation to investment.

Psychosynthesis is positioned within the Humanistic and Integrative Psychotherapy section of the UKCP. It is a transpersonal approach, which values and explores what is spiritually, emotionally, intellectually, culturally and relationally meaningful to people, as an integrated part of examining the more psychopathological issues that bring them to therapy. Fundamentally, psychosynthesis as an approach is interested in placing a person in their wider contexts, seeking to discover what connects them to others and the world around them, with a view to exploring existential issues and experiences of the world, and with a growing emphasis on the interpersonal field that the client occupies. There is an increasing interest in the concepts of field theory, and intersubjectivity, understanding the nature of the therapist's impact on the field between client and therapist, and the subjective impact both bring to bear. There is often substantial enquiry into transference and countertransference as a way of opening the dialogue about the interpersonal forces at play.

There are therefore many aspects to psychosynthesis that separate it from CBT. Although practitioners will often appear to use cognitive and behavioural approaches in their work, the fundamental difference is likely to be one of models, values and attitude towards the client, their world and the therapeutic relationship. Therefore, it is not so much what is 'done' in therapy that defines and distinguishes practitioners, as much as the way in which therapist's perceive their clients, and the effect that perception has on the client, and on the work.

World view and model of the person

Roberto Assagioli (1990) was an Italian psychiatrist, deeply interested in the psychoanalytic movement. He was a member of the psychoanalytic group, formed in 1910 by Jung, and received psychiatric training under Paul Eugen Bleuler. His doctoral thesis presented the original concepts that formed psychosynthesis, challenging what he considered to be the limitations of Freud's views, and exploring the possibility of using analytical insight to not only understand dysfunction, but also the realms of human potential, inspiration and motivation. In this respect the model he developed was not focused on a reductive interpretation of the human psyche by breaking it down to its constituent problematic parts, but in discovering what was generative within not just the individual psyche, but in terms of connection and interaction with the world around it.

Assagioli's interest extended beyond the realm of what constituted a healthy ego, towards the realm of transpersonal experience in which the individual moves beyond a purely personal experience of themselves in the world, into a unitive and universal dimension of reality. The approach he envisioned therefore incorporated a dimension of personal and transpersonal growth, the two arenas being seen as distinct developmental stages within a larger context of what he called self-realization.

The psychosynthesis model hypothesizes that the psyche exists within a field of interaction that Assagioli, like Jung, termed 'the collective unconscious'. This is an important distinction, as many schools, including CBT, are solely interested in the intrapsychic world of the individual, and in their capacity to analyse, and control the 'content' of that psyche. Psychosynthesis, along with other transpersonal approaches, acknowledges the impact of collective themes, which can also be described as 'archetypes'; patterned ways of being that are inherited and passed down through the generations. In this respect, transpersonal therapists do not perceive a client as operating independently of the collective field in which they live, and the influences at play internally are in many ways intimately connected with their larger environment. In this respect, individuals are not seen as separate, and the mechanistic model of the Cartesian era that spawned such approaches as CBT, which is interested in cause and effect, and the capacity of an individual to identify the cause of a disturbing symptom through the erroneous thought that produced it, is a far cry from the more intersubjective, contextual, connective view that psychosynthesis takes of the individual.

In line with the majority of therapeutic approaches, psychosynthesis hypothesizes that an infant's 'reality' is co-created through the relational experiences of early childhood, and that fundamental wounding occurs on the level of empathic failures in that relational world. A child's developing sense of self is derived from the many mirroring connections that are internalized and form the blueprint from which an individual evolves. There have been interesting developments in psychosynthesis theory in the defining and exploration of the concept of 'primal wounding' (Firman and Gila, 1997), exploring the effects of empathic failures and the resultant repression of the parts of the psyche that were threatened by that wounding.

This relational view of child development posits that as children we need the empathic mirroring of 'external unifying centres' (Firman and Gila, 1997) in our lives that operate as 'fields of influence', welcoming, normalizing and encouraging the various parts of our emerging personalities, and our essential 'selfhood' into the world in its many forms. If there are elements of ourselves that are neglected, traumatized, rejected or in some way denied, there will be a resulting primal wounding in which we split off and suppress or repress that element within the unconscious, while simultaneously establishing survival strategies for avoiding those elements and the pain that comes with them. These survival strategies, which are commonly known as defence mechanisms, can coagulate into a survival personality, which we come to identify with as 'who I am'. This identity becomes like a fortress against the hostile and pain-making influences of the wider experiential landscape (the unconscious), and this potential war between 'who I am' and 'who I am not', rather than being a healthy differentiation of personal boundaries, can become a struggle that is echoed in our wider lives as a perceived tension and potential threat from the world at large.

A model of 'health' from a psychosynthetic viewpoint would therefore involve the evolution of our identity into a widening, broadening and increasingly inclusive identification with banished elements of the psyche. Softening those rigid identifications and allowing a permeability that increases awareness of who we are, in order that inner and outer prejudices towards humanity (both in self and others) are examined, is an essential part of healing. It is in the 'field' of the therapeutic relationship that such splits, and denied, ghettoized elements often emerge, largely through transference, as both therapist and client engage in the deeper challenge of the hated and shamed parts of the unconscious, and in so doing, support a kind of 'homecoming' to that which has been excommunicated. Therapy is therefore a mutual space of discovery, rather than a one-sided exploration where therapist as expert imparts the wisdom of how to move towards health and 'normalcy'. In fact, the more the therapist sets him or herself up as being 'healthier' than the client, the more the client is forced to carry shadow elements for both the therapist and him or herself.

A core element of the psychosynthesis model is the concept of an I–self connection in the psyche. The 'I' is a reflection of the deepest parts of ourselves, the self, both imminent and transcendent of the content of the psyche, the source of feeling authentically alive, closer to a sense of rightness and connectedness both to ourselves and others. The self is considered to be a transpersonal source, both intimately connected with our individuality, but equally connected to the collective unconscious. Thus, the self is considered to be a deep source of wisdom and compassion as well as having volitional qualities of transpersonal will, often experienced as a drive towards that which feels purposeful and meaningful in life. This sense of deeper direction is seen as fundamental to experiencing well-being in life, and without it, there can be feelings of lostness, loneliness and the pain of living a life without integrity to one's own values. Thus, psychosynthesis considers that many symptoms of psychopathology are fundamentally rooted not only in erroneous thought processes or meaning-making functions within the mind, but from a sense of disconnection from our deepest authentic sense of self, and the world around us. Without that connectedness, we are destined to feel alienated from, and afraid of, ourselves, and the world in which we live.

Generalizing about human experience?

> Moreover, although this manual provides a classification of mental disorders, it must be admitted that no definition adequately specifies precise boundaries for the concept of 'mental disorder.' The concept of mental disorder, like many other concepts in medicine and science, lacks a consistent operational definition that covers all situations.
>
> (Taskforce on DSM-IV, 1994: xxiii)

Although psychosynthesis has a 'model of the person', it is very careful in its approach to constantly remind both students and practitioners that there is no such thing as absolute truth or certainty when it comes to the human psyche. The unconscious is a vast and mysterious landscape and although psychological structures that might create familiar landmarks are useful, to use them as absolutes is to stand on the illusion of solid ground that perhaps is more for the therapist's need to feel secure and knowledgeable, rather than serving the unique unpredictability of the client. The mind is not an objective entity like the body, and therefore psychosynthesis would suggest that it does not lend itself to categorization as easily as the body. Despite this, there is of course a need to carve out ways of categorizing and treating symptoms; in other words, to recognize the repetition of certain patterns that seem to collect around certain conditions and respond favourably to particular treatment interventions. This is to be wise, and to learn from others' experience and from past experimentation. But as with everything, attitude and perception are everything, and to hold theory lightly as a reference rather than a rule is vital.

Coherence with medical-model thinking?

Psychosynthesis training institutions, like most serious schools of psychology and psychotherapy, include a rigorous exploration of the field of psychopathology as fundamental to their courses. All psychosynthesis UKCP-accredited trainings require students to attend clinical placements within a mental health setting that exposes them to the assessment and diagnosis of patients and to the multidisciplinary teams that treat them. Assagioli was a psychiatrist first and foremost, and he wished for psychosynthesis to be taken seriously within the medical establishment, and increasingly in the modern world; all psychotherapeutic approaches that are regulated and accredited by either the BACP or UKCP are required to be versed in the vocabulary of the medical model. I have seen students in training gain depth and a greater capacity to work with increasing levels of disturbance through their exposure to mental health settings and the rigour of learning the concepts of psychopathology.

However, the most important element within this increased capacity is in the application of theory to practice. Clinicians who rely solely on theory run the risk of using mental concepts to shield themselves from the true mystery and uncertainty of the therapeutic relationship and the unconscious. Skilful therapists allow themselves to use their theory as metaphorical references that can describe, and create connections in the service of, mutual discovery with their clients. Taskforce on DSM-IV (2004) itself states that diagnostic categories and criteria are not meant to be applied mechanically, and that it is the use of clinical judgement that justifies the application of a certain diagnosis to an individual.

The possibility of objectivity and the question of intersubjectivity

In the twentieth and twenty-first centuries, we have been plagued by alienation between consciousness and matter, a sense that we are strangers in this world. These roots can be traced back to Plato's distinction between the realm of ideas and experience, Christianity's favouring of the soul over the body (or at the cost of the body as somehow a vessel for sin), and the seventeenth-century philosophical and scientific revolution that ushered in Cartesian doubt and Newtonian physics. The living cosmos of the Greek and mediaeval times in which the universe was filled with mystery, intelligence and purpose was replaced by a sense of the universe as a clockwork machine (Zohar, 1990).

The paradigm that emerged from the scientific, economic and industrial revolutions of the seventeenth and eighteenth centuries was therefore one that viewed the world as predetermined, potentially predictable and that the whole could be objectively understood by examining the parts. It was considered that life was made up of isolated, independent objects. Descartes' theories added to this sense of separateness by splitting the mind off from the body, claiming that mind and matter are essentially separate and that we must therefore set out with the objective power of our mind to control nature. This paradigm puts forward the myth of rational thinking that claims the only worthwhile knowledge or truth is that which is quantifiable and can be empirically proven.

It was not until the 1960s that this prevailing paradigm was truly questioned with the emerging sense that we are interconnected with each other and life. It was in the 1960s among such radical changes in society that Assagioli's teachings began to be internationally accepted. His theory of psychosynthesis created a way of working with fragmented parts in order to enable an increasing experience of wholeness.

Science in particular has come to challenge our deepest-held notions of objectivity. Atoms were presumed to be unchanging and indestructible until the nineteenth century when the atom was split and a number of subatomic particles were identified. Einstein developed his theory of relativity in the early years of the twentieth century and the basic tenets of Newtonian physics were severely rocked. He concluded that instead of space and time being separate entities, they are connected in a way that he called spacetime continuum (curved by the influence of gravity). All objects relate relative to the curved nature of the spacetime continuum. Energy and mass were no longer seen as separate, but two aspects of the same phenomena. His theory opened up a world in which mass is not an inanimate, indestructible form, but is instead a living form of energy that is capable of change. Things could now only be understood in relation to each other and interdependently (O'Murchu, 1997: 24).

There were also new perceptions about movement. Movement used to be seen as something quantifiable, consisting of a body of certain density moving at a certain speed through the space defined between the point of departure and the point of arrival. In quantum reality there is no real 'space' between things, and therefore movement is more a series of leaps in which electrons jump from one energy state to another depending on the amount of quanta (energy packets) they have absorbed or released. There is no separateness and all things and moments touch each other at every point. This accounts for the phenomenon of non-locality at a subatomic level; correlation experiments of pairs of correlated photons show us that two events can be related across time and space in an 'in tune' way (simultaneously). In other words, there is no simple cause and effect (Zohar, 1990).

Most schools of psychotherapy are part of the global paradigm shift towards viewing reality as a vast system in which all things, including the observer, are included, rather than as being composed of isolated objects interacting in space. Einstein's discoveries, family system's theory, Heisenberg's uncertainty principle all point towards life as fundamentally relational. The isolated individual is now coming to be seen as an integral part of a larger whole and this relational stance is now evident in intersubjective psychology, object relations theory and self-psychology (Firman and Gila, 2002).

Conception of change

> Although it may not be made explicit as a goal of the therapeutic process, psychosynthesis psychotherapy aims to achieve something more while working with the client's problems and predicament: the discovery and expression of an increasingly purposeful and creative life, rich with meaning and value.
>
> (Whitmore, 1991: 19)

A psychosynthesis therapist will seek to understand the change a client is seeking, and it is often through the exploration of the specific nature of the client's hopes and dreams for change that the very process of disidentifying from the current state that is holding them captive begins. However, there is something larger than the presenting issue at play, and psychosynthesis as a transpersonal approach also encourages therapists to seek a contextual change, rather than just addressing their immediate problems. The context illuminates and gives meaning to the issues that the client brings in, and ultimately addresses their fundamental relationship to themselves and the world around them.

The psychosynthesis therapist will address the client's concerns and while doing so will ask the question, 'What is trying to emerge through this symptom?' The question's purpose is to evoke the deeper meaning and potential that may be seeking expression through the symptom that is being presented. In this respect, even the deepest, darkest issue hypothetically contains an element of the client's psyche that is seeking liberation and connection to the wider whole of the client's life. There is an underlying assumption that given the opportunity, the wisdom of the self will emerge as an integrating, healing force (Whitmore, 1991). Therefore, psychosynthesis is not so much concerned with solely solving particular problems, but through the establishment of an empathic attachment between therapist and client, which is termed as an external unifying centre (Firman and Gila, 1997).

It is hoped that within this mutual field of engagement, unconscious elements, without which the client is impoverished, can emerge. The therapist must continually examine his or her own prejudices towards experience in order to be able to welcome the wide-ranging disowned material that may be constellated. As the pain of original wounding is experienced and the shame, guilt and fear that comes with it is tolerated, a greater sense of 'and I am this too' deepens the I–self connection. From an interconnected perspective, as the client deepens their contact with themselves, so does the therapist, in a mutual field of awareness and affect.

The nature of change within psychosynthesis is also viewed in terms of the unconscious, the survival personality and the defence mechanisms that seek to sustain, support and protect the authentic self. Therapy can seek to draw out these unconscious defences and their purpose through the transference, interpersonal dynamics, and through intrapsychic enquiry. There is a realistic perspective that while we can seek to make more conscious the nature of our defences, that they are also profoundly and deeply part of our unconscious, and that therefore while we can change behaviour, attitude and most importantly, the depth of compassion and acceptance we have towards ourselves, deep and lasting change is something that emerges over time as we respectfully work with the defences that are present.

It is also important to question the very nature of the concept of 'change'.

Many clients come to therapy hoping to get rid of symptoms and parts of themselves that are causing distress. A heroic 'going to war' with our own personality is itself a Western narcissistic attitude reflecting the belief that we can and should be the god of our own world, and the master of our own universe. This attitude is part of the popular 'you create your own reality' thinking that is increasingly prevalent in our culture today, and is not one that belongs to the psychosynthesis perspective, which instead seeks, within the humility of the therapy room, to face the vastness of the mystery of the psyche, and the nature of relationship.

The materialism/transpersonal continuum, and notions of happiness and well-being

> The full picture of human intelligence can be completed with a discussion of our spiritual intelligence – SQ for short. By SQ I mean the intelligence with which we address and solve problems of meaning and value, the intelligence with which we can place our actions and our lives in a wider, richer, meaning-giving context, the intelligence with which we can assess that one course of action or one life-path is more meaningful than another. SQ is the necessary foundation for the effective functioning of both IQ and EQ. It is our ultimate intelligence.
>
> (Zohar and Marshall, 2000: 3)

Western society has become increasingly dominated by the concept of individualism, and with that has come a neglect of community and connectivity. Therefore, change as a concept within the therapy room needs to consider the implications of not just 'getting the client what they want' but healing some of the more profound ills of our time, if it is to be relevant in our world today.

Therapeutic relationship has the task of enabling people to reconnect at deeper levels of themselves with what is not just vulnerable, but also interdependent, and interconnected. This lends value to our humbler and more primal needs such as relationship, kindness and love that have become so lost in our mechanistic, materialistic age, where people often focus on how to have more, and to get more, rather than to 'be' more or give more.

In this climate, transpersonal therapy is not so much part of the spiritual supermarket of 'create whatever you want', but is rather an opportunity to seek beyond our 'wants' that are so rarely satisfied towards a deeper connection with a source that provides experiences of belonging, welcome, acceptance and comfort that are the more profound needs hidden within the materialistic consumption that so often fails, ultimately, to fulfil us.

How might psychosynthesis respond to the 'Layard thesis'?

The economist, Richard Layard, argued that happiness can be measured, and that despite the West getting richer over the last 50 years, we are no happier. He urged the government to invest in CBT as a way of saving money by getting people off incapacity benefit and back into the workforce (Layard, 2005).

Layard surmises that the factors needed for happiness are: good family relationships; enjoyable work; community engagement and friendships; enough money to avoid poverty; a clear personal value system; and personal freedom and good health. Interestingly, these conclusions support a more transpersonal approach within therapy, which might enable people to address the lack of meaning in their lives and to relate differently to the larger whole.

However, Layard appears to take an attitude of uncritical trust towards the bodies of knowledge on which he relies (being an economist not a psychologist), and fails to take into account the power relationships between the disciplinary interests and academic disciplines from which he draws (Pilgrim, 2008). Layard invests much face-value trust in psychiatric diagnosis, and the economically viable approach of antidepressants alongside the quick fix of CBT.

Psychosynthesis as an approach might respond to Layard's battle cry that happiness for all is a human right, with the perspective that suffering in and of itself is an integral part of human experience and ought to be approached with an attitude of enquiry and respect, rather than reductionism. To attempt to classify human misery as a bad thing that ought to be attacked with pharmaceuticals and short-term talking therapy, with the underlying assumption that the vast canvass of unhappiness can be reduced to such a broad-brush approach, seems naïve in the extreme. Yes, we can agree that basic human conditions of safety and security economically and physically are necessary for happiness in life. However, psychosynthesis views suffering as a deep existential and transpersonal arena where experiencing the heights and depths of life are a necessary part of the journey towards wholeness. To assume that the creation of a life of 'no pain' where people are drugged up and taught to rectify faulty thinking patterns conjures up visions of machine-like automatons, and suggests that 'being happy' is somehow a required part of being a useful human being.

History is littered with extremely talented people who have suffered from dark periods in their lives, and it seems that an attempt to enforce a happy mode of functioning takes us dangerously close to overlaying normative expectations on humanity, where not only are we told how many hours a week to work but how we will be expected to feel while we do it. A truly transpersonal perspective takes the view that within all suffering lies the signpost towards what is meaningful and valuable to us, that along the road of pain-making we can rediscover that which matters most to us. 'Happiness' is not simply an absence of pain, but the discovery of something far vaster, and more meaningful.

Perspectives on the alleged 'cost-effectivness' and evidence/research-based efficacy of CBT

If we take a field theory approach to the question of evidence-based research, we would have to start asking whether we find the results we want to find due to the attitude that we take to the subject, and indeed whether any kind of truly objective research is ever possible. Enquiry into the human psyche is unfathomable, and any measurements that are used are themselves constructs that represent a set of beliefs and assumptions that are already shaping outcomes. Therefore, while research is helpful in terms of highlighting trends, in order to keep practitioners reflective, it must only ever be a tool for enquiry, not an absolute to be applied generally.

If you give a client a questionnaire and ask them to rate their attitudinal changes as a result of therapy once they have completed it, the majority of the time they will report some degree of favourable change, no matter what the approach. However, much of the outcome-based research in psychotherapy points to the fact that the simple experience of having an interested, empathic, inquiring relationship is a cause for an increased sense of well-being. In the scientific, technical age of assessing what psychological content has changed in a client, it is easy to overlook the simple and human need for contact, and mutual meaning-making, the pure feeling of not being alone in one's perspective on the world, of being witnessed in the most painful places, and the experience of being welcomed and accepted for who you are, rather than who you are meant to be. Transpersonal therapy is therefore sometimes grand in its vision, but humble in it approach, because it respects the profound mystery that lies at the heart of human nature. It knows what it does not know, but wishes to discover.

Advantages and disadvantages of psychosynthesis in relation to CBT, and the potential for alignment

It is always important to respect a client's perspective on what is helping them. And if CBT is getting good results, all for the good. I am sure there are complex academic arguments for and against the nature of such research, which others can outline much more effectively than I. Being essentially inclusive by nature, psychosynthesis already incorporates a profoundly pragmatic approach at times, understanding underlying thought processes, unearthing core beliefs, trying on for size new ways of looking at a problem (we would call 'disidentification'), visualizing potential positive outcomes, addressing fears rather than analysing them, and most efficient of all, getting to the heart of what a person values and is seeking to protect, and finding new ways to risk expressing what is precious in the world, and risking pain or disappointment in doing so.

CBT is by no means the only effective psychotherapeutic orientation being used in therapeutic environments where short-term interventions are offered in order to produce cost-effective, maximum impact to the largest number of people. Psychosynthesis therapists are working in a myriad of environments where clients are offered a standard number of sessions, such as GP surgeries, hospitals, low-cost counselling centres and schools. In these short-term environments 'outcomes' and the concept of maximum impact to generate change within a short time frame brings out elements of psychosynthesis that have similarities to the CBT approach.

The concept of the transpersonal Will in psychosynthesis is one that encourages our capacity for assessment and to make choices that serve us more fully. Psychosynthesis considers that it is possible to work at depth in the short term because it is able to take a structured and pragmatic view of presenting issues, and is inherently optimistic in its perspective of a person's capacity, no matter how latent to move towards that which is meaningful for them, even if this goes against normative views of 'health'.

Fundamentally though, the greatest difference and strength in psycho-synthesis in relation to CBT is the premise that it is the therapist's presence, and ability to be empathically present, which denote the depth that is to be reached. The development of the psychosynthesis therapist is considered to be at the core of their readiness to work with others, and it is expected that they be much more than a developed mind, but that they are able to sit with, contain and relate to the breadth and depth of what their clients will bring, and that they will resist the temptation to reduce their client's material to a manageable problem. This is ultimately an expression of a core value that views the therapeutic relationship as the catalyst for meaning and healing, rather than a clever technician seeking to mend what is broken.

References

Assagioli, R. (1990) *The Act of Will*, London: Thorsons Publishing.
Firman, J. and Gila, A. (1997) *The Primal Wound*, New York: State University of New York Press.
Firman, J. and Gila, A. (2002) *A Psychology of the Spirit*, New York: State University of New York Press.

Layard, R. (2005) *Happiness: Lessons from a New Science*, London: Penguin Books.

O'Murchu, D. (1997) *Quantum Theology*, New York: The Crossroad Publishing Company.

Taskforce on DSM-IV (1994) *Diagnostic and Statistical Manual of Mental Disorders*, 4th edn, Arlington, VA: American Psychiatric Association.

Whitmore, D. (1991) *Psychosynthesis Counselling in Action*, London: Sage Publications.

Wilkinson, H. (2008) 'Can you regulate psychotherapy?', *The Times*, 15 July.

Pilgrim, D. (2008) 'Reading happiness: CBT and the Layard thesis', in R. House and Loewenthal (eds), *Against and For CBT: Towards a Constructive Dialogue?*, Ross-on-Wye: PCCS Books, pp. 256–68.

Zohar, D. (1990) *The Quantum Self*, New York: William Morrow and Company, Inc.

Zohar, D. and Marshall, I. (2000) *SQ – Spiritual Intelligence, the Ultimate Intelligence*, USA: Bloomsbury Publishing.

10 Critically engaged CBT

Howard Paul

I have had the good fortune to be part of the growth of behaviour therapy (BT), cognitive behaviour therapy (CBT), mindfulness and acceptance as well as the new trend of returning to behavioural roots interestingly coupled with an increased focus on emotion, interpersonal openness and the therapeutic relationship. Early on, I took great pride as empirically supported treatments emerged forming a concrete foundation of validated therapeutic procedures that, with careful selection, made provision of efficient and effective patient care more possible. In the 1960s and 1970s, validation meant demonstration of stimulus control. Multiple baseline and ABA (Baseline – Behavioural – Intervention – Baseline) designs were the accepted strategies for 'proof'. The early texts and journals contained new and important procedures and incrementally expanded the impact of therapy.

In the 1960s and 1970s the stimulus–response contingencies developed by the founders of BT (Skinner, 1938; Bijou, 1954; and Azrin and Lindsley, 1956 to cite only a few), along with social learning theory (Bandura, 1961), provided both a theoretical and empirical base. When dealing with children or with the developmentally delayed, these procedures were most potent and effective. Often, after successfully dealing with a child's behavioural problem, parents would return and wish to deal with their issues. It was humbling to realize that while behaviour therapy provided a technology to manage a broad range of problems, a good deal of the existential pain being presented by adults seemed poorly managed by contingency management and the social learning theory provided by my training.

I greeted the nascent development of CBT with great excitement. While I had been trained to carefully analyse antecedents and understand the valance and potency of reinforcements and consequences and extend this to social consequences and modelling, people actually wanted to *talk* to me. This was distracting to my provision of BT, yet it was compelling.

With CBT, there emerged a new set of procedures more fully available to help adults and adolescents. Importantly, CBT, in my mind, provided an important step towards expanding and integrating BT with other then forbidden and eschewed theories. The so-called 'black box' seemed to be opening up. When BT was growing in the 1950s and 1960s, there was considerable contention between the psychoanalytically dominant ideas of the time and the pioneers of BT. Seemingly arcane issues such as symptom substitution and even the ethics of funding research in behaviour therapy (Bandura, 2001) were very much alive. There were two very opposing camps and ways of looking at the relationships between human behaviour and the environment. As can be seen from many of the chapters in this book, these differences persist and along with that persistence, there is continuing misunderstanding of what CBT currently represents.

Many sophisticated persons when asked, 'Where do feelings come from?', respond that they are derived from our background, history and parenting and represent an internal process. This is an entirely non-behavioural conceptualization. When most people are asked to explain the 'where' of feelings (where do they come from), they give a psychodynamic (not necessarily psychoanalytic) response, such as from my background (early learning) and experience. What is fascinating is that when most people are asked about the 'why' of emotion, they become entirely behavioural and will detail antecedent conditions and actively avoid any internalizing explanation!

Early theorists recognized that there were many instances where similar antecedents led to very disparate emotional consequences. This represented a behavioural dilemma in that when antecedents and consequences are apparently identical, affective reactions can be worlds apart. The only variable that is predictive is the knowledge of internal process. From this recognition, the cognitive-behavioural age was born. Antecedent (A), Belief (B) and affective and behavioural Consequence became the new ABCs. The concept that belief predicated emotion represented a leap forward and CBT grew exponentially. Interestingly, by opening up the 'black box', clinical dynamics, untouched in behaviour therapy, began to be more openly discussed in the hallways of convention meetings. Antecedents and consequences were observable, however, unseen, and often unheard; beliefs needed to be understood and accounted for in order to understand and predict behaviour. These internal beliefs, from within behavioural conceptualization, were (and are) thought to operate at the level of habit. Habits operate automatically. Many could not see that 'automatic thought' became a behavioural synonym for the unconscious. Early learning creates our significant base of beliefs and, as habits do, operated on a level below awareness. In one stroke CBT had resurrected the unconscious (although labelling it as habit) and recreated the notion of early experience and learning as important psychological developmental variables. It was seldom discussed that this, at some level, paralleled someone else's theory; however, this insight guided me towards a more integrative approach and helped reduce (in me) the almost xenophobic stance being taken within behavioural circles towards anything dynamic.

By adding talking, believing and thinking to the behavioural repertoire, CBT not only grew, it flourished. However, even with the addition of previously eschewed concepts (talking, believing and thinking), CBT stayed true to its behavioural roots and maintained a dedication to empiricism and validation of treatment efficacy. From within, there has been some challenge to and maturation of the CBT model. Both Zajonc (1984) and LeDoux (1996) note that the ABC model of antecedent, belief and resultant emotion and action may not be accurate and that cognition is not necessary to have emotion. Stimuli, when they present themselves are first processed by subcortical brain systems within the amygdala and hippocampal areas. They are processed at an automatic, precognitive level and then sent to neocortex for further differentiation. LeDoux proposes an AEBC model where antecedents (A) produce an autonomic (and automatic) emotional reaction (E), which is then modified by cognitive processing (B), which then leads to a differentiated affective and behavioural reaction (C).

The original ABC analysis is a heuristic tautology in that it fosters the creation and testing of hypotheses and, while not fully accurate, does enable the development of effective concepts and procedures. These more mature conceptualizations are more physiologically accurate and enable the development of more potent and effective methodologies. Most importantly, it repositions emotion as more primary in the behavioural schema and has helped in the development of more affectively focused treatments. While there has been advancement in concepts, we are limited with the lack of a collateral change in descriptive language. Anger represents a good example. When we are confronted with something noxious, unappealing or not to our liking, there will be a primary arousal, representing autonomic activation. Whether this arousal is more mediated by epinephrine or norepinephrine determines, to some extent, whether our propensity will be to flee or attack. This primary arousal is then mediated in expression by involving our neocortex and it is at this level that our cognitions serve to modify and shape our ultimate expression of arousal. When CBT practitioners speak of irrational emotion, they are referring to this second-order level of feeling, not the primary, irreducible level of biological arousal. Many often miss this crucial distinction.

By the early 1990s randomized controlled trials (RCTs) replaced stimulus control as the accepted method of proof to document the efficacy of CBT interventions. Nathan and Gorman's (1998) first book on *A Guide to Treatments that Work* was released, followed by the second edition in 2002, along with other evidence-based books (Barlow, 2001; Kazdin and Weisz, 2003) touting the broad range of effective interventions developed in CBT and related therapies. While all of this progress was being made, grumbling and rumblings also developed in parallel to these notable achievements. On the one hand, randomized controlled trials (RCTs) used manualized approaches, anathema to many therapists who believe in the need for flexible management and creating of interpersonal engagement to enhance therapy.

Practitioners knew that there was a fundamental base of empiricism, yet much of what was being seen 'in the office' did not match what was being presented in the books on empirically supported treatments (ESTs) and evidence-based procedures (EBPs). Without careful reading of the studies, it sometimes seemed that patients were not getting as well as the ESTs said they should! Also, patients came into treatment with problems not addressed in the EBP literature. For those that did present with problems addressed by EBPs, after appropriate treatment many patients saw improvement, yet, they were still symptomatic. Some received little or no benefit. Clearly, something was either wrong or missing. Even with EBP, only 70 per cent of patients showed improvement (50 per cent in generalized anxiety disorder). Of the 70 per cent who improved, 70 per cent still had symptoms (Paul, 2004a). I have termed this the '70 per cent conundrum'.

The Division of Psychotherapy of the American Psychological Association believed that what was missing was a focus on the interpersonal; something hard to find and little addressed within the early behavioural community. Norcross (2002), an esteemed researcher, was given the formidable task to organize data supportive of the effect of the therapeutic relationship on therapy outcome. Most therapists, including myself, wanted this book to meet its charge. Sadly, the book is thick, the evidence thin. This is a puzzle. Most psychologists or psychotherapists (of all schools) will attest to the potency of the therapeutic relationship and its central role in positive outcome. Initially, the therapeutic relationship was never mentioned within the behavioural literature. It is mentioned in more recent behavioural- and cognitive-behavioural texts as integral to a good outcome.

Traditional CBT seemed to hit a plateau and could not get past the 70 per cent conundrum. Recent (and some not so recent) work has added to the utility and flexibility of behaviour therapy and CBT. Tools such as motivational interviewing (Miller and Rollnick, 1991), emerging from the substance abuse and alcoholism tradition and interpersonal psychotherapy (Klerman et al., 1984), have received empirical support and have been added to the list of expanding, efficacious CBT procedures. The work of the functional analytic psychotherapy movement (Kohlenberg and Tsai, 2003) along with other radical behavioural research (radical insofar as they disagreed with Skinner's conceptions about language) became (re)discovered and more available to mainstream CBT practitioners. Presentations on acceptance and commitment therapy (ACT) (Hayes et al., 1999), mindfulness and other aligned procedures (Linehan et al., 2001) with a lesser focus on direct change emerged.

While all of behaviour therapy and a significant proportion of CBT is aimed at primary change, these newer therapies see the need to induce and produce change more as the problem than the solution. They directly target those who remain symptomatic or resistant to traditional CBT and, what is most interesting, they see the therapeutic relationship as core. Many of these therapies derived from radical behaviourism are intensely interpersonal and, unlike early behaviour therapy and CBT, focus on the nature and quality of the therapeutic relationship.

There are additional emerging theories and therapies serving to round out the armamentarium of behaviour therapists. There used to be a belief (not from within the behavioural tradition) that behaviour therapy or CBT was only good for 'the simple cases' and when personality disorder or serious psychopathology due to trauma and abuse existed, a referral to a more dynamically oriented therapist was needed. Fortunately (more for our patients than for us as therapists) this is no longer the case.

To further expand on one such theory, Young et al.'s (2003) schema therapy is a good example of the maturation of behaviour therapy and CBT treatments. Young has been developing schema therapy since the early 1990s, believing that the presence of an Axis II disorder contributes to some of the reasons why CBT does not work well with more impaired patients. He believes that addressing early trauma as well as the results of poor parenting is required along with traditional CBT. Young sees schema therapy as evolving from traditional CBT, integrating elements of Gestalt and more dynamic treatments noting that, for many patients with characterological problems, their complicated motivations and approaches to therapy make them poor candidates for traditional CBT. Additionally, he notes that certain patients with characterological problems have difficulty observing their thoughts and feelings accurately, which is a requisite for successful CBT. Young believes that core CBT strategies such as empirical analysis, logical discourse, experimentation, gradual steps and repetition are often insufficient to alter the distorted thoughts and self-defeating behaviours of individuals with certain characterological challenges. Such individuals are often exceptionally rigid and rarely able to respond to short-term treatments. They have difficulty in establishing a collaborative relationship with the therapist, making focus on the relationship more important.

Young et al. (2003) additionally argue that such patients may have difficulty in pinpointing precise targets of treatment; instead, presenting with vague, unspecified and existential problems of unhappiness. Schema therapy, unlike traditional CBT, places much greater emphasis on exploring the childhood and adolescent origins of psychopathology. In exploration, early maladaptive schemas and coping strategies are identified. This, according to Young, assists in making sense of chronic and pervasive problems, organizing them within his system in a comprehensible manner. His theory states that these patterns, or schema, represent memories, emotions, cognitions and bodily sensations that coalesce to form broad patterns that are resistant to change, developing during childhood and adolescence and elaborating throughout one's lifetime, leading to dysfunctions regarding self and/or relationships. Young believes that to survive, individuals who were subjected to abandonment, abuse, neglect or rejection developed survival patterns, which ultimately become maladaptive when their environment changes and adjustments are no longer necessary. He believes that such early maladaptive schemas are resistant to change and fight for their survival, making them not conform to typical extinction paradigms. Paralleling the beliefs of Young, Borkovec (2006) has developed a therapy focusing on emotional processing. This therapy includes procedures for emotional deepening, not typically focused on in traditional CBT. Emotional deepening is combined with CBT as well as with mindfulness, interpersonal skills training and experimental challenges (akin to exposure procedures) as well as empathy training.

Within the behavioural tradition, there finally seemed to be a rounding out of therapeutic procedures consisting of behavioural, cognitive, emotional focus and mindfulness/acceptance tools to more fully deal with the wide array of presenting problems brought into therapy by patients. Most importantly, there is an acceptance of and focus on the importance of the therapeutic relationship, while the therapeutic relationship, dynamics and emotion have become more forefront. All these treatments and the theorists who are developing them maintain a core commitment to empiricism and research, separating them from many psychoanalytic practices. Combining sensitivity to what emerges in the therapy session with a research emphasis has created an ever-expanding set of tools for therapists to learn and use. Behaviour therapy and CBT are far from mature, however; there has been significant growth leading to ever-increasing efficacy and the ability to deal with more seriously impaired patients. It is with this knowledge and background that I address the points raised in this book by contributors aiming to critically engage CBT.

The core points of those critical of CBT seemingly revolve around issues reflecting concerns about the applicability of science and empiricism to psychotherapy, umbrage over the use of RCTs as an indicator of efficacy, the elusiveness and unmeasurability of the therapeutic relationship, the issue of manualized, mechanistic treatment, overreliance on the *Diagnostic and Statistical Manual of Mental Disorders (DSM)* and a somewhat self-serving notion that CBT is practised in a non-humanistic, non-systemic, narrow and myopic fashion. Many criticize the 'medical model' that they mistakenly believe is central to CBT theorists and practitioners. Millichamp (Chapter 9) goes so far as to say that the practice of therapy is only an art and *not* a science, somehow believing that science 'threatens to dilute the richness of diversity' and the 'right' of every person to find a therapist 'tailored to their own specific needs, world view and preferences'. Such eschewing of empiricism and rejection of science is anathema to anyone trained as a scientist-practitioner and cannot serve to legitimize the practice of psychotherapy. Indeed, psychotherapy is part art. To divorce it, however, from science is reckless and irresponsible. To state that research cannot be objective and that inquiry into the human psyche is unfathomable is to create a sheltered arena within which to maintain beliefs without question.

Millichamp, as do many other psychoanalytically trained practitioners, states that the goal of therapy is *understanding*, not *alteration* of maladaptive behaviour. The reality is that understanding does not change behaviour; alteration of habit changes behaviour. We are, in fact, not creatures of knowledge. We are creatures of habit. To create long-lasting improvement in behaviour, new habits must be facilitated, rehearsed and strengthened. Millichamp additionally mistakenly states that CBT is 'solely interested in the intrapsychic world of the individual, and in their capacity to analyze, and control the "content" of that psyche'. Many current CBT practitioners have a very different view of the mind, noting that the mind often cannot be controlled and acceptance and other non-change based strategies are called for.

I believe that there is a hierarchy of potency of therapeutic strategies. When systems and antecedents can be altered, therapists have the most power and leverage to promote growth and change. When antecedents cannot be altered, modification of reinforcement and consequences leads to the next level of potency. Beneath that is alteration of cognition using the many CBT approaches. For those who have had failed experience with CBT (delivered by a skilled and sensitive therapist), acceptance and commitment as espoused in ACT (and other related therapies) come into play. Rather than 'going to war' with our own personality, CBT does provide a range of interventions based on individual need and character structure. Millichamp concludes by stating, 'the greatest difference and strength of psychosynthesis in relation to CBT is the premise that it is the therapist's presence, and the ability to be empathically present, that denotes the depth to be reached'. CBT also sees the therapeutic relationship as necessary and vital. It is, however, not sufficient. When coupled with actual procedures of proven efficacy, patient care is enhanced.

Ryle (Chapter 3) notes that CBT lacks a serious developmental model. He is only partially correct. Most CBT practitioners do rely on attachment theory and Piagetian stages of development, along with other developmental theorists, accepting them as a valid base, and feeling they do not need to 'reinvent the wheel'. Ryle incorrectly states that CBT 'takes little account of early development and its effects upon psychological structure.' As noted in my introduction to this chapter, the development of erroneous cognitions and schema are based on early development and it is by virtue that all of us start out as infants that there is such ubiquity and uniformity of distortion of cognition. CBT practitioners would agree with Ryle that habit, when combined with temperament, forms a powerful basis for defining future behaviour. What he calls reciprocal role procedures can be easily translated into early-learned habit patterns, such that it may well be that his point of difference is, in fact, a point of similarity. Since identifying underlying faulty schemata also involves the bringing into awareness of unheard and 'unconscious' thinking, Ryle's belief is not supported that Cognitive Analytical Therapy (CAT) is different from behaviour therapy because it targets 'hitherto unrecognized patterns of thought and action which therapy would seek to modify'. Interestingly, Ryle infuses many behavioural terms into his presentation, noting that stability of role procedures is maintained by eliciting reinforcing reciprocations from others. Ryle also restates much of early social learning theory in his discussion of the social formation of individuals. He separates himself from the empiricism of CBT by his belief that 'studying humans as objects, is inappropriate . . . and must include intersubjective understanding'. Another self-serving notion includes his statement that '. . . manualized therapy seems to me to be incompatible with humanely respectful therapy'. If, in fact, procedures can be developed that are so robust that, even with limiting individual variability, positive effects can be repeatedly demonstrated, then a very potent intervention is at hand.

Ryle criticizes CBT due to what he terms a naïve belief that RTCs are the only way to document proof. In my (Paul, 2004b) review of RTCs and empirically supported treatments, I noted that until lately it took both fortitude and perseverance to be a researcher in the field of psychotherapy efficacy. This was true not only because of the public hue and cry, but also because of the fact that no treatment provided compelling data as to its efficacy. While today there is consensus (within the CBT literature) that there are specific treatments for specific problems that are empirically supported, there remain significant rifts between researchers and practitioners and practitioners and policy-makers. The pendulum has swung in favour of ESTs; however, the prudent practitioner needs to maintain a scientific mind, even towards ESTs and EBPs. Key questions need to be addressed, including the pragmatic validity of the EST guidelines, the purpose and use of EST findings and the real-world applicability of the findings, including their acceptance and transfer into the therapeutic process. Nathan and Gorman, in both their initial (1998) and now second edition (2002), as well as Norcross, are careful to look at the EST guidelines and delineate their strengths and weaknesses. ESTs follow a medical model of double-blind studies. Nathan and Gorman outline the now classic levels of research study detailed in their book and developed by the American Psychological Association (APA) task force. Type 1 studies are the most rigorous and involve randomized prospective clinical trials with comparison groups including a valid placebo, random assignment and blind assessment. Studies must also define clear exclusion and inclusion requirements, detail their diagnostic criteria, be of sufficient size to have statistical power and have clearly specified and valid statistical processing.

Interestingly, within the behavioural tradition, many studies of high research calibre are excluded as they utilize small group or single case studies using multiple baseline designs. Applied behavioural analysis was a corner-stone of early behavioural research and literature. Multiple baseline designs became the foundation of much of the behavioural strategies now at the very core of behavioural management. Early groundbreaking studies such as Zeilberger et al.'s (1968) study detailing the procedures of time out and Paul and Miller's (1971) study on reduction of extreme deviant behaviour in a developmentally disabled child would not be considered as reaching the level of proof needed to qualify for EST research. Ironically, Type 2 studies, which lack some of the aspects of a Type 1 study and are of lesser power than an ABA study, have found their way into the EST literature where no Type 1 studies exist. Interestingly, as patient pathology becomes more profound or more typically represents the type of patient found in real-world outpatient practice, being based on Axis II variables or V code problems, fewer Type 1 studies exist. Most EST research is targeted towards a single diagnosis with dual diagnosis being an exclusionary factor. This may be one of the reasons for the tepid acceptance of EST data into the treatment office as few patients come into therapy with singular disorders as addressed in the EST and EBP literature. Below are some of the pros and cons I detailed:

Pros:
- emphasizes utilization of protocols with proven efficacy;
- enhances use of scientist-practitioner model;
- enables the clear explication of treatment methods;
- emphasizes the reproducibility of results among various treatment sites;
- encourages research into efficacy and component analysis of critical procedures;
- enables comparison of diverse treatments;
- leads therapists to look at supported treatments from alternative schools of therapy.

Cons:
- Even where EST/EBP has shown efficacy, there remains a substantial (approximately 30 per cent) number of individuals who are non-responders and of responders, many who are still symptomatic.
- Manualized presentation eliminates patient and therapist variables from treatment variance.
- Presentation of EST data can inadvertently lead to an overzealous presentation of real-world efficacy and potentially can lead to untoward insurance company demands for specific procedures when they are not appropriate.
- Reliance on RCT occasionally leads to ignoring alternative research strategies with documented efficacy.

- The impact of ESTs has limited impact on 'problems of living', personality disorders and V code complaints.
- RCTs may inadvertently lead to unwanted government or insurance company meddling into the business of therapy.

Not all CBT practitioners worship at the altar of RCT. Stating that CBT has a naïve understanding of research may, in and of itself, be naïve.

In the mid–1970s I founded the Institute for Behavior and Family Therapy in New Jersey. Over the last few years, I have been an Editor for the *Journal of Child and Family Behavior Therapy*. As such, much of Stratton's presentation on 'Systemic family and couples therapy' (Chapter 5) resonates as compatible with my views. I view the individual from a systems standpoint using Lazarus's (1976) multimodal approach, looking not only at cognition, but behaviour, affect, sensations, imagery, ideation and drugs. (As an aside, even as early as the 1970s Lazarus (1971) espoused integration noting that technical eclecticism was a positive, as long as it was coupled with theoretical monadism.) I further break down data into the biological by taking into account central nervous system functioning, autonomic signatures as they relate to stress responses and enquire about neurohumoural, endocrine and musculoskeletal status and reactivity. We are indeed psychobiological beings and assessment must be multifocal and systemic, both within and without the individual.

Stratton notes that the self is not fixed and fluidly adapts in each encounter. From a CBT perspective, this relates to the controlling power of discriminative stimuli (S^D). Those working with distressed couples may relate to times when couples in conflict go away on vacation and have a blissful time, only to resume their bickering as soon as they return home.

Stratton sagely states that 'although we reject the idea of one perspective being true and others being false, we do not see all perspectives as equally useful'. BT does not have ownership of the truth. It is, however, committed to try, even if in a flawed way, to get closer. Stratton, as do many other contributors, see their theories as not 'lend(ing) themselves to standard paradigms of evidence'.

Stratton also wrongly believes that CBT is 'married to the DSM' and targets its treatments to it. Knowing the DSM diagnosis in *some* cases does lead to utilization of specific procedures. More often than not, a comprehensive multimodal behavioural and cognitive assessment forms the basis for accurate treatment planning. The DSM is more a function of the economics of providing therapy. If a DSM diagnosis is not used, there is no 'illness' and therefore no reimbursement. There are many flaws in the DSM and there is a movement to change from a discrete nosology to one that is more representative and scalable, using dimensions, which takes into account the marked comorbidity of many disorders. CBT actually does not like the medical model; however, pragmatism dictates that it be recognized and, due to the politics of our time, be maximized and used to the advantage of patients. CBT agrees with Stratton that most of what goes on within the walls of therapy rooms deals with problems of living, not disease. That being said, there are clear cases where the medical model does apply, insofar as there is a compelling biological base for some disorders. This is most true for schizophrenia, major depression, bipolar disorder and obsessive–compulsive disorder (OCD). Even in these instances, a behavioural/ cognitive analysis is in order to craft an individualized treatment plan.

Just as I found much to agree with in Stratton's chapter, Holmes's chapter (Chapter 2) has much to commend it. His confluence of theory mirrors some of the thinking that led me towards integration. I joined the faculty of the Institute for Integrative Training in psychotherapy in the mid-1980s and lectured (to those who would listen) on gaining the most from the wisdom of others and highlighting where I believed there was commonality between CBT and more psychodynamic positions.

Holmes accurately depicts the extant contentions between the behavioral and analytic camps. His understanding of CBT's mechanism of action is aimed more at older models of CBT and does not take into account CBT's maturation and current understandings. For example, currently, changes in behaviour are thought to be central in changing affect. Changing cognitions serves to augment and motivate changes in behaviour, which seems to be emerging as primary.

Parker (Chapter 6) writes about Lacanian psychoanalysis. It strikes me that he may be a fearful and angry person in that he had difficulty not falling into a school-based attack against CBT (against the guidelines of the editors) noting that CBT is based on a 'fake materialism' and rendering it essentially illegitimate. I am personally unfamiliar with the CBT he attacks and therefore at some loss to constructively respond. I teach my patients to only talk when they have a pair of ears ready to listen. As such, little further will be said.

Casement (Chapter 8) discusses critically engaging CBT from a Jungian perspective. Positively, she includes ongoing research meant to empirically support Jungian interventions, citing studies based on the long-term (100+ sessions) application of such treatment. While positive change is noted, 100+ sessions seems to be a current luxury. Outcome would best be compared to parallel CBT/BT approaches to gain true insight in cost-effectiveness. Casement cites Brazier (2008) noting that 'real healing is required of the gradual erosion of standards and mounting ruthlessness of our culture'. I agree. Too many cultures induce neuroses, and in fact, it may be impossible in today's age not to do so. There will always be the need for healers of the mind and it seems, given the limited resources available, that it is a moral imperative to do all that we can to find and provide the most efficient treatments.

Psychotherapy deals with at least two levels of problem. On the one hand, we deal with real illness and biologically based disorders. On the other, we deal with problems of living, existential pain, disconnectedness, the search for meaning and the seeking of happiness. I personally believe that when individuals seek happiness, they probably will not find it as it requires one to open oneself up to its presence (and paradoxically, let it find you). Happiness can exist even when there is pain. There exists a continuum of feeling, from joy to sorrow, which is part of the human experience. These feelings (sorrow) are not to be avoided. Some see CBT as working to suppress feeling, rather that to align feelings along that dimension. When feelings are orthogonal to the joy – sorrow dimension, neurosis, or 'faulty cognitions' from within the CBT framework, are at play. As the goals of therapy leave the arena of reducing 'symptoms' from psychobiological disorders to managing more existential issues, the differences in application between CBT and other practitioners most likely reduces.

It is interesting that the eight contributors who were asked to critically engage CBT were supplied guidelines and particular questions to address. Those of us who were to respond were only asked to participate in reviewing the opinions of others and respond. It did become apparent that 'happiness', more a philosophical than traditional psychological issue, was to be significantly addressed. Happiness, as a construct, is not generally addressed within the CBT literature; however, as it is a central theme in this book, here is one CBT practitioner's take on the issue.

Happiness appears to be a much misunderstood issue. Patients often see happiness as a state to enter and then never leave, like moving into the house on the hill and living there happily ever after. As I look at the issue, happiness has many levels and dimensions. On an appetitive level, brief happiness comes from simply getting what you want, whether from sex, a good meal, a promotion, a good grade, seeing a good movie, and so on. This aspect of happiness has led many people to define happiness as 'getting what they want'. This, perhaps, harkens back to our infancy when we cried when we wanted food, or to be cleaned, and felt happy when our basic needs were met. Most of us, as infants, did succeed in getting most of what we wanted, at least through our first year. Of course, this does not last and we are soon frustrated with a new, strange two-letter word, heretofore not heard! It takes most of us until age two to rebel against this tyranny (of no) and go to war with our parents, entering 'terrible twos'. Terrible twos is that stage when we try to restore happiness, to make the world revert to the truth and beauty we once knew when we did get almost all of what we wanted. In actuality, we all spend the rest of our lives trying to outgrow 'terrible twos'. Perhaps the current state of the world, with its consumerism, 'bigger is better' ideation, me first trends and loss of contact with the greater good represents how few people actually transcend this stage leading to the corrupt notion that getting what you want equals happiness. Moreover, there is an unfortunate entitlement that has grown wherein people think they are due happiness and that happiness can only be achieved when others assume responsibility for their comfort and well-being.

Happiness, as noted by many of the contributors to this book, is an existential issue. It has a higher level than simply satisfaction of need and desire. It is enhanced by involvement in relationships. These relationships involve joining with others in value-guided activities. These relationships can be with another person or community. Happiness best emerges from living a valued life and performing acts of giving and kindness.

Buddhist tradition, frequently referred to by many contributors, has also influenced many CBT practitioners. Happiness, it appears, comes not from getting what we want, but instead, comes from making peace with what we do not have. Most CBT writing is not philosophical, and as such, philosophical and existential issues are little addressed. Since CBT does try to operationalize and define that which it attempts to deal with, here are my notions about happiness. Happiness is achieved by living a value-based life. Much time is spent in therapy in assisting individuals to define and clarify their own values and then use them to create goals and assist in decision-making. Happiness comes from making adult choices and being able to appreciate these choices as representing our ideals. We are often confronted with the choice between what we wish and what we think may be best. There are some times when these are congruent, however; there are many times when what might be the most fun or most enjoyable differs from what our values dictate. Seeing this difference and recognizing that 'doing the right thing' is a choice, places us on an adult footing, which can contribute to a sense of self-satisfaction different from the more base 'getting what we want'. Another key contributor to happiness rests on realizing that we are the equal of others and therefore cannot dictate their behaviour. Anger, a spoiler of happiness, at least from within the cognitive-behavioural tradition, comes from taking our wishes and elevating them to some level of demand; developmentally, being two years old, and demanding our way. Being able to identify when our desires are being expressed as demands and being able to reverse this error is another key aspect of being adult.

Many years ago I assisted a depressed young adult overcome his depression. He was a poet and was fearful that if he lost his pathology, he would lose his gift. He produced poems detailing his sojourn through therapy, which lasted about four months. Space does not permit reproducing (with permission) all of his poems; however, three will well make the point. This first poem was written shortly before therapy started.

> **THEM**
> *Beware of them,*
> *   They created evil.*
> *Use caution,*
> *   They kill and stifle.*
> *Suspect them,*

> *They betray friends.*
> *Distrust them,*
> > *They mock and torture.*
> *Shun them,*
> > *They tempt to corrupt.*
> *Love them,*
> > *They are you and me.*

This next poem was written after about 4–6 weeks of therapy. A good rapport had been established, trust issues had been dealt with and the patient began to be more comfortable with CBT notions and began to feel somewhat liberated when he grasped his own power in being able to alter his many years of depressive ideation.

> *In the black of early morning,*
> > *All is quiet, all is at rest.*
> *A beam of light gently breaks the darkness.*
> *Ever so slowly, ever so softly.*
> *Trees begin to appear; so strong, so proud,*
> > *With glistening bark, and bright colored leaves*
> > > *Rustling in the autumn breeze.*
> *Birds begin to sing;*
> > > *breaking out in a rage of brilliant song,*
> > > *filling the air with a rainbow of tones.*
> *As the fiery red ball continues to rise,*
> > > *it illuminates things with a warm glow*
> > > *giving life to all it touches.*

This last poem was written after about 10 sessions (about three months) of CBT. It is remarkable in that it contains irony, but not anger, wryly commenting on what he now saw as the generators of his despair and his separation from it, enabling his approaching happiness.

> *We are told of the promised land,*
> > *Where all is, and we are one.*
> > *Where beauty is more than we*
> > *Can possible perceive in physical form*
> *We are told of heaven and hell . . .*
> > *That we are created in the*
> > *image of god.*
> > *And how Adam created Eve.*
> *We are told of the revelation*
> > *When the superior souls will rise*

> *in total bliss.*
> *And when the lower beings will live*
> *In eternal hell.*
> *This is not a place in time,*
> *But a place in mind.*
> *Be conscious of it.*

Happiness is not real. It is a mindset. It has some teachable components. It is more a philosophical and existential issue than one directly based on the psychopathology of the individual, but may be more directly linked to the pathology of our cultures. Since much of what is actually dealt with in therapy stems from the existential angst of our times, it becomes fair game for any therapy and certainly one that deserves more thought from within a CBT perspective.

Conclusion

It strikes me that some of the criticisms aimed at CBT may be accurate; however, many are no longer reflective of where CBT is today. It is somewhat akin to being angry at the young adult, because he was once an adolescent. Many contributors have noted that CBT proves elusive as it is no longer a simple, mechanistic process, differentiating itself into many empirically based strategies and theories. Over the last few years, CBT has matured; it has more fully embraced the value and centricity of the therapeutic relationship and has been more willing to look, not only at its successes, but also at those areas where its results are less than stellar. It is felt that by not placing itself above empiricism and by embracing, not eschewing, data-driven paradigms and research, that gains will also be more forthcoming in these elusive areas.

Truly, patients seen in the office are not often reflective of the samples in RCT studies. As Axis II pathology rises, so does the complexity and length of treatment. As CBT develops, ESTs, even for these challenging populations, are slowly being formulated and tested.

Many of this book's contributors seem fearful and angry that CBT has larger political aspirations to eliminate psychotherapeutic competition. It is true that there has been an unforeseen outcome of RCTs and ESTs, which is unwanted government and insurance company intrusion. This is a function of our times and the limited resources for health care, not a structured agenda within the CBT movement (at least not in the USA). While there may be some truth in the notion that CBT is enjoying some adolescent pleasure at the current discomfort being felt within psychoanalytic circles, one only hopes that the ultimate interest of our patients will overcome acting out by both sides. Hopefully, one aim of this book is mutual learning, which can only benefit all.

References

Azrin, N.H. and Lindsley, O.R. (1956) 'The reinforcement of cooperation between children', *Journal of Abnormal Psychology*, 52(1): 100–2.

Bandura, A. (1961) 'Psychotherapy as a learning process', *Psychological Bulletin*, 58: 143–59.

Bandura, A. (2001) 'Swimming against the mainstream: the early years in chilly waters', in William T. O'Donohue, Deborah A. Henderson, Steven Hayes et al. (eds), *A History of the Behavioral Therapies: Founders' Personal Histories*, Reno, NV: Contect Press, pp. 163–82.

Barlow, D.H. (ed.) (2001) *Clinical Handbook of Psychological Disorders*, 3rd edn, New York: Guilford Press.

Bijou, S.W. (1954) 'Therapeutic techniques with children', in L.A. Pennington and I.A. Berg (eds), *An Introduction to Clinical Psychology*, 2nd edn, New York: Ronald Press.

Borkovec, T. (2006) 'CBT plus emotional processing for worry and GAD'. Master lecture series, NJ-ACT.

Brazier, D. (2008) 'CBT in historical perspective', in R. House and D. Loewenthal (eds), *Against and For CBT: Towards a Constructive Dialogue?*, Ross on Wye: PCCS Books, pp. 72–6.

Hayes, S.C., Strosahl, K.D. and Wilson, K.G. (1999) *Acceptance and Commitment Therapy: An Experiential Approach to Behavior Change*, New York: Guilford Press.

Kazdin, A.E. and Weisz, J.R. (eds) (2003) *Evidence-based Psychotherapies for Children and Adolescents*, New York: Guilford Press.

Klerman, G.L., Weisman, M.M. and Rounsaille, B.J. (1984) *Interpersonal Psychotherapy of depression*, Northvalle, NJ: Jason Aronson.

Kohlenberg, R.J. and Tsai, M. (2003) *Functional Analytic Psychotherapy*, New York: Springer.

Lazarus, A.A. (1971) Personal communication.

Lazarus, A.A. (1976) *Multimodal Behavior Therapy*, New York: Springer.

LeDoux, J. (1996) *The Emotional Brain*, New York: Simon & Schuster.

Linehan, M.M., Cochran, B.N. and Kehrer, C.A. (2001) 'Dialectical behavior therapy for borderline personality disorder', in D. Barlow (ed.), *Clinical Handbook of Psychological Disorders, A Step-by-Step Treatment Manual*, 3rd edn, New York: Guilford Press.

Miller, W.R. and Rollnick, S. (1991) *Motivational Interviewing: Preparing People to Change Addictive Behavior*, New York: Guilford Press.

Nathan, P.E. and Gorman, J.M. (1998) *A Guide to Treatments that Work*, New York: Oxford University Press.

Nathan, P.E. and Gorman, J.M. (2002) *A Guide to Treatments that Work*, 2nd edn, New York: Oxford University Press.

Norcross, J.C. (ed.) (2002) *Psychotherapy Relationships that Work: Therapist Contributions and Responsiveness to Patients*, New York: Oxford University Press.

Paul, H.A. (2004a) 'Recent texts on empirically based psychotherapy and the issues and controversies that surround them', *Child and Family Behavior Therapy*, 26(3): 37–51.

Paul, H.A. (2004b) 'Issues and controversies surrounding recent texts on empirically based psychotherapy: a meta-review', *Brief Treatment and Crisis Intervention*, 4(4): 389–99.

Paul, H. and Miller, J. (1971) 'Reduction of extreme deviant behaviors in a severely retarded girl', *Training School Bulletin*, 67: 193–7.

Skinner, B.F. (1938) *The Behavior of Organisms*, New York: Appleton-Century-Crofts.

Young, J.E., Klosko, J.S. and Weis, M.E. (2003) *Schema Therapy: A Practitioner's Guide*, New York: Guilford Press.

Zajonc, R.B. (1984) 'On the primacy of affect', *American Psychologist*, 39: 117–23.

Zeilberger J., Sampson, S. and Sloan, H. (1968) 'Modification of a child's problem behaviors in the home with the mother as therapist', *Journal of Applied Behavior Analysis*, 1(1).

11 CBT, happiness and evidence-based practice

Michael Proeve

The first chapter in this book, by House and Loewenthal, outlines the interest-ing political context of the discussions that follow in the modality chapters of the book. As a resident of a country far from the UK, I was not pre-viously aware of the 'Layard thesis'. I was a little surprised at the boldness of promoting a particular psychotherapy approach as a public policy issue. Like some contributors to the book (Ryle, Chapter 3; Heaton, Chapter 4), I am sceptical about the idea of improving society by prescribing wholesale psychotherapy rather than examining the aspects of society that contribute to human misery. The dismay that some contributors to the modality chap-ters feel towards the 'Layard thesis' was very clear, particularly the idea of excluding other psychotherapy approaches in favour of cognitive-behaviour therapy (CBT).

I found that the authors of the modality chapters raised many thought-provoking issues for me. The discussion of psychoanalysis and CBT by Holmes (Chapter 2) outlined many thought-provoking points of correspondence between the approaches. The relationship between black-and-white thinking and defensive splitting seems clear but, for example, the description of the difference between schema-focused and psychoanalytic approaches to trauma was interesting. Ryle's outline of the development of cognitive-analytic ther-apy (CAT) (Chapter 3) is a valuable account of a psychotherapy approach that offers significant help to people who experience borderline personality dis-order (BPD). I am unconvinced about the value of CBT for the treatment of BPD. However, dialectical-behaviour therapy (DBT), which I describe further on, does show encouraging evidence of effectiveness with BPD. The theoretical innovations of DBT set it apart as a distinct therapy from CBT. My lack of further comment on Stratton's Chapter 5 on systemic family and couples ther-apy does not signify disinterest in what he has to say. In my opinion, systemic approaches occupy a helpful niche that overlaps little with other therapies, including CBT. Few other therapy approaches have the framework to enable therapists to work directly with more than one person. It is encouraging that systemic therapists have increasingly sought to evaluate their approaches, despite the methodological challenges presented.

Heaton (Chapter 4) and Tudor (Chapter 7) contributed particularly helpful discussions of happiness, which are contrasted with Layard's particular view of happiness. Heaton comments on types of reasoning in CBT but makes little comment about CBT beyond that. In my later description of CBT, I hope to show that CBT is concerned with more than reasoning. Tudor's discussion of person-centred therapy renewed my already considerable appreciation of Rogers. His contribution to psychotherapy theory as well as research was immense and perhaps too often forgotten by therapists of other therapeutic persuasions.

Casement (Chapter 8) contrasts the Jungian emphasis on uniqueness and individuation with a normalizing approach in CBT. Although an emphasis on the value of the individual is important, a normalizing approach also has its uses. To know that others have experienced similar distressing thoughts and feelings and that they have addressed that distress using CBT interventions is a helpful aspect of a normalizing approach. Casement also comments on the silence of CBT concerning meaning. I agree with this point and return to it later. Similarly, Millichamp (Chapter 9) addresses the issue of meaning in her account of psychosynthesis. She also suggests that a strength of psychosynthesis relative to CBT is the therapist's empathic presence. In reply I note that Beck's cognitive therapy approach has always acknowledged the importance of Rogerian therapist qualities, including empathy. However, I do think that the importance of an empathic relationship is honoured more in the practice than in the theory of CBT. Parker (Chapter 6) gives a strong critique of CBT in his account of Lacanian psychoanalysis. He attacks CBT for its normative prescriptions and limiting control over thinking and behaviour. In response, I suggest that some degree of normative prescription and control over thinking and behaviour is helpful to enable people to get along with others. Parker also notes that CBT can be useful and sometimes sufficient when it helps individuals to question their conception of the world and think through alternatives. I suggest that, at its best, CBT helps clients to do exactly that.

Aside from this admittedly brief response to the modality chapters, I decided that it was not the best use of this chapter to engage in a prolonged defence of CBT, responding point for point to issues raised in the modality chapters. It would be possible to engage in detailed discussion of research findings regarding the effectiveness of CBT, which were particularly raised by Holmes (Chapter 2) and Tudor (Chapter 7). However, such a discussion would require consideration of a large body of literature about which eminent researchers cannot agree. Instead of following these options, I decided to organize my chapter in the following way. First, the portrait of CBT reflected in some of the modality chapters seems overly mechanistic and coldly cognitive. Therefore, I give a brief account of some changes in emphasis in CBT that have occurred since the original models of CBT practice. I also draw attention to the trend of eclecticism in CBT, which I hope is not too much of a projection of my own eclectic inclinations. I finish this section with a brief description of the so-called third-wave behaviour therapies, DBT and ACT, which are related but separate from CBT.

In the following section, I respond to particular themes raised in the modality chapters concerning CBT. I discuss some perceived shortcomings of CBT, including case formulation, personal therapy experience and questions of meaning, before I comment on two strengths of CBT: its responsiveness to research and its adaptability.

In the next sections, I discuss notions of happiness, particularly the utilitarian view promoted by Layard. I conclude that advocates of psychotherapy need to work within a utilitarian framework, which is associated with evidence-based practice. However, evidence-based practice does not necessarily mean a restricted focus on randomized controlled trials. In the final section, I suggest that restriction of psychotherapy practice to CBT is undesirable and make suggestions for desirable developments in CBT.

Development and change in CBT

As House and Loewenthal note in Chapter 1, CBT seems increasingly difficult to define. CBT has undoubtedly changed, I would say expanded, over time. I want to draw attention to three trends in CBT. I want to first consider the changing roles of cognition and the therapeutic relationship in CBT. Second, I want to describe the trend of eclecticism or integration in CBT. I finish this section with a brief description of the so-called third wave behaviour therapies, DBT and ACT, which are related to but separate from CBT. These therapies demonstrate a third trend, towards acceptance of experience.

Role of cognition in CBT

As Holmes observed (Chapter 2), CBT is concerned particularly with three types of phenomena: emotions, thoughts and behaviours. Although the relationship between emotions, thoughts and behaviours is the concern of CBT, the founders of cognitive therapy, Aaron Beck and Albert Ellis, give primacy to the role of cognition. According to Beck's cognitive therapy, cognition is organized into deep cognitive structures called 'schemas', which contain ideas about oneself or the world. Schemas are triggered by particular situations and lead to negative automatic thoughts, which are thoughts about a limited range of situations. Negative automatic thoughts are cognitions that are closest to the surface of consciousness. Therefore, CBT therapy proceeds from awareness of negative automatic thoughts towards the deeper cognitive territory of assumptions, rules and schemas. Although the goal of cognitive therapy is to relieve emotional distress, the means of doing so is by focusing on misinterpretations of situations, dysfunctional attitudes and self-defeating behaviour (Beck et al., 1979). Clients are encouraged to treat their beliefs as hypotheses, which can be disputed by examining evidence from the client's life. Although cognitive therapy frequently employs behavioural techniques, its purpose is to facilitate changes in cognition. Behavioural 'experiments' are employed as a means of testing out predictions about situations that follow from problematic beliefs, or from newly formulated and more adaptive beliefs.

Rational-emotive behaviour therapy (REBT), developed by Albert Ellis, converges with Beck's approach in its focus on cognition. However, REBT is concerned with disputing common philosophical errors, according to Ellis's view. These 'irrational' beliefs include equating needs with preferences and demanding that the world should conform to our wishes. REBT tends to make more eclectic use of behavioural interventions than Beck's cognitive therapy. For example, contingency contracts that include donations to a despised organization for failing to follow through homework assignments are not particularly tied to testing or disputing beliefs, but rather employ behaviour modification techniques such as response cost to directly change the behaviour of completing homework.

More recent trends in cognitive therapy show changes in emphasis concerning the relationship between thoughts, emotions and behaviours in the practice of CBT. For example, a recent cognitive therapy text (Sanders and Wills, 2005) emphasizes the reciprocal relationship between thoughts and emotions, where emotions and behaviour affect thinking, so that a vicious cycle develops. Second, the idiosyncratic nature of a client's approach to appraising events, because of unique personal circumstances, is emphasized in contrast to the notion that CT applies generalized categories of information-processing errors.

Another recent trend in CT practice involves a focus away from cognitive content towards cognitive processes. For example, many members of the general population experience intrusive worries that are characteristic of generalized anxiety disorder. However, people who experience this particular problem may focus more time and attention than members of the general population on worrying (Sanders and Wills, 2005). The meta-cognitive approach of Wells (2002) distinguishes between the content of worries and beliefs about worries. Beliefs about the positive benefit of worrying to prevent catastrophes can reinforce the problem of worrying. Therefore, the therapeutic focus may be on beliefs about the value of worrying rather than evaluation of specific worries. A focus on beliefs about the behaviour of worrying represents a slight shift towards process, using CBT to influence clients' use of and unhelpful process that generates continuing anxiety.

The focus on process rather than content is taken much further in mindfulness-based cognitive therapy (MBCT). The originators of this approach (Segal et al., 2002) pondered the outcome of numerous studies concerning attitudes characteristic of depression. Although these depressive attitudes are elevated during an episode of depression, people who have recovered from depression did not differ in their levels of depressive attitudes from never-depressed people. However, people who had been formerly depressed showed an exaggerated cognitive bias towards depressive thinking, compared to never-depressed people, when a sad mood was induced. Therefore, sad mood could easily reinstate thinking patterns that people had experienced when depressed. The evidence that cognitive therapy reduces the rate of relapse for depression were explained as follows: although the emphasis in cognitive therapy is on changing thought content, its useful effect may be to change a person's relationship to their thought and feelings. In other words, the *process* of challenging distorted thinking is the mechanism of change. The founders of MBCT turned to Jon Kabat-Zinn's mindfulness-based stress reduction approach for useful techniques consistent with their goal of changing people's relationship to their thoughts. Although MBCT includes some familiar CBT techniques such as exploring the relationship between thoughts and emotions and encouraging pleasant events, its practice is much more experiential and process-oriented and less didactic than typical CBT.

These recent changes in the role of cognition in the recent history of CBT lead to changes in practice in several directions. On one hand, increased emphasis on the reciprocal relationships of cognition, emotion and behaviour and the resulting vicious cycles leading to emotional disorders leads to increased possibilities of intervening with unhelpful cognition, emotion and behaviour relationships using behavioural or emotional changes as well as cognitive interventions. On the other hand, the meta-cognitive approach brings an increased and sophisticated focus on cognition by its attention to levels of information-processing and brings an emphasis on more nuanced cognitive interventions. MBCT leads to changes in practice in a third direction. The practice implication of MBCT is to de-emphasize engagement with cognition in favour of a more observing approach to cognition and an increased focus on the body and on sensory experience.

Therapeutic relationship in CBT

Although the focus of Beck's cognitive therapy is on cognition, it is important to note that Beck also paid attention to desirable therapist qualities. Beck and colleagues considered that Rogerian therapist characteristics of warmth, accurate empathy and genuineness facilitate cognitive therapy. According to Beck, these characteristics are necessary but not sufficient to produce the best therapeutic effect (Beck et al., 1979). The desirable therapeutic stance is described as collaborative empiricism in which the therapeutic relationship, with the client and therapist as a team, facilitates the completion of therapy goals. REBT advocates a different therapist approach than cognitive therapy. Although unconditional acceptance of clients is advocated, warmth or liking towards the client is not considered necessary for successful treatment (Prochaska and Norcross, 2009).

Later developments in CBT have changed the role of the therapeutic relationship. Safran and Segal (1990), with some debt to Bowlby's concept of attachment, emphasized attachment schemas and interpersonal core beliefs and assumptions. Interpersonal patterns based on attachment schemas may be played out in the therapeutic relationship, so that the therapy relationship becomes a place where interpersonal schemas may be observed and addressed.

Integration in CBT

The integration trend has been present in CBT for a long time, perhaps best exemplified by Arnold Lazarus. Lazarus began as a student and collaborator of the behaviour therapist Joseph Wolpe but their collaboration foundered over the issue of Lazarus's integrative approach. Lazarus took a pragmatic approach to psychotherapy, borrowing what he believed were helpful techniques from other psychotherapies in order to decrease relapse after psychotherapy. He promoted the approach of technical eclecticism, which means borrowing techniques from other psychotherapies without necessarily subscribing to the underlying theory. Technical eclecticism defined the approach of Lazarus's multimodal therapy (Lazarus, 1976). Multimodal therapy rests on a theoretical base of social learning theory, but happily borrows techniques from Gestalt therapy, systemic therapies, and makes use of imagery approaches.

Although many CBT practitioners do not advocate a technically eclectic approach that is as far-reaching, the integrative tendency is recognizable in recent developments in CBT. For example, MBCT incorporates sitting and walking meditations as well as such attitudes as non-striving and acceptance of experience from Buddhism. Two other so-called third-wave behaviour therapies also demonstrate eclectic borrowing of practices and concepts from Buddhism.

DBT (Linehan, 1993) is a pragmatic and structured therapy approach for the treatment of BPD. DBT is designed to be more intensive and of longer duration than typical CBT and promotes a combination of group skills training and individual therapy. DBT proceeds from an understanding of BPD as dysregulation of affect, behaviour, cognition and self. There is a focus on decreasing parasuicidal and interpersonal behaviour that interferes with therapy, balanced with acceptance, compassion and validation of the client's experiences. DBT employs the notion of dialectics. For the therapist, there are dialectics such as unwavering centeredness versus flexibility, and nurturing versus having expectations of the client. For clients, dialectics include trust versus suspicion of others and regulation of affect versus tolerance of distress. In addition to behavioural skills approaches such as problem-solving,

DBT includes mindfulness interventions, which are less intensive than the mindfulness meditations that are characteristic of MBCT. Various intervention studies have supported the superiority of DBT compared to treatment as usual, treatment by experts and person-centred therapy. DBT has been implemented in diverse regions of the world including Australasia, North and South America, Europe and Japan.

Acceptance and commitment therapy (ACT) (Hayes and Strosahl, 2004) is a recent form of eclectic behaviour therapy that enjoys modest research support and an increasing level of interest from psychologists in Australia. ACT started from a Skinnerian analysis of language. The core theory in ACT is relational frame theory, which explains phenomena such as the fear of events not previously experienced by association with language and cognition. A stated goal of ACT is to undermine the verbal content of cognition. Like MBCT and DBT, ACT promotes acceptance of psychological problems such as anxiety rather than struggle against them. ACT emphasizes two particular problems: avoidance of unwanted experiences and cognitive fusion. According to ACT, suppression or avoidance of unwanted thoughts and emotions can increase their impact. The concept of cognitive fusion concerns the relationship that individuals have to verbal rules and evaluations of the world rather than with here-and-now experiences. To address avoidance, ACT promotes acceptance rather than struggle against psychological problems. To address cognitive fusion, contact with the present moment, which may be enhanced through mindfulness exercises, is recommended. ACT also has a forward-looking aspect that is summed up in the second two letters of the acronym. The letter C stands for choosing. Here ACT shows a distinctly existential influence. Clients are encouraged to explore and choose life values that enhance purpose and meaning, perhaps by death awareness exercises. Finally, the T refers to taking action by committing to actions consistent with chosen values. Clients may take action using behavioural strategies such as problem-solving and skill-building.

Characteristics of CBT considered

In this section, I consider three areas in which CBT is less well-developed than some other psychotherapy approaches: case formulation, personal experience by therapists and questions of meaning. I also consider two positive characteristics of CBT: its responsiveness to research and its adaptability.

Case formulation

Case formulation seems to receive little explicit attention in earlier CBT literature. However, contemporary CBT gives more emphasis to formulation.

Case formulation in CBT occurs at two levels. The first level of case formulation occurs at the assessment phase. A good case formulation, according to Persons and Tompkins (2007), is parsimonious and evidence-based. A nomothetic formulation, or research-based understanding of a particular disorder, is the foundation for the development of an individualized idiographic formulation. Client symptoms and problems are given DSM diagnoses because this provides a link to empirical literature including empirically supported treatments. The clinician then chooses an 'anchoring diagnosis,' which is usually the diagnosis that accounts for the largest number of client problems. A nomothetic formulation is chosen from research literature concerning the 'anchoring' disorder as a basis for an individual formulation. The nomothetic formulation is individualized using the client's particular history and presentation, usually in terms of vulnerability factors for development of the problems, precipitating factors for the current problems and maintaining factors for the problems. Although this case formulation approach works well enough when the research literature provides good guidance, for example, with anxiety disorders, it can be problematic for under-researched disorders. Indeed, in my experience there are some cases of sexually deviant behaviour where a cognitive-behavioural approach seems to offer little help in developing a formulation, but a more Freudian formulation beckons with a helpful answer.

The second level of case formulation in CBT takes place within CBT therapy. Formulation helps to involve the client actively in therapy and so aids the 'collaborative empiricism' advocated by Beck. It also helps client and therapist to understand the client's current problems and to focus the therapy. Formulations may be of many types. At the basic level, a formulation may show how thoughts, emotions and behaviour link together in a cycle to perpetuate the client's problem. Other basic formulations may link thoughts, emotions and distressing physical symptoms. More detailed formulations link childhood experiences, the development of core beliefs or maladaptive schemas, and rules for living, which develop from the schemas with critical life incidents, leading to current problematic emotions, thoughts and behaviours. These detailed formulations may be developed early on in therapy or may evolve where the client experiences complex problems (Sanders and Wills, 2005). Case formulation in the course of therapy is both individualized and important for building a collaborative therapy relationship during CBT.

Personal experience by therapists

Unlike some other therapies, such as psychoanalysis and analytic psychology, there is little tradition in CBT of requiring trainees to undergo therapy. Indeed, as Parker (Chapter 6) noted, it is unusual for CBT therapists to have undergone CBT themselves. Personal experience of CBT is likely to have a number of benefits for the therapist. First, there are the general benefits gained from training therapies of many persuasions: an awareness of one's own issues and their significance for the therapeutic relationship, as well as the experience of being a client. Second, personal experience of CBT may confer specific benefits for the CBT therapist, including greater empathy for clients in their struggles with monitoring and challenging their own thinking, and changing behaviour. Personal CBT experience may also lend greater conviction to the therapist's recommendation of CBT. Bennett-Levy (2001) provides one approach to personal CBT using a combination of therapy with a training partner and written reflections on the process. It is to be hoped that personal therapy in the CBT tradition will be more frequently advocated in future. In contrast to the situation with standard CBT, MBCT has a strong expectation that MBCT therapists undergo the standard MBCT group programme as part of the training. In addition, MBCT therapists are expected to continue the personal practice of meditation.

Questions of meaning

Questions of meaning and purpose are prominent in some psychotherapy approaches such as existential and analytical therapy. Casement (Chapter 8) provides a quote from analytical psychologist Andrew Samuels, who stated that CBT is silent around questions of meaning but attempts to address meaning in the case of MBCT. Although exploration of idiosyncratic thinking patterns with clients in the course of CBT does touch on issues of personal construction of meaning in the world, I tend to agree with Samuels that CBT has little to say about ultimate meaning and purpose. However, REBT in its stronger or 'elegant' form is inclined to give the answer that the pursuit of ultimate meaning is itself meaningless. Instead, meaning is found in aspects of the world that make life more enjoyable and minimize pain. I also do not think that MBCT is particularly concerned with meaning. However, MBCT may tend to bring questions of meaning to the fore; for example, when the notion of non-striving is promoted, which is discordant with goal-driven Western societies. The third-wave behaviour therapy approach of ACT is an exception among CBT approaches with regard to meaning, as examination of values and acting according to chosen values are explicit aspects of ACT. The focus of most forms of CBT on the relationships between the phenomena of cognition, emotion and behaviour has tended to exclude questions of meaning, which lie outside the connections between these phenomena.

Responsiveness to research

It is difficult to dispute that there is a large body of research supporting the effectiveness of CBT. Certainly, characteristics of CBT make this therapy easier to evaluate than some other therapy approaches. For example, the behavioural tradition of operationalizing targets of change and the relative brevity of CBT are factors that mean CBT interventions can be evaluated within a reasonable time period and outcomes of therapy can be readily measured. The behaviourist commitment to evaluation is a strength of the CBT tradition that has contributed to the volume of CBT research. In addition, openness to change in response to research findings may be a discernible theme in CBT (although see Holmes, Chapter 2, for a less charitable view of this point). For example, the theoretical reflections that preceded the development of MBCT occurred in response to findings that dysfunctional attitudes were not greater in formerly depressed people, as would be predicted from the original cognitive theory of depression. Partly in response to these findings, Teasdale and colleagues developed a process-oriented rather than content-oriented explanation for the effect of CBT.

The adaptability of CBT

A final characteristic of CBT I want to mention is its potential for adaptability. Research and practice in CBT has used the notion of cognitive specificity, that different disorders have specific profiles of problematic cognition, to develop specific combinations of interventions for specific disorders. For example, the usual interventions for CBT treatment of depression differ from those used for social phobia or for obsessive-compulsive disorder (OCD). As a result there is large body of research supporting the application of CBT to the treatment of a variety of different disorders. However, characteristics of CBT mean that it is also adaptable in another sense for diverse groups of clients. The change-oriented focus in CBT on the connections between psychological phenomena and relative lack of concern for theory development, together with its silence about issues of meaning, have the interesting effect that CBT is potentially very accessible for religious clients, where meaning is already assumed. Hodge (2006) reviewed outcome studies of spiritually modified cognitive therapy. He described some examples of effective spiritually modified CBT treatment of depression. One study reported superiority for Christian-informed CBT over standard CBT in the treatment of depression. In another study, Islamically modified CBT for depression was effective compared to a control group. The comments of Badri (2007) show an approach by which CBT is assimilated into an Islamic perspective, by giving examples of behaviour therapy and cognitive therapy interventions described in the writings of prominent Islamic physicians.

CBT and happiness

The concept of happiness has been explored eloquently by other contributors to this book, particularly Heaton (Chapter 4) and Tudor (Chapter 7). I could not hope to improve on these contributions. I do not personally endorse the Epicurean view of happiness that underlies REBT, but am more attracted to the views of Carl Rogers concerning happiness described by Tudor and to the comment of Viktor Frankl that happiness ensues but cannot be pursued (quoted in Yalom, 1980). I do not believe that psychotherapy can be directly linked to happiness. Psychotherapy should, however, reduce misery and help people to live their lives in such a way that happiness is more likely to ensue.

In contrast, Layard's (2005) book *Happiness: Lessons from a New Science* assumes a clearly utilitarian view of happiness, as Tudor points out, and links it directly to psychotherapy. Layard defined happiness as enjoying life and unhappiness as feeling bad and wishing things were different. He argued that happiness is a suitable ultimate goal for society because it is self-evidently good. Layard (2005) affirmed Bentham's greatest happiness principle that the right action is the one that produces the greatest overall happiness. His advocacy of CBT is a consequence of his view that that psychiatric drugs and cognitive therapy have helped to reduce misery more than any other changes in the last 50 years (p. 230).

The utilitarian goal of greatest happiness for the greatest number of people leads to particular practical considerations when comparing psychotherapy approaches, including evidence of effectiveness, duration of psychotherapy and accessibility for clients. A utilitarian psychotherapy should have strong evidence of effectiveness, be brief, be easily learned and be acceptable to a wide range of clients. On these grounds, CBT is an attractive option. It has an extensive research literature, is designed to be brief in duration, has less extensive training than some other approaches, and is adaptable to a wide range of clinical problems and clients.

The alternative to utilitarianism is to take a deontological position by arguing that a particular approach is inherently good or bad. However, a deontological approach may not be an attractive option in a postmodern world. How then can psychotherapy approaches be compared? One option is for advocates of particular psychotherapy approaches to compile a comparative list that shows the particular world view, therapeutic goals, therapist approach, as well as effectiveness evidence or attitude towards such evidence for each psychotherapy approach. Such a document could be given to potential clients to assist them in making informed choices about psychotherapy. Although this approach may be a good idea for educating the general public, it is unlikely to satisfy policy-makers who fund psychotherapy services. I doubt there is a viable alternative to comparing particular psychotherapy approaches within a utilitarian framework. In my view, the world of evidence-based practice is unavoidable. Although evidence-based practice may be conflated by some with CBT, they are not the same thing.

Evidence-based practice

In an effort to promote evidence-based psychotherapy practice, the American Psychological Association in 1995 developed criteria for assigning psychotherapy approaches to the category of *empirically supported* (EST) or *empirically validated* therapies. The EST criteria promoted features of good experimental method, including comparison of treatments with psychological placebos or established credible treatments, careful selection of participants and manualized treatment. Westen and Morrison (2001) assessed high-quality studies of interventions, many of which were CBT interventions, for three common disorders: depression, panic and generalized anxiety disorder. Although the empirically supported treatments provided substantial benefits in the short term, the majority of clients did not show sustained improvement over one to two years. One could conclude from such results either that interventions should be similar but longer in duration, or that different interventions should be tried. Within a utilitarian framework, one could argue from these findings that briefer interventions may not be necessarily better in achieving the greatest possible good.

Westen et al. (2004) provided an extensive critique of the use of randomised controlled trial (RCT) methodology to validate empirically supported treatments, which it is not possible to outline in detail here. For example, features of RCT trials such as a focus on single client problems and adherence to treatment manuals are not characteristic of real world or necessarily effective practice. Westen et al. advocated more limited use of RCT designs as well as more use of practice-based research approaches based on unselected treatment samples in the community. In a more recent development, the American Psychological Association (2005) report on evidence-based practice in psychology (EBPP) made a clear distinction between evidence-based practice and empirically supported treatments. According to this report, EBPP integrates the best available research with clinical expertise in the context of patient characteristics, culture and preferences. The list of useful research approaches endorsed in EBPP is considerably longer than just RCTs, including studies of interventions in naturalistic settings, single case experimental designs, systematic case studies and qualitative research. Therefore, a narrow focus on RCTs is not supported by the dominant American Association of Psychologists. The narrow focus on RCTs as the sole focus of research evidence is likely to give a distorted reflection of effective practice.

Conclusion and future directions

In my opinion, the concept of evidence-based practice in psychotherapy, perhaps broadly defined in the manner of the recent American Psychological

Association report, has to be acknowledged. Advocates of psychotherapy approaches will find it difficult to influence public policy without using the language of evidence. It is important to challenge the one-sided reliance on RCT methodology while acknowledging that this methodology has a particular contribution towards inferring causal influences of psychotherapeutic intervention. It is particularly important to promote research based on less selected groups of psychotherapy clients that has the particular strength of external validity, or evidence of generalization of interventions beyond the artificial setting of RCTs.

Restriction of psychotherapy approaches other than CBT at the present time would be unreasonable for three reasons. First, it is more or less beyond question that factors common to psychotherapies account for a significant proportion of psychotherapy outcome, whatever the additional contribution of features specific to CBT or other psychotherapies. The arguments about whether the apparent superiority of CBT in particular areas is due to allegiance effects or bias in interpretation are likely to continue for some time yet. Second, there is evidence for the effectiveness of non-CBT therapies for conditions such as BPD, where standard CBT has less to offer. Finally, the eclectic history of CBT suggests that CBT itself benefits from the opportunity to assimilate concepts and techniques from other approaches.

I suspect CBT will develop in useful directions from further attention to one of the sets of phenomena with which it is primarily concerned. CBT concerns relationships between cognition, behaviour and emotion. Cognitive therapy built a particular focus on cognition on a base of knowledge about behaviour and behavioural technologies. CBT can be further enriched through increased focus on emotion. Shame is a particular example of the usefulness of focusing on particular emotions. Shame has been the object of theory and phenomenological study in psychodynamic traditions, philosophy and general psychology. Gilbert (1998) has usefully incorporated the emotion of shame into CBT approach for treating depression. The identification of strong feelings of shame during the treatment of depression may make sense of a client's behaviour in the therapeutic relationship and lead to a modification of the therapist's usual CBT approach. A second use of shame with CBT occurs in the context of criminal behaviour such as sexual offending and introduces a moral dimension to CBT. The differentiation of moral shame from moral guilt can assist clients to take constructive steps towards rehabilitation without avoiding distress concerning their reprehensible behaviour (Proeve and Howells, 2006).

Finally, CBT clients and therapist are likely to benefit from engaging with the question of meaning. The question of meaning has already emerged in a circumscribed form in the behaviour therapy area with the development of ACT, where an exploration of values is followed by commitment to behaving in accordance with those values. However, broader approaches to exploring meaning may be needed. At least in some cases where clients experience anxiety, depression or other common problems in the purview of CBT, issues of meaning will be relevant or highly relevant. Useful approaches to the question of meaning may be borrowed from other approaches such as existential or analytic therapy. If this occurs, CBT will once again exercise its eclectic tendency in the service of meeting the needs of its clients.

References

American Psychological Association (2005) *Report of the 2005 Presidential Task Force on Evidence-based Practice*, Washington, DC: APA.

Badri, M.B. (2007) *Can the Psychotherapy of Muslim Patients be of Real Help to them without being Islamicized?* Available online at www.islamicworld.net/psychology/psy.php?ArtID=204 (accessed 28 July 2009).

Beck, A.T., Rush, A.J., Shaw, B.F. and Emery, G.D. (1979) *Cognitive Therapy of Depression*, New York: Guilford Press.

Bennett-Levy, J. (2001) 'The value of self-practice of cognitive therapy techniques and self-reflection in the training of cognitive therapists', *Behavioural and Cognitive Psychotherapy*, 29: 203–20.

Gilbert, P. (1998) 'Shame and humiliation in the treatment of complex cases', in N. Tarrier, A. Wells and G. Haddock (eds), *Treating Complex Cases: The Cognitive Behavioural Therapy Approach*, London: Wiley, pp. 241–71.

Hayes, S.C. and Strosahl, K.D. (eds) (2004) *A Practical Guide to Acceptance and Commitment Therapy*, New York: Springer.

Hodge, D.R. (2006) 'Spiritually modified cognitive therapy: a review of the literature', *Social Work*, 51: 157–66.

Layard, R. (2005) *Happiness: Lessons from a New Science*, London: Penguin Books.

Lazarus, A.A. (1976) *Multimodal Behavior Therapy*, New York: Springer.

Linehan, M.M. (1993) *Cognitive-behavioral Treatment of Borderline Personality Disorder*, New York: Guilford Press.

Persons, J.B. and Tompkins, M.A. (2007) 'Cognitive-behavioural case formulation' in T.D. Eells (ed.), *Handbook of Psychotherapy Case Formulation*, 2nd edn, New York: Guilford Press, pp. 290–314.

Prochaska, J.O. and Norcross, J.C. (2009) *Systems of Psychotherapy*, 7th edn, Belmont, CA: Brooks/Cole.

Proeve, M.J. and Howells, K. (2006) 'Shame and guilt in child molesters', in W.L. Marshall, Y.M. Fernandez, L.E. Marshall and G.A. Serran (eds), *Sexual Offender Treatment: Controversial Issues*, London: Wiley, pp. 125–39.

Safran, J.D. and Segal, Z.V. (1990) *Interpersonal Processes in Cognitive Therapy*, New York: Basic Books.

Sanders, D. and Wills, F. (2005) *Cognitive Therapy: An Introduction*, 2nd edn, London: Sage Publications.

Segal, Z.V., Williams, J.M.G. and Teasdale, J.D. (2002) *Mindfulness-based Cognitive Therapy for Depression: A New Approach to Preventing Relapse*, New York: Guilford Press.

Wells, A. (2002) *Emotional Disorders and Meta-cognition: Innovative Cognitive Therapy*, Chichester: Wiley.

Westen, D. and Morrison, K. (2001) 'A multidimensional meta-analysis of treatments for depression, panic, and generalized anxiety disorder: an empirical examination of the status of empirically supported therapies', *Journal of Consulting and Clinical Psychology*, 69: 875–99.

Westen, D., Novotny, C.M. and Thompson-Brenner, H. (2004) 'The empirical status of empirically supported psychotherapies: assumptions, findings, and reporting in controlled clinical trials', *Psychological Bulletin*, 130: 631–63.

Yalom, I.D. (1980) *Existential Psychotherapy*, New York: Basic Books.

12 What can CBT therapists and other psychotherapists learn from one another?

Windy Dryden

Introduction

As the editors note, in devising this book, they had an ambitious purpose. It was to invite eminent British non-CBT therapists to engage critically with CBT. In carrying out their task, contributors were given a 'broad organizing framework' that they were invited to use, but flexibly so, according to their approach's own position on the validity and helpfulness of the framework's elements.

The editors see the current book as building on their previous publications, which initiated a constructive dialogue between CBT and other psychological therapies. These earlier publications focused on 'paradigmatic, epistemological, political and cultural perspectives' (House and Loewenthal, 2008a; House and Loewenthal, 2008b). The editors note that a 'relatively small part of that book' (i.e. House and Loewenthal, 2008a) was given over to what they termed 'clinical perspectives', and it is this initial exploration that we have made the entire focus of this book. This statement helps the commentator. *The Compact Oxford English Dictionary* defines the word 'clinical', thus: *adjective* relating to the observation and treatment of patients (rather than theoretical studies). I return to this issue presently.

The stimuli for these three connected texts are a number of related cultural developments in the UK:

1   An increasing political focus on happiness stimulated by the work of Lord Layard (2005) whose book on the subject recommended the extensive use of CBT therapists in the NHS. This suggestion came from his reading of the research literature.
2   The recommendations of the National Institute of Clinical Excellence (NICE) whose reading of the research literature also suggested the

extensive use of CBT (and to a lesser extent a few other therapies) as empirically supported treatments for a wide range of psychological problems.

3 The initiative known as 'Improving Access to Psychological Treatment' (IAPT) where large numbers of people with a range of psychological problems are to have easier access to psychological treatment, which is to be basically CBT in nature. Large numbers of therapists are to be trained to be either 'low-intensity' CBT workers (for milder problems) or 'high-intensity' CBT workers (for more serious problems).

As the editors note, much debate has occurred within what they call the 'psy' field on the issues that the above developments have spawned and they see this book as taking the debate forward, particularly on 'clinical' matters.

As you will see, I am one of three CBT practitioners who have been invited to 'offer authoritative and penetrating commentaries on the eight preceding modality chapters'. I did suggest to the editors that I might coordinate the efforts of the three CBT commentators so that we did not duplicate our efforts. However, the editors preferred us to work independently and to choose our own focus. Therefore, this is what I have done.

As I have been asked to write to a tight word limit, I have chosen to focus on what contributors have to say about 'clinical' matters (which are the focus of the book) and more specifically their thoughts about what CBT therapists and other psychotherapists can learn from one another. In doing so, I am particularly interested to see what CBT work the contributors cite in their chapters.

The task that contributors have chosen to undertake is a very challenging one. In order to engage critically with CBT from the perspective of their own orientation, contributors have to understand CBT internally, otherwise we will be given their view of CBT, based perhaps on ignorance, on hearsay or even on prejudice. Thus, in my view, contributors do need to demonstrate that they understand CBT to the satisfaction of CBT therapists and considering what sources they have cited is one way of doing this.

The parallel here can be seen in the consulting room. In order to engage with a patient critically, the therapist first needs to understand the patient from the patient's perspective to the patient's satisfaction. Only when the therapist can understand the patient from his or her internal frame of reference, can he or she engage with that client critically and offer an external frame of reference that may help the patient to move forward.

Let me also be clear about what I am not going to discuss and the reasons for this decision. While CBT lends itself to being a prime therapeutic player in the 'happiness', 'empirically supported treatments' (EST) and 'IAPT' developments, CBT predates these developments and is practised not only in Britain in the NHS (within which context much of the current debate has been located), but also in Britain in other settings including social services, the voluntary sector and in private practice. CBT is also practised throughout the world in a variety of settings. Thus, the practice of CBT is much broader than the current preoccupation with its perceived favoured position as the treatment of choice within the NHS in Britain. In short, my decision to see what contributors have to say about how their modality can inform the practice of CBT and vice versa is in line with the avowedly 'clinical' focus of this book.

What is CBT?

Before I undertake my task, it should be pointed out that nobody in this book has attempted to offer a definition of CBT. It is as if there is a shared underlying assumption subscribed to by the editors and the contributors that they and you all know what CBT is, so we do not have to define it. I would question this assumption and thus, I will offer a definition of CBT that appears on the website of the British Association for Cognitive and Behavioural Psychotherapies (BABCP). You might find it useful to refer to this as you read my commentary and those of my two CBT colleagues.

What is CBT

Cognitive and/or behavioural psychotherapies (CBP) are psychological approaches based on scientific principles and which research has shown to be effective for a wide range of problems. Clients and therapists work together, once a therapeutic alliance has been formed, to identify and understand problems in terms of the relationship between thoughts, feelings and behaviour. The approach usually focuses on difficulties in the here and now, and relies on the therapist and client developing a shared view of the individual's problem. This then leads to identification of personalised, usually time-limited therapy goals and strategies which are continually monitored and evaluated. The treatments are inherently empowering in nature; the outcome being to focus on specific psychological and practical skills (e.g. in reflecting on and exploring the meaning attributed to events and situations and re-evaluation of those meanings) aimed at enabling the client to tackle their problems by harnessing their own resources. The acquisition and utilisation of such skills is seen as the main goal, and the active component in promoting change with an emphasis on putting what has been learned into practice between sessions ("homework"). Thus, the overall aim is for the individual to attribute improvement in their problems to their own efforts, in collaboration with the psychotherapist. Cognitive and/or behavioural psychotherapists work with individuals, families and groups. The approaches can be used to help anyone irrespective of ability, culture, race, gender or sexual preference. Cognitive and/or behavioural psychotherapies can be used on their own or in conjunction with medication, depending on the severity or nature of each client's problem.

Grazebrook, Garland and the Board of BABCP (2005: 1)

I have provided this definition, not because I am in full agreement with it, but because it has been authorized by the BABCP, the foremost organization of CBT therapists in Britain. With this in mind, let me turn to my commentary.

The commentary

I have provided my commentary below on the modality chapters in the order in which they appear in the editors' introduction.

Jeremy Holmes on psychoanalysis and CBT

Jeremy Holmes (Chapter 2) lists 44 references of which 9 are clearly on CBT. Of these, one appears to be practice-based (Kuyken et al., 2005). Interestingly, Holmes is the only one of the eight contributors to refer to a piece co-authored by Aaron T. Beck, perhaps the most influential figure in CBT. What would be the reaction if of eight contributors to a similar book entitled 'Critically Engaging Psychoanalysis', only one cited Freud?

In his chapter, Holmes argues that there are areas of theoretical compatibility between CBT and psychoanalysis. He quotes Kuyken et al. (2005) who advocate a consideration of maladaptive beliefs in depression as they are 'shaped through formative developmental experiences'. He notes that CBT's focus on the 'maladaptiveness of depressive thinking is consistent with psychoanalytic defense analysis, in which patterns of self-protection appropriate to childhood persist into adult life to the subject's disadvantage'.

While the latter may be the case, I note the language that Holmes uses here and wonder to what extent CBT therapists would be encouraged to pursue the relevant literature as a result of such language. A more stark example of this occurs when Holmes cites the CBT term 'catastrophizing' that 'arises when a single setback is taken as a signal of general disarray' and says that it can also be seen as 'a failure of Bionic "K" – the lack of processing of beta into alpha elements due to the absence of an internalized "thinking breast" (Bion, 1967)'. In using such language, does Holmes hope to persuade CBT therapists to look to the work of Bion as a possible source for widening their theoretical perspective on thinking errors? This is one of the problems of this book. Just who do the contributors think their audience is? Will CBT therapists be critically engaged with such language? I doubt it.

Holmes notes the loosening of the traditional boundaries between psychoanalysis and CBT by stating that contemporary psychoanalysis is 'more concerned with the "present transference" than reconstructions of the putative past' and that CBT approaches stress the important role that invalidation in childhood (dialectical behaviour therapy (DBT)) and early maladaptive schemas (EMS) (schema-focused therapy) play in the development of psychological problems. However, he does not speculate on what contemporary psychoanalysts can learn from DBT therapists and schema-focused therapists and vice versa.

One area of difference between the modalities that Holmes notes concerns the focus of therapeutic work with respect to Freud's dictum that 'effigies cannot be destroyed in absentia' with the 'transcendence of these false Gods' taking place outside the consulting room through experiments in CBT's case and inside the room in the case of psychoanalysis where these false Gods are 'brought to life and then reworked in the therapeutic relationship'. I think that the 'in here' and 'out there' focus of therapeutic work is worthy of future attention with both psychoanalytic and CBT therapists sharing their respective skills with one another to the enhancement and advancement of their respective therapeutic practice. Sadly, Holmes does not offer any suggestions about how this might be done. In this respect, I was surprised that he did not quote the seminal work of Paul Wachtel (1977) who, over 30 years ago, suggested coherent ways of synthesizing the practice of psychoanalysis and CBT.

One thought-provoking idea that Holmes introduces is that while the opening and closing of psychoanalytic and CBT sessions may be very different from one another, they may be less dissimilar in the work that happens in the middle of sessions. With regard to the beginnings and ends of sessions, Holmes observes that psychoanalysts adopt a waiting role at the beginning of sessions and are content to just note the end of sessions, while CBT therapists are more structured at the beginning and the end with negotiated homework assignments being reviewed and negotiated accordingly. If psychoanalysts are to learn from one another on this point, the following questions need to be addressed:

1   When in psychoanalysis might it enhance the work to introduce structure at the beginning of sessions and to make a deliberate attempt to encourage generalization from 'in here' to 'out there'?
2   When in CBT might it enhance the work to adopt a waiting role at the beginning of sessions and not to negotiate homework sessions at their end?

I end my comments on Holmes by noting that of all the contributors he was the one (together with Ann Casement) who, in my opinion, engaged best with the task and he was the one who showed most evidence of citing the CBT literature.

Anthony Ryle on cognitive analytic therapy (CAT) and CBT

In 1985, I returned to London from Birmingham and spent some time working in Tony Ryle's clinic at St Thomas's Hospital. He was welcoming and respectful of my rational emotive behaviour therapy (REBT)/CBT orientation and I enjoyed the interdisciplinary atmosphere of the clinical sessions he convened. Thus, I was particularly looking forward to reading his chapter. Sad to say, then, I admit to being disappointed with his contribution. He cites only one CBT article and this was one written by Dave Richards, a past president of the British Association of Behavioural and Cognitive Therapies (BABCP) who was critical of some of the current preoccupations of the CBT field.

The tone and content of Ryle's Chapter 3 are unlikely to take forward the possibility of CBT and CAT therapists learning from one another. Ryle uses every opportunity to cite the superiority of CAT over CBT and since he does not cite any CBT texts, it is difficult to understand just how knowledgeable he is about CBT. When considering the advantages of CBT, he mentions 'the use of patient self-monitoring to identify the events associated with symptoms' as one such advantage, but then quickly goes on to say how this technique was extended by CAT.

Ryle's assertions that CBT therapists do not know how to deal with patients' persistent negative behaviours, especially when they undermine therapy, is not correct as a cursory search reveals core texts on the subject by Beck (2005), Leahy (2003) and Ellis (2002).

Ryle also appears reluctant to show how the insights of CAT could benefit CBT so let me do this for him. CBT therapists have much to learn from Ryle and his colleagues concerning the concepts of 'snags', 'traps' and 'dilemmas', the sending of letters at the beginning of therapy that address the formulation and suggested reformulation of patients' problems, the schematic representation of how patients perpetuate their problems and the sending of 'good-bye' letters at the end of therapy (Ryle and Kerr, 2002). Hopefully, there are other CAT therapists who are more interested than Ryle in critically engaging with CBT in a way that encourages mutual respect and learning. The really sad thing for me is that the Tony Ryle of the mid-1980s would have written a very different and more inclusive chapter than the Tony Ryle of 2009. Even in a book that he edited in 1995, Ryle included a chapter that compared CAT with CBT and which noted areas of convergence and divergence (Marzillier and Butler, 1995). Although it was written almost 15 years ago, I am puzzled why Ryle does not refer to this chapter as a point of comparison in his contribution to the present book. Kingdon (2001) has also considered the relationship between CBT and CAT and what he had to say could also have been discussed by Ryle.

John Heaton on existential therapy and CBT

John Heaton notes that CBT has many different approaches and finds it 'impossible to generalize about CBT'. It is strange, therefore, that he has chosen to accept an invitation that asks him to do just that! Instead, he chooses to focus on a discussion of happiness and does not engage with the issue of how CBT therapists and existential therapists can learn from one another. He can be forgiven for doing so, however, since, as I noted above, the book originally had '. . . in the age of happiness' in its working title and the editors seem content to publish the contribution as it is. As such, I have little to say about his chapter. He cites 11 references and none are on CBT. He could have cited and discussed Albert Ellis's (2002) points on how REBT and CBT can be integrated. This would have done two things. First, it would have given his chapter a more clinical focus, which is the stated focus of this book, and it would have demonstrated an awareness of relevant literature. Ironically, a recent discussion on the social website, 'Facebook' (July 2009), addresses the very issue neglected by Heaton and I close my commentary by reproducing this as an example of a debate that would have enhanced the clinical focus of Heaton's contribution. I have removed the names of the four people to protect their confidentiality.

Person 1 wrote:
What do you think? Is CBT something that Existential Therapists could use or is it at odds with Existential ideals?

Person 2 wrote:
One of our basic assumptions is that there is always already a connection between thinking, doing and feeling which is in line with where CBT is coming from. So this is not at odds with existential thinking. One of the things that is at odds is the powerful role of the therapist in CBT.

This, of course, can be very attractive and I am sure it is helpful for many people who want to get to grips with their symptoms with a therapist who is very much like a doctor/expert; a person who gives homework, makes suggestions and leads rather than follows the client.

Person 3 wrote:
It depends, I think. If the CBT therapist takes the approach that things like

anxiety, depression, OCD, (the difficulties that CBT can work well for) are 'bad' and need to be 'got rid of' then I firmly believe that this is unhelpful. Far better that CBT techniques can be used to help the client 'manage' better these 'surface' anxieties and feelings, which are after all manifestations of deeper, existential anxieties, I believe. Once helped to better cope with these feelings the client can then, if they choose, move on into deeper, analytical work, looking at these existential anxieties. An integrative CBT approach is the way forward. Incorporating and integrative CBT techniques into general therapeutic practice rather than rigidly following CBT principles only.

Person 4 wrote:
Agreed. I think anxiety is a good 'test case', and good CBT doesn't see anxiety as something to just 'get rid of', but to change your relationship to (more specifically, your beliefs and assumptions about). In fact, a central theme in CBT for anxiety is acceptance of uncertainty and the limits of our control over our lives . . . sounds fairly existential!

Peter Stratton on systemic family and couples therapy (SFCT) and CBT

Peter Stratton (Chapter 5) keeps to the chapter structure that he was asked to use very well, but you will have seen that he is more expansive in describing systems therapy than he is in considering its possible relationship with CBT. When he does address this latter issue, he largely stresses the differences between SFCT and CBT. Thus, he notes that a 'CBT therapist may sometimes see a parent and child together, but we would claim that the four year intensive training for SFCT, its focus on working with multiple generations (and not just working with a child in the presence of his/her parent) and the widespread use of a therapeutic team make the work very different'.

CBT therapists do work with couples and families, but are less likely than SFCT therapists to focus on multiple generations and to make widespread use of a therapeutic team. It is true that CBT therapists are more likely to focus on individuals than SFCT, but are keenly aware of and utilize the interpersonal context of individuals' problems (Dattilio, 1998). At the end of his chapter, Stratton notes three attempts to create systemic CBT (Dummett, 2006; Rhodes and Jakes, 2009; and Treasure et al.) that sadly he neither describes nor discusses. These are the only three CBT references out of a total of 45.

In this regard, Stratton fails to mention some older North American work on synthesizing systemic and cognitive perspectives on couple and family therapy (Dattillio, 1998) and on providing a systems perspective on rational-emotive family therapy (Huber and Baruth, 1989).

Stratton concludes his piece as follows: 'Given how SFCT welcomes diversity and has detailed structures for putting alternative world views alongside each other, there should be further scope for the two approaches to benefit from each other. Even when CBT takes account of a client's relationships, its practitioners may do well to adopt the theoretical positions and skills that SFCT has developed to work equally strongly for the benefit of all the people in that relationship.' These are fine words, but Stratton has wasted an opportunity to lay the foundations of this mutually beneficial relationship by failing to describe and discuss past and current attempts to do just this. I was hoping to learn how CBT therapists might use a systemic perspective to broaden our view of our patients, but I came away dissatisfied.

Ian Parker on Lacanian psychonalysis and CBT

Parker (Chapter 6) makes the error to which I referred earlier in my chapter. He seems to equate CBT with its practice in the NHS and particularly within an IAPT setting. However, CBT is not to be equated with its practice in these contexts. There is much more to CBT than that.

Of the 23 references that Parker cites, 6 have a CBT focus. However, a closer examination of these shows that one is from House and Loewenthal (2008a), three from House and Loewenthal (2008b) and two appear to be psychoanalytic critiques of CBT. Thus, Parker does not cite a single CBT reference that is written by an advocate of CBT. Consequently, can Parker be said to critique CBT from an informed or biased perspective? Let us see.

Parker states that CBT therapists know what patients should think and that CBT 'stipulates how the subject should and should not understand reality'. I simply do not recognize his portrayal of CBT here and without knowing what his evidence is, it is difficult to know whether he is genuinely misinformed or has a psychotherapeutic axe to grind.

Elsewhere, Parker states that CBT therapists view dissatisfaction and discontentment as 'something faulty into which the individual should have insight so that it could be repaired'. I hold that he is wrong here too. Thus, in REBT, an approach within the CBT tradition that has been in existence for over 50 years, an important distinction is made between emotions that are negative in tone and largely disturbed in their consequences (e.g. depression, anxiety and shame) and emotions that are negative in tone and largely functional in their effects (e.g. sadness, concern and disappointment). Thus, CBT therapists would not generally see dissatisfaction and discontent in the way portrayed by Parker. They would generally see them as healthy responses to an adversity, such as unemployment, untainted by rigid and extreme belief systems that would turn healthy discontent into disturbance.

However, I do share Parker's views and those of other contributors to this book about the relationship between CBT and happiness. Let me take this opportunity to state my position on this issue. There are three levels that CBT therapists address in therapy and they are best targeted in the following order:

disturbance, dissatisfaction and development (Dryden, 2009a). Let me elaborate. If a person enters therapy disturbed about an adversity, in general the CBT therapist will suggest that patient and therapist focus on this disturbance before tackling issues of dissatisfaction and development and will proceed with this order only with the active agreement of the patient. This disturbance is deemed to be underpinned by a set of unhealthy schemas and other forms of distorted thinking. If the patient addresses her (in this case) disturbed feelings effectively, then with the CBT therapist's help, she is better placed to explore whether she can change the adversity about which she is discontented. If she can, then she is again better placed to deal with issues of development and answer such questions such as 'How can I live more resourcefully and meaningfully?'. If the patient cannot change the adversity about which she is discontented, then she may be encouraged to accept (but not like) this fact and move on to issues of developments as best she can. So, despite what Parker says, discontentment is not pathologized in CBT when it is about an adversity. When it is a more general feeling about life, then this would warrant a more thorough exploration before treatment decisions are collaboratively made between patient and therapist.

Following on from the above, Parker consistently demonstrates a misconception about CBT by implying that it is not a collaborative therapy. Thus, as discussed above, CBT therapists are viewed by Parker as knowing how patients should see reality and knowing how they should think. Earlier in his chapter, he also says that 'CBT in the name of prediction and control, the subject is encouraged to predict and control how they will think and behave, but within circumscribed limits. Limits defined by what the CBT practitioner thinks the problem is and how the manual indicates it should be tackled'. Parker's view of the therapeutic relationship in CBT is that the therapist knows what is correct, details how and what the patient should think and that the patient has no voice. Unfortunately, he provides no evidence to substantiate his claims. In truth, we are offered 'Parker-created CBT', which is then criticized. If Parker was curious enough about CBT to read some of the CBT literature, he would find a very different picture. He would find that the CBT therapist is encouraged to listen carefully to the patient's concerns and offer a CBT-based formulation of them and that the patient would be an active participant in this process. If a CBT way of construing the patient's concerns made sense to the patient, the two would proceed. If not the therapist would seek to effect a referral to a therapist whose model would better fit the patient's view of his or her issues and how these can be best tackled.

All therapeutic modalities (including Lacanian psychoanalysis) adopt a view concerning how patients' problems can be best understood and best addressed and the differences among the modalities are implicitly seen in the eight modality chapters in this book (for a more explicit presentation of therapeutic approaches, see Dryden, 2007).

The relevant points here, which have been neglected by all contributors to this book (and not just Parker), are as follows:

- CBT therapists are explicit about their conceptualizations and treatment plans.
- Patients are active participants in such matters. Thus, collaboration is a key principle in CBT.
- Referrals are made when the 'fit' between patient and CBT is not good.

My concern about the last point that I have made elsewhere (Dryden, 2009b) is what are the options for patients within the NHS who do not resonate with CBT?

To end my commentary on Parker on a positive note, I share his concerns abut CBT's place in the NHS, but this is a political matter and should not be confused with clinical matters concerning CBT.

Keith Tudor on person-centred therapy (PCT) and CBT

Keith Tudor (Chapter 7) has chosen to concentrate on a person-centred view of happiness in his chapter. He gives an interesting philosophical background to the concept of happiness taking in Buddhism, Greek philosophy, a Maori world view (Tudor has located to New Zealand that perhaps explains its inclusion here), empiricism, romanticism and utilitarianism. He then discusses happiness as a process and focuses on Rogers' views on 'the good life' and the fully functioning person. We have to wait until over halfway into the chapter before CBT makes an appearance and even then it is only in the context of Tudor's views on 'the Layard thesis', the medical model and what constitutes evidence in the psychotherapies. What Tudor does not do is to deal with and discuss any clinical perspectives. These were supposed to be the focus of the book as stated by the editors in their introduction.

As is the case with Heaton, I do not blame Tudor here. He may have been influenced by the book's working title (i.e. 'Critically Engaging CBT in the Age of Happiness'). Second, in their enthusiasm for encouraging contributors to write in their own way, the editors have neglected their editorial task to have contributors like Tudor and Heaton address these clinical perspectives. Tudor says at the end of his chapter 'in what is a profession comprising theoretical diversity, it is important (a) to make serious and informed comparisons between approaches . . . and (b) to take up opportunities for critical engagement between approaches'. Indeed! It is a puzzle why Tudor did not take up such an opportunity in his own chapter!

For the record, Tudor cites four CBT references: two from House and Loewenthal (2008a) and two concerning mindfulness and CBT.

Ann Casement on analytical psychology and CBT

In Chapter 8, Ann Casement emphasizes the differences between analytical psychology and CBT in the following ways:

1   What she sees as the emphasis on clinical competences, particularly when they are manualized, is anathema to the Jungian approach because the resulting standardization stunts clinical creativity.
2   CBT neglects focusing on the unconscious, especially the creative unconscious, so integral to the Jungian approach.
3   CBT focuses exclusively on the ego and neglects consciousness of other archetypal components.
4   The Jungian approach has an introverted orientation while CBT is extraverted.

I think Casement overstates her case in her views of CBT. Thus, while CBT can be manualized, it does not have to be and there is plenty of evidence in the literature of the clinical creativity of CBT therapists (e.g. Dryden, 1990; Leahy, 2003). CBT therapists do recognize and work with unconscious processes, particularly where these processes can fairly easily be brought to the patient's awareness (Ellis, 1994), although they do not seek to work with deeply buried unconscious phenomena. Without knowing what Casement means by other 'archetypal components', it is difficult for me to comment on her third point. Also, while I am not sure what she means by her extraversion–introversion categorization of CBT and the Jungian approach, what I can say is that CBT works well with both extravert and introverted patients (DiLoreto, 1971).

Despite emphasizing the differences between the Jungian approach and CBT, Casement notes that the two approaches can be integrated and, like Jeremy Holmes, she makes reference to existing attempts to consider how Jungian and CBT therapists may learn from another. For example, she cites Albert Ellis (2002), the founder of REBT, who lists four ways in which REBT and CBT can be integrated with the Jungian approach. Unfortunately, Casement does not specify these so let me do so:

• helping patients to see that meaning and purpose are more important than their drives;
• helping clients 'to achieve holistic individuation and to reclaim their undeveloped and unused parts of themselves';
• helping clients, once they are less disturbed, to focus on how they can actualize themselves;
• helping clients by using creative therapy (including dance, art and music therapy).

Casement also cites a case study by Silverstein (2007) where the Jungian technique of archetypal amplification was modified and used in CBT with a young male with schizophrenia who refused to engage in what Casement calls 'standard CBT treatment'. However, she provides no information about how this was done.

Again, for the record, Casement cites five CBT-related references. One written by Albert Ellis (2002), the House and Loewenthal (2008a) edited book, two contributions from that book and the Silverstein (2007) case study.

Stacey Millichamp on psychosynthesis and CBT

Millichamp (Chapter 9) does not include any references on CBT of the eleven that she cites. Thus, it is not clear on what she bases her statements about CBT. She makes the interesting point that it is not necessarily what is done in therapy that distinguishes psychosynthesis practitioners and CBT therapists 'as much as the way in which therapists perceive their clients and the effect that perception has on the client and on the work'. She then goes on to expand this point as follows:

1   She claims that in psychosynthesis, the client is viewed within the collective field in which he or she lives and that CBT is 'solely interested in the intrapsychic world of the individual'. This is not the case as in CBT the person is always viewed contextually although not the archetypal context stressed in psychosynthesis.

2   In psychosynthesis, Millichamp claims it is 'the therapist's presence and the ability to be empathically present that denotes the depth that is to be reached'. In addition, therapists from this modality 'are able to sit with, contain and relate to the breadth and depth of what their clients will bring' and that they will resist the temptation to reduce their clients' material to a manageable problem. This is ultimately an expression of a core value that views the therapeutic relationship as the catalyst for meaning and healing, rather than a clever technician seeking to mend what is broken.' Thus, Millichamp sees CBT therapists as clever technicians who do not prioritize the therapeutic relationship. This is a misconception about CBT. While CBT therapists are problem-focused, this is not invariably the case and they regard the therapeutic relationship as very important, but often insufficient to promote lasting change for a variety of clinical problems.

Millichamp does not address what practitioners of CBT and psychosynthesis might learn from one another. While there is little written on this subject, there are a number of practitioners who claim on the Internet to integrate the two. In addition, the Institute of Psychosynthesis advertises a course entitled 'CBT+' that is designed for CBT therapists who wish to 'develop a deeper and values-based context for their CBT work'. These developments offer an encouraging antidote to Millichamp's misconceived views of CBT and lack of consideration of possible mutual learning between the two modalities.

Conclusion

When I first agreed to comment on the modality chapters, I had four fears:

1   Contributors would use their chapters as an opportunity to show the superiority of their approach over CBT.
    This was the case with Ryle, Stratton, Parker and Millichamp.
2   Contributors would not portray CBT accurately.
    This fear was generally realized, although some were more guilty of this than others (e.g. Parker and Millichamp).
3   Contributors would 'diss' CBT.
    This was particularly the case with Parker and Millichamp.
4   Contributors would ignore the possibilities of mutual learning between CBT and non-CBT therapists.
    This was the case with Heaton, Tudor and Ryle.

As I said earlier, only Holmes and Casement write meaningfully on possibilities for mutual learning between the modality they represented and CBT.

I think the editors have to take their fair share of responsibility for setting up an opportunity for respectful, informed critical engagement and then, in my opinion, wasting it. They are both critical of CBT (House more so than Loewenthal) and what the book lacks is the participation of an advocate of CBT on the editorial team to provide balance and ensure fair play in the sense of encouraging contributors to portray CBT accurately and to keep to their 'clinical' brief.

On a more positive note, in the course of writing this commentary, I did discover a number of people on the Internet who are exploring the links between CBT and modalities represented in this book. These people are less well known than the illustrious names of the contributors. Perhaps the future of mutual learning between CBT therapists and other psychotherapists lies not in the hands of the 'big names', but in the hands of less well-known people more open to the possibility of communicating with CBT therapists.

However, let me close by providing balance. Do not run away with the idea that CBT therapists are actively being encouraged to learn from other psychotherapists. We are not! For example, I am an accredited British Association for Behavioural & Cognitive Psychotherapies (BABCP) therapist, but BABCP would not accept as continuing professional development (CPD) the hours that I spent going to non-CBT events to further my learning. It is only when our professional associations actively encourage and promote mutual learning will the kind of critical engagement between CBT and other modalities hoped for by House and Loewenthal really take root.

References

Beck, J.S. (2005) *Cognitive Therapy for Challenging Problems: What to Do When the Basics Don't Work*, New York: Guilford Press.

Bion, W. (1967) *Second Thoughts*, New York: Jason Aronson.

Dattillio, F.M. (ed.) (1998) *Case Studies in Couple and Family Therapy: Systemic and Cognitive Perspectives*, New York: Guilford Press.

DiLoreto, A.E. (1971) *Comparative Psychotherapy: An Experimental Analysis*, Chicago: Aldine-Atherton.

Dryden, W. (1990) *Creativity in Rational-emotive Therapy*, London: Gale Centre Publications.

Dryden, W. (ed.) (2007) *Dryden's Handbook of Individual Therapy*, London: Sage Publications.

Dryden, W. (2009a) *Rational Emotive Behaviour Therapy: Distinctive Features*, London: Routledge.

Dryden, W. (2009b) 'The importance of choice in therapy: from the perspective of a, hopefully flexible, CBT practitioner', *European Journal of Psychotherapy and Counselling*, 11: 311–22.

Dummett, N. (2006) 'Processes for systemic cognitive-behavioural therapy with children, young people and families', *Behavioural and Cognitive Psychotherapy*, 34: 179–89.

Ellis, A. (1994) *Reason and Emotion in Psychotherapy*, revised and expanded edition, New York: Birch Lane Press.

Ellis, A. (2002) *Overcoming Resistance: A Rational Emotive Behaviour Therapy Integrated Approach*, New York: Springer.

Grazebrook, K., Garland, A. and the Board of BABCP (2005) 'What are cognitive and/or behavioural psychotherapies'. Paper prepared for a UKCP/BABCP mapping exercise, Bury: BABCP.

House, R. and Loewenthal, D. (eds) (2008a) *Against and For CBT: Towards a Constructive Dialogue?*, Ross-on-Wye: PCCS Books.

House, R. and Loewenthal, D. (eds) (2008b) 'CBT in question', *European Journal of Psychotherapy and Counselling*, 10(3): 181–279.

Huber, C.H. and Baruth, L.G. (1989) *Rational Emotive Family Therapy: A Systems Perspective*, New York: Springer Publishing Company.

Kingdon, D. (2001) 'Commentary', *Advances in Psychiatric Treatment*, 7: 243–56.

Kuyken, W., Watkins, E. and Beck A. (2005) 'CBT for mood disorders', in G. Gabbard,

J. Beck and J. Holmes (eds), *Oxford Textbook of Psychotherapy*, Oxford: Oxford University Press, pp. 111–26.

Layard, R. (2005) *Happiness: Lessons from a New Science*, London: Penguin Books.

Leahy, R.L. (ed.) (2003) *Roadblocks in Cognitive-behavioral Therapy: Transforming Challenges into Opportunities for Change*, New York: Guilford Press.

Marzillier, J. and Butler, G. (1995) 'CAT in relation to cognitive therapy', in A. Ryle (ed.), *Cognitive Analytic Therapy: Developments in Theory and Practice*, Chichester: Wiley, pp. 121–38.

Rhodes, J. and Jakes, S. (2009) *Narrative CBT for Psychosis*, London: Routledge.

Ryle, A. and Kerr, I.B. (2002) *Introducing Cognitive Analytic Therapy: Principles and Practice*, Chichester, Wiley.

Silverstein, S.W. (2007) 'Integrating Jungian and self-psychological perspectives within cognitive-behavior therapy for a young man with a fixed religious delusion', *Clinical Case Studies*, 6: 263–76.

Treasure, J., Schmidt, U. and MacDonald, P. (2009) *The Clinician's Guide to Collaborative Caring in Eating Disorders*. London: Routledge.

Wachtel, P. (1977) *Psychoanalysis and Behavior Therapy: Toward an Integration*, New York: Basic Books.

13 Conclusion

Del Loewenthal and Richard House

> Many of this book's contributors seem fearful and angry that CBT
> has larger political aspirations to eliminate psychotherapeutic
> competition . . . [U]nwanted government and insurance company
> intrusion . . . is a function of our time and the limited resources
> for health care. . . .
>
> (Paul, Chapter 10, p. 142)

It is tempting to take the editorial opportunity in this concluding chapter
to review in detail the commonalities and incommensurabilities (and the
balance between them) that have emerged both between the various modality
chapters and the cognitive-behaviour therapy (CBT) commentaries, and –
perhaps somewhat more surprisingly – between the CBT respondents themselves. What this points to is something that we have suspected all along;
namely, that the traditional 'schoolist' boundaries between the various therapy modalities are sometimes more apparent than real, and are certainly
far more permeable than the partisan positionings of the various modality
schools would tend to suggest. We feel it is more important to leave readers
themselves to reach their own conclusions about both the various critiques of,
and commonalities with, CBT identified by the eight chosen modality authors,
and also about the comparative analyses so ably articulated by our three
CBT respondents. Such a 'light-touch' approach sits very well with the spirit in
which this book was conceived; that is, a pluralistic *opening-up* of a (hopefully
constructive) cross-modality engagement in ways that have never really happened in the literature before, rather than engaging in a crass modernist
attempt to account for and pronounce on differences in a closing-down way.

   Rather, in this brief concluding chapter we highlight just a few of the
themes, in particular as a rejoinder to our three CBT respondents (Dryden,
Paul and Proeve) who also, usefully, have provided us with, respectively,
a definition of CBT and accounts of its early and more recent developments.
The selected themes are those that strike us as being especially prominent and

poignant, and which have emerged from this book's unique incursion into the world of comparative cross-modality engagement. It is important to acknowledge that the 'post-existential' (Loewenthal, 2008, 2010), deconstructionist position (House, 2003) that we tend to adopt will inevitably colour our own particular reading of the issues, and what we choose to highlight here. However, as with other strongly held theoretical standpoints, such positions are potentially always a cover story for our own unexplored projections.

Having said this, we would like to respond to Dryden's (Chapter 12) criticisms about some of this book's editorial directions. Dryden is right, first, that we declined to offer a definition of CBT; yet we believe this editorial decision to be more than vindicated by the repeated argument made in the book – and not least by the CBT writers themselves – that 'CBT' is a very broad church indeed, with such a range of diverse practices and associated theoretical underpinnings that it really makes little sense even to attempt *a* definition. And in any case, embracing such a task would also be colluding with the modernist fantasy that it is in principle even possible to define 'CBT' in an objective, coherent way – an assumption that we would strongly question.

We are also told that we have neglected our editorial task to have contributors address clinical perspectives, and that we have 'set up an opportunity for respectful, informed critical engagement and then wasted it'.

Yet from our perspective, which privileges the phenomenological stance of *allowing these things to emerge* rather than programmatically controlling them from the outset, we believe that the way in which our contributors have responded to our remit is *in itself* very interesting in terms of current cultures of therapy, and what it reveals about the field's current schisms and possibilities for dialogue; and to have interfered unduly in this process would actually have stopped this important information emerging from the project.

We are told further that 'what the book lacks is the participation of an advocate of CBT on the editorial team to provide balance and ensure fair play in the sense of encouraging contributors to portray CBT accurately and to keep to their "clinical" brief'. In our view, this is a 'modernist' viewpoint with which we simply do not identify; for it tacitly assumes that there exists one 'fair, objective "reality" ' of CBT; yet it seems clear to us that there simply exists no such thing; rather, there are multiple realities, and multiple fantasies about them – and fantasies can often be at least as illuminating as so-called 'objective' descriptions or attempts at representation. It is the former that we have encouraged in this book; and of course there are further stories to be told about the origins of these multiple fantasies and representations of CBT, which are alas beyond the current discussion.

As is made clear at other points in the book, Dryden points out strongly that 'the practice of CBT is much broader than the current preoccupation with its perceived favoured position as the treatment of choice within the NHS in Britain'. In commenting critically on Ian Parker's Chapter 6, he writes that

'I share [Parker's] concerns about CBT's place in the NHS, but this is a political matter and should not be confused with clinical matters concerning CBT'. Similary, Dryden also states that 'Parker makes the error [of equating] CBT with its practice in the NHS and particularly within an IAPT setting. However, CBT is not to be equated with its practice in these contexts. There is much more to CBT than that.' However, we are not nearly as clear as Dryden seems to be that it is legitimate to make such a sharp distinction between CBT-labelled therapy that is increasingly common in modern society, and the more 'legitimate' clinical CBT that Dryden is referring to.

Whether Dryden's strong critique of Parker's chapter is valid, or based on a misunderstanding of the Lacanian approach, is an issue that will need to be addressed elsewhere. Thus, we wonder, for example, whether a Lacanian would agree with Dryden's assertion that 'All therapeutic modalities (including Lacanian psychoanalysis) adopt a view concerning how patients' problems can be best understood and best addressed.'

Dryden does very usefully outline at some length his view on CBT and happiness, which gives sufficient information for the various modalities to enter into an interesting and enlightening dialogue about the place of happiness in therapeutic work.

Overall, one is struck in particular by the diversity of the three CBT responses – not least in terms of their differing views on the status of the various critiques of CBT – which we find both interesting and reassuring, to the extent that CBT is by no means seen, by at least some of its theorists and practitioners, as a uniform, conformable practice; and that it is open to innovation and change. However, this welcome flexibility must cut both ways, of course, in that such diversity therefore behoves proponents of 'CBT' to specify precisely what approach they *are* advocating, and its nuanced dimensions – something that is perhaps very far from happening in the mass-delivered IAPT programme with the accompanying language of being 'rolled out' and 'delivered' across the UK. There is, moreover, a difficulty in specifying what might or might not be a legitimate criticism of CBT, for again we are faced with confusion and conflation in just what is being criticized, and the generalizability of the criticisms. For on the one hand, while it is no doubt a move of dubious fairness to imply that a given critique of an aspect of one kind of CBT is necessarily generalizable to CBT more widely, it is also surely unfair for any critique of CBT to be rejected out of hand merely because one can invoke some kind of 'CBT' approach to which the given criticism does not apply! We see this kind of problem clearly visible, for example, when Dryden writes that 'While CBT therapists are problem-focused, this is not invariably the case' – thus effectively rendering 'CBT' as a conformable modality approach immune from any meaningful criticism.

It seems to us that we are only at the beginning of injecting this kind of nuanced precision and clarity into these comparative modality discussions;

and perhaps all we can hope for in this book is to begin to lay out the parameters of the disputes, and what a good-enough clarification or resolution of them would need to look like. Paul (Chapter 10) certainly does concede that some criticisms of CBT are indeed valid while others are not; and this is just one of the many clarifications that are sorely needed in the field.

First, from a certain perspective, CBT can be argued to be a particularly cost-effective way of 'managing' the mental health problems of advanced industrial society in the twenty-first century, whereas the other therapy modalities represented in this book might be seen as resonating more with the twentieth-century culture. So to what extent, we might provocatively ask, do at least some of our modality respondents' offerings represent the envious attacks of 'has-beens', whose erstwhile relatively comfortable empires or power bases may now be crumbling, and who are left, at best, with sentimental nostalgia for a bygone, golden therapy age which, to some extent, may have never really existed?

Seen somewhat differently, to what extent might these more twentieth-century approaches reflect an essential humanity that we are, perhaps, in grave danger of losing in an increasingly technocratic, managerialist age? It would appear that there has indeed been a significant shift in cultural patterns, whereby previous attempts at and commitments to increased self-awareness are being replaced with a greater focus on taking people's minds off that which they find troubling. Thus, while we have some sympathy with Dryden's exploration of the extent to which other modalities might be willing to come alongside CBT, there may well be differences in the fundamental assumptions and world views underlying the two cultures that make such a meeting particularly problematic, if not highly unlikely.

These differences in the two cultures, and their resulting psychotherapies, with their contrasting underlying assumptions, can perhaps usefully be explored in the British Association for Behavioural and Cognitive Physiotherapies (BABCP) definition of CBT, provided by Dryden in his chapter (pp. 162–3) of this book. This begins, 'Cognitive and/or behavioural psychotherapies (CBP) are *psychological* approaches based on *scientific principles* and which *research has shown* to be effective for a wide range of problems' (own emphasis). As indicated in Chapter 1, one of the fathers of psychology, Wilhelm Wundt ([1902] 1904), considers that the essence of psychology is to marry the empirical with the cultural and historical. However, Wundt was misrepresented in English-speaking countries, because only his empirical, laboratory-based work was emphasized in English translations. So the inappropriate and limiting positivistic move only to consider 'evidence' in terms of that which can be quantified was already in strong evidence by the early twentieth century.

We are also routinely told – in a 'power move' in the face of which we are presumably meant to be unquestioningly impressed! – that these 'psychological approaches', as mentioned above, now called CBP rather than CBT in this definition without explanation, are based on 'scientific principles' – as if by merely asserting that something is 'scientific', in the complete absence of any critical awareness of how philosophically problematic and culturally constructed the term 'scientific' can be – any possibility of a critical, wide-ranging conversation about therapeutic efficacy is inevitably curtailed and closed down, rather than opened up to reflective thinking. Indeed, psychology as a discipline and profession can be seen to be rife with such 'psychologisms', whereby what is asserted to be a scientific *technique* replaces, and becomes conflated with, what might constitute a 'scientific' approach in the much broader, post-positivistic sense of that term. Dryden, while stating that he is not in full agreement with BABCP definitions, examines the extent to which other modalities are seriously interested in coming alongside CBT by counting how many CBT references are cited at the end of their chapters. This interesting procedure does certainly have the genuine potential for encouraging us to think, but not if it excludes by definition the possibility of a modality author having something very significant to say about CBT, even though not a single CBT reference is evident. There may be resonance here with the next part of this sentence, defining CBT, as it does, as involving a totemic phrase that has become emblematic of our culture; that is, '. . . which research has shown to be effective'.

Yet what is 'research'? Again, it would appear to be a cultural practice that is subject to shifting fashions. Thus, for example, in the twentieth century, it was far more acceptable for a doctorate to focus on exploring theory; whereas now in psychology, and increasingly in psychotherapy, our impression is that doctorate theory sections seem to be increasingly sparse, to the benefit of method (though this would require empirical verification), but not *methodology*. Similarly, there would appear to be a trend towards increasing emphasis on aspects like larger sample size (sometimes buying into the modernist fantasy that this will somehow confer greater legitimacy and *certainty* on the findings), rather than epistemological, ontological and/or methodological explorations. Increasingly, what was previously regarded as 'theory' is now arguably being categorized as 'philosophy' – and therefore more easily dismissed from a positivistic perspective. This in turn is part of a wider cultural, paradigmatic story about what is happening to our taken-for-granted conceptions and assumptions about what 'research' consists in, in late modernity (House and Bohart, 2008; Loewenthal, 2009a; House, 2010).

One argument for CBT is that it is particularly helpful in taking one's mind off one's problems. Indeed, some of the founders of behavioural approaches, for example, William James (Cotkin, 1994) and Aaron Beck (Weishaar, 1993), are known to have suffered from severe depression. So what better therapeutic approach could there be for a world that has arguably become so alienated that it is too frightened to experience its alienation (Loewenthal, 2009b)? –

with society's currently favoured therapy approach faithfully parallelling the cultural anomie to which we are currently subject in late modernity (Levin, 1987). It follows that this can then be true for our twenty-first century researchers who, like the psychological therapist and client they are research-ing, may be terrified of allowing thoughts to come to them, and therefore, all must learn forms of CBT techniques in order to change their natural, some-times disturbing way of thinking. In this context, the BABCP definition of CBT as 'inherently empowering in nature, (focusing) on *specific psychological and practical skills'* [own emphasis] could perhaps be seen as an antidote to allowing thoughts to come freely to us.

Thus, people perhaps *appear* to be open to research, but this is only research conducted within very narrow notions of evidence that suit a particu-lar, easily quantifiable therapeutic technique, and our impoverished cultural moment more generally. In such a paradigm, it tends to be assumed that phenomena like love and intimacy do not exist unless they can be measured and quantified. This then raises the question of what is meant in the second sentence of the BABCP definition which starts: 'Clients and therapists work together once the *therapeutic alliance* [our emphasis] has been formed . . .' What is this 'therapeutic alliance' referred to here? There do seem to be very different ideas of this notion between the different modalities. It would appear that 'the relationship' is central to the therapeutic endeavour (Beutler and Harwood, 2002), which common factor might account for a substantial part of 'improvement' with both CBT and other therapies. However, an important question that arises is that if 'the relationship' is indeed such an important factor in CBT, then why is it not a requirement in the training of CBT therap-ists to have personal therapy? Again, when the next sentence of this BABCP definition starts with 'the approach generally focuses on the here and now', why is this not assumed, in CBT, to be what is taking place between the therapist and client? There is a similar issue with such derivatives of CBT as in the UK Department of Health national roll-out programme training 'high-' and 'low-intensity' therapists in the name of improving access to psychological therapies (Department of Health, 2007).

Even if we do confer scientific status on CBT, there is what C.P. Snow described as 'a gulf of mutual incomprehension' between scientists and what he terms 'literary intellectuals'. 'If scientists have the future in their bones then the traditional culture responds by wishing the future did not exist' (cited in Robertson, 2005: 107). We therefore have at least two groups of approaches that have very different paradigmatic world views (Kuhn, 1962), and very different assumptions about what it means to be human (Woodhouse, 1996; Bohart and House, 2008; Loewenthal and House, 2008). So-called third-wave CBT (as referred to particularly in Proeve's Chapter 11) appears particularly adroit at being able to add on new aspects, for example, the importance of relationships to a CBT framework (Gilbert and Leahy, 2007), although we would still question the underlying assumptions. For many non-CBT approaches, such a fundamental mind-shift would be required to include aspects of CBT that there is perhaps an understandable resistance, as well as a less understandable one, perhaps deriving from envy and an inability and/or an unwillingness to change.

To be more provocative still, there is even the possible argument that most non-CBT approaches are, in effect and in all but name, either cognitive or behaviour-modification programmes, where there is the tacit aim of the client/ patient successfully completing therapy only when they think and/or behave in a certain way. Thus, criticisms of CBT could therefore be seen, for example, psychoanalytically as a reaction formation by psychological therapists who are not clear for themselves or their clients as to the CBT aspects of what is, in fact, inherent in their work. For example, many of us talk about when our patients do and do not appear ready to leave therapy. Perhaps we are all engaged in a massive quasi-CBT programme . . .? On this kind of view, the CBT practitioner could then be seen to be far more honest and explicit than other modalities who have a vested interest to stay with their modality-specific delusions. What we are doing here, of course, is to be as open as we can be to deconstructing our own position on CBT; and if the modality engagement that we are encouraging in this book is to have legs in the future (being a crucial test of the maturity of our 'profession' perhaps), then we all need to be open to deconstructing, and exposing to reflexive scrutiny, our own (more or less) entrenched modality positions and associated ideologies and practices. And as will be clear from the above, it would be a major and self-serving error merely to expect this of CBT alone. It will perhaps come as no surprise to the reader at this juncture to state that we are deeply (and, we believe, healthily) suspicious of all psychotherapeutic 'frame-ups', considering that they are frequently only there for the benefit of the client to the extent to which they succeed in keeping the psychological therapist (apparently) in one piece. We therefore think that a further shift in our culture around all these issues is desperately needed.

As psychological therapists, surely we need to have an understanding of the world in which we are living and bringing up our children (House and Loewenthal, 2009). And here, we are in agreement with Michael Proeve, and other contributors, where he says that he is 'sceptical about the idea of improving society by prescribing wholesale psychotherapy rather than examining the aspects of society that contribute to human misery' (p. 145). Furthermore, in common with most of our contributors and in the spirit of a postmodern diversity, we do not consider that any one therapeutic approach can by any means possess all the answers. Indeed, we would wish to write a robust 'critically engaging' book about *any* current modality, including our own favoured ones, that government would propose as some kind of universal, standarization-driven panacea. Unfortunately, because each and every therapeutic approach stands on such shaky ground, just as we are all ontologically insecure as individuals, it has become more difficult for us to speak to each other – which is just one reason why this book and its radical comparative approach could have such cultural importance.

We would like to take the opportunity here to respond to a review of our earlier book *Against and For CBT* (House and Loewenthal, 2008) by David Smail (2009), in which he questions whether we think any form of psychotherapy is effective. While agreeing with Smail that the enhancement of well-being in society will sometimes, and even often, require interventions other than those of individual psychotherapy – see, for example, Loewenthal (forthcoming) – our respective experiences over several decades as both therapists and clients, together with our reading of a wide range of research outcome literature, lead us to believe that all approaches to psychotherapy and counselling can potentially help to alleviate individual human suffering. However, we also view questions regarding what is taken to be legitimate 'evidence' and appropriate research methods in terms of culturally rooted practices that are commonly dependent on the very conditions that can cause societal ill-health (e.g. the sole reliance on positivistic research methods).

An interesting recent development in the field of psychological therapies is the move towards exploring 'common factors' in the psychological therapies (Wampold, 2001; Norcross, 2005). However, there may be problems in subscribing, as Proeve does in his chapter, to the technical eclecticism that Lazarus (1976) has proposed, where one is 'borrowing techniques' from other psychotherapeutic approaches without necessarily subscribing to the underlying theory' (p. 150). For example, Proeve does not see it as problematic that by talking about changing our relationship to our thoughts, this might create further splits in the client – as if one's thoughts and who one 'is' could be unproblematically different. There is also a welcome move by the National Institute of Clinical Excellence (NICE) in association with the Medical Research Council in the UK to start to consider approaches to research other than randomized controlled trials (National Institute of Clinical Excellence, 2009).

Once we have a less positivistic approach to our being and its interrogation and exploration, then perhaps this can open the way to considering other, previously neglected dimensions of human experience; for example, Kierkegaard's 'education by dread' (e.g. Lowrie, 1973), as well as Layard's and Seligman's notions of 'happiness' (Seligman, 2003; Layard, 2005). Hopefully, there will also be more opportunities for the various psychological therapies to venture out from their defensive conceptual fortresses. To date, too few opportunities are being created for inter-modality cooperation where we could openly discuss what we think are the foundational assumptions underpinning our various approaches and whether it is possible or even advisable to attempt to legislate between them – a key aspect of which process would be exploring just how CBT and other modalities might help in informing and deepening our practice. A major hope for this book is that it will assist in enabling such future praxis-enhancing conversations to take place.

References

Beutler, L.E. and Harwood, T.M. (2002) 'What is and can be attributed to the therapeutic relationship?', *Journal of Contemporary Psychotherapy*, 32: 25–33.

Bohart, A.C. and House, R. (2008) 'Empirically supported/validated treatments as modernist ideology, I: Dodo, manualization, and the paradigm question', in R. House and D. Loewenthal (eds), *Against and For CBT: Towards a Constructive Dialogue?*, Ross-on-Wye: PCCS Books, pp. 188–201.

Cotkin, G. (1994) *William James: Public Philosopher*, Chicago, IL: University of Illinois Press.

Department of Health (2007) 'Improving access to psychological therapies: specification for the commissioner-led pathfinder programme', available online at www.mhchoice.csip.org.uk/psychological-therapies/-iapt-commissionerled-pathfinder-sites/resources.html (accessed 10 October 2009).

Gilbert, P. and Leahy, R.L. (eds) (2007) *The Therapeutic Relationship in the Cognitive Behavioural Psychotherapies*, London: Routledge.

House, R. (2003) *Therapy Beyond Modernity: Deconstructing and Transcending Profession-centred Therapy*, London: Karnac Books.

House, R. (2010) ' "Psy" research beyond late-modernity: towards praxis-congruent research', *Psychotherapy and Politics International*, 8(1): 13–20.

House, R. and Bohart, A.C. (2008) 'Empirically supported/validated treatments as modernist ideology, II: Alternative perspectives on research and practice', in R. House and D. Loewenthal (eds), *Against and For CBT: Towards a Constructive Dialogue?*, Ross-on-Wye: PCCS Books, pp. 202–17.

House, R. and Loewenthal, D. (eds) (2008) *Against and For CBT: Towards a Constructive Dialogue?* Ross-on-Wye: PCCS Books.

House, R. and Loewenthal, D. (eds) (2009) *Childhood, Wellbeing and a Therapeutic Ethos*, London: Karnac Books.

Kuhn, T. (1962) *The Structure of Scientific Revolutions*, Chicago, IL: Chicago University Press.

Layard, R. (2005) *Happiness: Lessons from a New Science*, London: Penguin Books.

Lazarus, A. (1976) *Multimodal Behavior Therapy*, New York: Springer.

Levin, D.M. (ed.) (1987) *Pathologies of the Modern Self: Postmodern Studies on Narcissism, Schizophrenia and Depression*, New York: New York University Press.

Loewenthal, D. (2008) 'Introducing post-existentialism: an approach to wellbeing in the 21st century', *Philosophical Practice*, 3: 316–21.

Loewenthal, D. (2009a) 'Editorial: ideology, research and evidence in the psychological therapies', *European Journal of Psychotherapy and Counselling*, 11(3): 245–50.

Loewenthal, D. (2009b) 'Childhood, wellbeing and a therapeutic ethos: a case for therapeutic education', in R. House and D. Loewenthal (eds), *Childhood, Wellbeing and a Therapeutic Ethos*, London: Karnac Books, pp. 19–35.

Loewenthal, D. (2010) 'Audit, audit culture and therapeia: some implications for wellbeing, with particular reference to children', in L. King and C. Moutsou (eds), *Audit Cultures: A Critical Look at 'Evidence Based Practice' in Psychotherapy and Beyond*, London: Karnac Books.

Loewenthal, D. and House, R. (2008) 'Conclusion: contesting therapy paradigms about what it means to be human', in R. House and D. Loewenthal (eds), *Against and For CBT: Towards a Constructive Dialogue?*, Ross-on-Wye: PCCS Books, pp. 289–96.

Lowrie, W. (1973) *Kierkegaard's 'The Concept of Dread'*, Princeton, NJ: Princeton University Press.

National Institute of Clinical Excellence (2009) 'NICE and MRC to collaborate on £2million methodology research programme', available online at www.nice.org.uk/newsroom/pressstatements/niceandmrctocollaborate. jsp (accessed October 2009).

Norcross, J.C. (2005) 'A primer on psychotherapy integration', in J.C. Norcross and M.R. Goldfried (eds), *Handbook of Psychotherapy Integration*, 2nd edn, New York: Oxford, pp. 3–23.

Robertson, M. (2005) 'Power and knowledge in psychiatry and the troubling case of Dr Osheroff', *Australian Psychiatry*, 13(4): 343–50.

Seligman, M.E.P. (2003) *Authentic Happiness*, London: Nicholas Brealey.

Smail, D. (2009) Review of *Against and For CBT* (eds R. House and D. Loewenthal), *Times Higher Education*, 19 February.

Wampold, B. (2001) *The Great Psychotherapy Debate: Models, Methods and Findings*, New York: Lawrence Erlbaum.

Weishaar, M. (1993) *Aaron T. Beck*, London: Sage Publications.

Woodhouse, M. (1996) *Paradigm Wars: Worldviews for a New Age*, Berkeley, CA: University of California Press.

Wundt, W. ([1902] 1904) *Principles of Physiological Psychology* (trans. E. Tichener), Harvard, MT: Harvard University Press.

Index